781.540973 Wol            180719
Woll.
Songs from Hollywood musical
 comedies, 1927 to the present.

| DATE | | | |
|---|---|---|---|
|  |  |  |  |
|  |  |  |  |
|  |  |  |  |
|  |  |  |  |
|  |  |  |  |
|  |  |  |  |
|  |  |  |  |
|  |  |  |  |
|  |  |  |  |
|  |  |  |  |
|  |  |  |  |
|  |  |  |  |
|  |  |  |  |

# Songs from Hollywood Musical Comedies, 1927 to the Present:

## A Dictionary

*Garland Reference Library in the Humanities (Vol. 44)*

# Songs from Hollywood Musical Comedies, 1927 to the Present:
# A Dictionary

**Allen L. Woll**

*Garland Publishing, Inc., New York & London*

Library of Congress Cataloging in Publication Data

Woll, Allen L
    Songs from Hollywood musical comedies, 1927 to the
present.

    (Garland reference library in the humanities ; v. 44)
    Bibliography:  p.
    1.  Music, Popular (Songs, etc.)--Dictionaries.
2.  Moving-picture music--Dictionaries.  I.  Title.
ML102.P66W64        782.8'1          75-24089
ISBN 0-8240-9958-3

*180719*

*Printed in the United States of America*

*To Myra*

# Contents

# HOW TO USE THIS BOOK

The film musical, once Hollywood's most popular art form, is currently experiencing a revival in interest. MGM's That's Entertainment (1974) has proved so successful that a sequel is being prepared. Countless books on the subject have appeared within the past few years. Soundtrack recordings of these films are also enjoying a boom, as long out-of-print albums are being re-released for younger fans. Songs from Hollywood Musical Comedies, 1927 to the Present provides a guide for these nostalgia buffs, allowing them to identify their favorite movie musical show tunes, and, if possible, find soundtrack recordings of them.

This compilation is divided into four parts. Section one ("The Songs") provides an alphabetical listing of more than seven thousand songs which appeared in Hollywood musicals since 1927. The item number follows the song title, and refers the reader to the musical film in which the song was performed. This information is included in section two ("The Films").

Section two lists the musical comedies produced in Hollywood since 1927. The item number is followed by the title of the film and the date of release. Next the major stars and the director of the film are listed. If a single composer and lyricist contributed the songs for the film, their names follow with the composer's name appearing first. Unlike Broadway shows, Hollywood musicals are rarely the product of one composer and lyricist. More often than not, several songwriters provide melodies for the film. These names are included in the listings of the songs in section two. Due to space restrictions, two categories of musicals have song listings included: (1) All musicals produced after 1950, since this information is not available elsewhere, and (2) All musicals with soundtrack recordings, in order that this text can guide the record buyer in his purchases.

Following the listing of songs is a reference to available soundtrack recordings of the score. The name of the company is listed first, followed by the album number. The album that is most easily available in record stores is listed in this section. For example, Good News (1947) was available in several formats (E-504, E-3229, E-3771) during the 1950's, all of which are currently out of print. However, MGM has recently re-released all of its soundtrack albums in deluxe two-record sets, all readily available in any record store. It is this number (2-SES-51ST) which is provided.

Also contributing to the recent surge in soundtrack recordings is the appearance of small companies (Curtain Calls, Soundtrack, etc.) which are releasing albums of previously unrecorded films of the 1930's and 1940's. These albums can be found primarily in the larger cities, while mail order houses can supply these recordings to those fans who do not live in New York, Chicago, or San Francisco. Perhaps the most reputable mail order firm is A-1 Record Finders, P. O. Box 75071, Los Angeles, California, 90075, which provides one of the largest selections of soundtrack recordings at reasonable prices.

Non-soundtrack recordings of selected songs by performers who did not appear in the film are also included if at least four selections from the score appear on the album.

A chronological listing of the 1187 musical comedies compiled in this book appears in section three. The final section of this book presents the composers and lyricists of these musical films. The item number once again refers the reader to section two for the films to which these songwriters have contributed their talents.

There must be a brief note concerning the definition of musical comedy that has been utilized in this text.

Any film that cannot be classified as a musical comedy or was not produced in the United States is not included in this listing. For this reason, no filmed operas or individual arias are classified herein. Similarly, the rock and roll films of the 1950's (Rock Around The Clock) and rock films of the 1960's and 1970's (Let It Be, Woodstock) are also absent from these pages unless based on a Broadway presentation. For this reason, Godspell and Jesus Christ Superstar are indexed in this text, while Tommy, based on a recording by The Who, is not. Likewise, any British musical comedy produced on Broadway (Oliver, The Boy Friend) and later filmed in Britain is incorporated in this listing. Animated and Western musical films are also excluded from this text. One final limitation restricts films with less than three new songs from classification as musicals unless the situation warrants.

I would like to thank several people who aided me in the preparation of this book. Susan Dalton and the staff of the University of Wisconsin Center for Theater Research arranged for the screening of all the Warner Brothers, RKO, and Monogram musicals listed in this book. The records of these companies, and the archives of United Artists provided a majority of the information for this compilation. Michael Fitzgerald of Films Incorporated, Skokie, Il-

xi

linois, and Patrick Sheean of the Library of Congress provided information and arranged screeings of several of the MGM films discussed herein. Thomas O'Brien Sr. and Thomas O'Brien Jr. provided
films, viewing facilities, and information concerning the Columbia
musicals. Rutgers University provided the computer facilities which
allowed the alphabetizing of the more than 8000 songs listed in
this book. Rutgers also arranged for the screening of several musical films in conjunction with a course on the History of the
Hollywood Musical. Lois Drapin encouraged me to begin this project.
Myra K. Woll nursed the book to completion and helped compile the
indices.

Whenever the archival sources or the films were found lacking,
the following printed sources provided valuable information:

A. BOOKS

Burton, Jack. Blue Book of Hollywood Musicals.(New York, 1953).

Croce, Arlene. The Fred Astaire and Ginger Rogers Book. (New York, 1972).

Fordin, Hugh. The World of Entertainment. (New York, 1975).

Green, Stanley and Goldblatt, Burt. Starring Fred Astaire. (New York, 1973).

Jablonski, Edward. Harold Arlen: Happy With the Blues. (New York, 1961).

---- and Stewart, Lawrence D. The Gershwin Years (New York, 1973).

Kimball, Robert. Cole. (New York, 1971).

---- and Simon, Alfred. The Gershwins. (New York, 1973).

Kobal, John. Gotta Sing! Gotta Dance! (London, 1970).

Kreuger, Miles, ed. The Movie Musical. (New York, 1975).

Lewine, Richard and Simon, Alfred. Songs of the American Theater. (New York, 1973).

xii

Mattfeld, Julius. _Variety Music Cavalcade_. (New York, 1962).

Mosher, W. Franklyn. _The Alice Faye Movie Book_. (Harrisburg, 1974).

----. _The New York Times Film Reviews_, 6 vols. (New York, 1971).

Shapiro, Nat. _Popular Music: An Annotated Index of American Popular Songs_. (New York, 1964-1969).

Taylor, John Russell and Jackson, Arthur. _The Hollywood Musical_. (New York, 1971).

Thomas, Lawrence B., _The MGM Years_. (New York, 1972).

Thomas, Tony and Terry, Jim. _The Busby Berkeley Book_. (New York, 1973).

Valliance, Tom. _The American Musical_. (New Jersey, 1971).

B. PERIODICALS

    _Billboard_.

    _Phonolog_.

    _Schwann Record Guide_.

    _Variety_.

# THE FANTASTIC WORLD OF THE HOLLYWOOD MUSICAL

## I. THE MUSICAL OF THE GREAT DEPRESSION

Studio executives tried repeatedly to cut "Somewhere Over The Rainbow" from the final print of The Wizard of Oz (1939). They argued that there was no reason for a young girl to sing a wistful ballad in the middle of a Kansas barnyard. No one complained about the evil witches, a talking lion, flying monkeys, a tin woodsman, or a dancing scarecrow. In the land of Oz anything could happen as all logic was suspended in that fantastic world. However, no one sings in a Kansas barnyard.[1]

Mervyn LeRoy's firm insistence on the matter eventually convinced MGM advisors to allow Dorothy to sing the lovely Harold Arlen - E. Y. Harburg ballad and the rest is history. However, this anecdote is revealing of the rigid bonds of logic governing the conventions of the Hollywood musical comedy. Despite talk of "fantasy" and "escapism" whenever the musical genre is considered, film musicals were inextricably bound to the real world.

Lorenz Hart noticed this problem when he and the young Richard Rodgers left Broadway for Hollywood in the early nineteen-thirties. Again studio executives expected the talented musicians to produce works similar to those that they had written for Broadway. However, when Hart attempted to insert rhythmic dialogue in such films as Hot Heiress (1931) and Love Me Tonight (1932), producers kept asking him why people were unexpectedly breaking into song. "How can you do this?," they asked. "Where's the cue?"[2]

The authors of Broadway musicals faced a different set of assumptions than the writers of film musicals. Song is expected on Broadway, and all denizens of the stage show may participate in the merriment no matter their background. For example, politicians may sing of presidential elections in Of Thee I Sing (1931); the Blacks of Catfish Row in Porgy and Bess (1935) may express their innermost feelings in song; and even Public Enemy Number One can recite the virtues of crime in lyric form in Anything Goes (1934). These occurences are not jarring to the Broadway audience, for, on the contrary, the immediate and unexplained recourse to song is expected.

In Hollywood, however, the reverse became true. The coming of sound to the hitherto silent world of the feature film heralded a new fidelity to the real world which had formerly been lacking. This new addition would allow the motion picture camera to reproduce the everyday reality of daily life with unparalleled accuracy, as both sound and image became one.

The Hollywood musical comedy was born with the birth of sound, and from that date it experienced logical restrictions that its Broadway parent never had to endure. Although not the first feature film to integrate song into its plot, The Jazz Singer (1927) was billed as the first all-singing, all-talking motion picture. This Warner-First National production featured Al Jolson as Jackie, the cantor's son, who becomes a world-wide celebrity. Jackie's father disowns his child when he discovers that his son would rather perform in nightclubs than sing in a temple. As a result, the cantor refuses to talk to his son ever again. Years later, the errant son returns to New York to assume the lead in a Broadway

show.  The elderly cantor falls ill on the show's opening night,
which also happens to be the most important Jewish Holy Day, Yom
Kippur.  Jolson is tormented by this event, but he ultimately decided to sing the Kol Nidre at the synagogue in order to please his
father.  The cantor hears his son's singing voice through an open
window, then he smiles and dies happily.

The musical numbers in The Jazz Singer were naturally tailored
for Jolson.  He mugs, cavorts, and twists in white-face and black.
But he is always performing, and he is always on stage.  Thus, there
is always a logical reason for Jolson's singing.  He is little
Jackie performing for pennies, the star on the Broadway stage, or
the substitute cantor in the synagogue.  He never breaks into song
without motivation.  This was no constraint for Jolson.  He performed as he did in night clubs or on Broadway.  However, it rep-
resented the constraints that prevented the film musical from developing beyond its initial logical assumptions, namely, that all
song and dance must be motivated.

Ironically, the musicals of the 1930's are often remembered
for the mad excesses of Busby Berkeley or the elegance of Fred Astaire and Ginger Rogers.  Despite the carefree memories of this
era, the musical seemed even more locked into the conventions that
Jolson and company had initiated.

Busby Berkeley rarely directed his own musical films in the
thirties.  More often than not Lloyd Bacon or Mervyn LeRoy directed
the "plot" sequences of the film, while Berkeley was called in for
the show-stopping finale, usually a sequence of dance numbers.
These two parts of the film were as different as night and day.

The narrative segment provided the explanation for the later musical scenes. The usual excuse for the extravagant dance numbers was
that Dick Powell was composing songs for a new musical or that James
Cagney was producing a new stage show. The same characters inhab-
ited most of the Warners' musicals; chorines, composers, lyricists,
tap-dancers, pianists, writers, producers, and choreographers. All
of these characters had a logical reason to participate in the song
and dance numbers. Rehearsals, backers' auditions, and out-of-town
tryouts provided the rationale for the musical numbers. Of all the
Warners' hits, only in Goldiggers of 1935 do Dick Powell and Ruby
Keeler sing an unmotivated song ("I'm Going Shopping With You") in
the lobby of their honeymoon hotel.

The plot sequences of these Warner Brothers' films proved sec-
ondary to the Busby Berkeley production numbers. Despite the fond
remembrances of the Berkeley extravagance, it must be remembered
that he, too, was constrained by the concept of the show, whether a
charity performance in Goldiggers of 1935, a series of musical
trailers for the new sound films in Footlight Parade, or a Broadway
show in Goldiggers of 1933 and Dames.

Habitually, the Berkeley numbers appear in the last reel of
the film. An audience is present, poised and quiet. The camera
pans the waiting audience. Cut to the stage. Suddenly the curtain
rises and the rules which limited the writers in earlier segments
of the film suddenly disappear. Even the stage itself seemingly
disappears and becomes a mythic space the size of three Grand Central Stations or several Olympic swimming pools.

The Berkeley stage demonstrates a nodding acceptance of the

rules governing the musical. But once the perfunctory curtain is raised all pretenses of reality disappear. This stage resembles no Broadway prototype, as space and scenes dissolve at a speed no Shubert Alley stagehand could ever hope to duplicate. While the actors of the first segment of the film are once again reunited in this supposed performance, they are no longer bound by the limits of logic. Ruby Keeler may divide into hundreds of identical twins in Dames, Al Jolson may fly through the heavens in Wonderbar (1934), and the laundry may dance with Joan Blondell in Dames.

The construction of Berkeley's dance numbers is not bound by the logic and reality of everyday life. More often than not, Berkeley's classic dance numbers resemble a game of free association, as the film progresses by repetitive images rather than by an orderly plot. For example, in the "Lullaby of Broadway" number from Goldiggers of 1935, the audience sees a working girl sharpening a pencil. Suddenly, as the work day ends, Berkeley shifts to the image of the organ grinder, cranking his machine in the same rhythmic motion as the girl at the pencil sharpener.

Similarly, the song lyrics might suggest an idea to Berkeley. In Harry Warren and Al Dubin's "I Only Have Eyes For You" (Dames), Dick Powell sings that "all others disappear from view" whenever he sees Ruby Keeler's face. Suddenly, all the people on a busy Manhattan street also "disappear from view" as if by magic. Likewise, the lyric continues, mentioning that "others join in song," and suddenly previously indifferent passersby begin to sing with him.

Yet, there is a sense of discomfort in these extravagant dance

sequences, as though the dance director is hindered by the know-
ledge that he must return to the reality of the stage on which the
number began.  Thus, despite these mad excesses, Berkeley always
realized that he must say goodbye to the displays of dancing pianos
or marble swimming pools and return his performers to center stage
of the pre-Broadway tryout.

Berkeley's standard method of return is the mere reversal of
the direction of the dance number, by retracing the illogical steps
that initially brought him to the fantastic configurations of his
greatest scenes.  For example, the "Lullaby of Broadway" number
ends as it began.  The fun-loving playgirl accidentally falls to
her death from the window of a celestial nightclub at the climax
of the scene.  Yet, the dance does not end at this point.  The scene
returns to the images of the woman's apartment, and her lonely cat
waiting for its milk.  The skyline of New York City reappears, and
the silhouette slowly transforms into the face of Winifred Shaw,
alone on a dark stage.  The face then floats in mid-air, and grad-
ually progresses backstage, disappearing from the view of the audience.  This sequence reverses the opening scenes of this number
and allows Berkeley to return the cast to center stage.  The curtain
falls and the audience applauds.

Thus, the screen audience is never allowed to forget that it
is watching a stage show, in which song, as a substitute for dialogue, is perfectly acceptable.  All the love songs that present
day audiences remember from the musicals of the 1930's were mainly
stage production numbers, such as "I Only Have Eyes for You."  Despite the romantic nature of such songs, the duet was the exception

rather than the rule, as an ensemble of performers were responsible for etching these songs indeliably in one's memory.

The nine Fred Astaire and Ginger Rogers films at RKO during this period would at first seem to be an exception to this trend, as duets in song and dance predominated in these motion pictures. Similarly, no one could repress Fred Astaire, as almost without notice, in living rooms, bedrooms, or city streets, he would unexplicably break into song and dance, and, if Ginger were present, she would join him.

Yet, despite this supposed freedom to break into song and dance, the Astaire and Rogers films were always hindered by excessive plot devices which attempted to rationalize such acts which would seem highly unusual in the everyday world. Thus Fred was invariably cast as a hoofer or a bandleader in these films. Such a device appeared necessary to explain Astaire's love for music and his penchant for dancing at the most inopportune moments. Interestingly, while Astaire was cast as a talented hoofer in the film version of The Gay Divorcee, the stage versions in both New York and London featured him as a noted novelist. On stage, no complicated plot device was found necessary to explain Astaire's continual dancing. Of all the RKO films, only in one, Carefree (1938), did Astaire not portray a musician or a dancer. Here he played Tony Flagg, psychiatrist. But even then he must rationalize his choreographic expertise by announcing to Ginger: "I always wanted to be a dancer. Psychiatry showed me I was wrong."

Ginger was never hampered by the same constraints. While part of the time she appears as a dance instructress (Swingtime), a pro-

fessional entertainer (<u>Carefree</u>), or a former vaudeville partner
of Astaire (<u>Follow the Fleet</u>), she is also presented in other films
as a woman of breeding who surprisingly possesses a unique ability
to follow the master's lead in dance and song.

Once these conventions were established, the writers, composers, and lyricists of the Astaire-Rogers films faced the dilemma
of integrating these now classic dance routines into the musical.
Mark Sandrich, who directed five of these films, reputedly hated
unmotivated dance numbers and avoided them like the plague. By way
of comparison, consider two of Fred and Ginger's classic routines,
"The Carioca" and "The Continental," just one year apart. In <u>Fly-</u>
<u>ing Down To Rio</u> (1933), directed by Thornton Freeland, Fred and
Ginger portray a band musician and a vocalist on tour in Brazil.
Fred lures the band leader to the Carioca Casino to hear the native
rhythms which are proving considerably more popular than the North
American melodies. The band members are both surprised and appalled
by the sensuous nature of the Latin dance, "The Carioca." Fred and
Ginger watch for a few minutes in a state of shock until Ginger
snaps: "We'll show them a thing or three," and they take to the
dance floor.

This reveals a marked contrast with "The Continental" number
from <u>The Gay Divorcee</u>, directed by Sandrich in 1934. No longer do
Fred and Ginger view the latest dance craze and immediately join
the natives and outshine them at their own game. Here, Ginger por-
trays a potential divorcee, about to be trapped with a correspon-
dent in a seaside hotel, so she can rid herself of her unwanted
husband. Fred complicates the situation by pursuing Ginger to her

hotel room. The gigolo prevents Fred and Ginger from leaving lest they sabotage his scheme. As a result, they hide in the bedroom where, hearing the music from the hotel night club, they pretend to dance. In reality, however, they perch two cut-out paper dolls atop the revolving turntables of the record player. Fred shines a bright light on the tiny dancing images, and their six-foot revolving shadows present the illusion of a dancing couple, thus fooling the gigolo. Only then are Fred and Ginger free to escape from the apartment and begin "The Continental." Thus, even in the carefree Astaire and Rogers musicals, plot considerations and the importance of logic came to overpower the potential freedom of the musical genre.

Ironically, these musicals which adhered to the basic realities of everyday life became the most popular and most remembered films of the 1930's, while those that attempted to expand or deny logical expectations were often dismal failures. These less successful, but often more ambitious, films hearkened back to the fantastic musical world created by the Frenchman René Clair. Clair's musical films were never populated with the backstage performers so common to Hollywood films. Clair's world presented common folk, bums, tailors, streetsingers, bartenders, and working men and women and allowed them all to be capable of song. The open nature of this assumption is revealed by the fact that Clair even permitted the non-human beings, such as flowers and animals to join in song in A Nous La Liberté. In Clair's films, music and song are accepted features of reality. There is no surprise if anyone (or anything) breaks into song. In this manner, Clair expanded the musical com-

edy tradition that had been inherited from Broadway, and suggested
that the musical film, a hybrid form, might break all the limita-
tions that the static Broadway stage had imposed.  The camera might
accomplish scene changes in a fraction of a second, and as a result,
the musical film need not be rooted in the linear and chronological
progression of the Broadway musical.

Few Hollywood musicals of this era recognized this potential.
Lorenz Hart argued that "the ideal musical comedy of the pictures
would kill the musical comedy of the stage."  Yet, he had no fears
that he would lose his main source of livelihood thanks to the pa-
rochial vision of film executives.  He criticized the irony that
"studios take stage writers to write stage stuff for the screen."
He tried to counter this expectation, but producers thought he and
Richard Rodgers were "blotto."

Hart attempted to pioneer a new form of film musical, but his
efforts were continually frustrated.  While other musical comedy
writers, such as Irving Berlin, devoted most of their attention to
the story conferences when they arrived in Hollywood, Hart was con-
sistently on the set and sticking his nose into all aspects of feature production.  He was most fascinated by the editing process,
and, as a result, believed that musicals "should be written for the
camera," and not be mere duplications of Broadway stage successes.

One of Rodgers and Hart's best film collaborations, Love Me
Tonight, directed by Rouben Mamoulian, reveals this new relation-
ship of music and song to the progression of the film.  Maurice
Chevalier, a tailor, sings "Isn't It Romantic?" in his tiny shop.
A Customer picks up the melody and sings quietly as he leaves the

shop and enters a taxi. The cab driver hears the tune, and, he,
too, begins singing. The song thus travels through the city as
different people are captivated by the clever melody. Eventually,
a troop of soldiers latch on to the melody, convert it to a marching rhythm, and carry it throughout the countryside. Finally, Jeanette MacDonald, at her distant castle, hears the song and begins
to sing. In this instance, the song has emerged as an editing device, allowing Jeanette MacDonald to be introduced to the audience
and her relationship to the tailor established. The music is thus
used to carry the film forward, and all necessity of dialogue is
eliminated.

Rodgers and Hart also attempted to pioneer yet another musical
form--rhythmic dialogue--in their first Hollywood films. This less
successful effort was based on the assumption that there should be
no clear division between the dialogue and musical portions of the
film. As a result, a rhythmic musical dialogue, almost a song,
emerged. At times the rhythm for the dialogue would be established
by a dominant thematic sound, as in Hot Heiress, where the noise
of the riveter's drill press supplied the pace and rhythm for the
film's opening dialogue. At other times, as in Fools for Scandal
(1938) or Love Me Tonight, this rhythmic patter would begin unexpectedly and be dropped just as suddenly. The themes of this rhythmic, but not always rhyming, dialogue was often commonplace. The
following example from Love Me Tonight illustrates the pacing and
brevity of this format. The doctor states to Jeanette MacDonald:
Now, my dear, remove your dress.
My what?
Your dress.
Is it necessary?

Very.

Rodgers and Hart had only one brief opportunity to expand the
concept of rhythmic dialogue to an entire film, Hallelujah, I'm a
Bum (1933), directed by Lewis Milestone.  Unfortunately, Al Jolson,
deprived of his typical mugging and eye-rolling, appeared restricted
in the title role.  The failure of this film and others which ex-
perimented with rhythmic dialogue soured Rodgers and Hart on Hollywood, and, as a result, their later films of the 1940's abandoned
this concept and merely duplicated the accepted stage conventions
of the Broadway shows.

Hallelujah, I'm A Bum failed for yet another reason.  It was
one of the few musicals to tackle the Great Depression as its main
theme.  The film was populated by a contingent of tramps who roamed
the streets of New York.  Some, such as Harry Langdon, even voiced
thoughts of social revolution.

Other musical films mentioned the Great Depression only in
passing.  In Goldiggers of 1933, the production which featured the
classic song, "We're in the Money," had to be suspended because the
producers could not find the backing for their show.  Otherwise,
few musical films acknowledged the presence of the traumatic state
of the American economy.  It is for this reason that historians
have considered the musical of the 1930's as an escapist delight.
It is argued that only in the darkened movie theatre could the members of the audience find relief from the problems of the everyday
world.  Ironically, musical production hit new lows during the first
years of the Great Depression.  Not until Roosevelt was inaugurated
and the New Deal well under way did the musical form become revived

in popularity.

It is this phenomena which seems most ironic. The form of the musicas film in the 1930's was dependent on the logic of the real world, however, in matters of content it was not. Thus, the musical film remained curiously divorced from the divisions affecting American society during this traumatic age. This division, however, was not to last for long. As the coming of World War II revived the flagging American economy, the mobilization for war also revived the musical comedy, giving it a definite commitment to the reality of the society it had previously ignored.

## II.  THE MUSICAL GOES TO WAR

By 1939 the Hollywood musical comedy seemed on the road to ex-
tinction.  Warner Brothers, the king of the Depression musicals,
quietly allowed Busby Berkeley and Dick Powell's contracts to lapse.
Irving Berlin, Ira Gershwin, and Rodgers and Hart returned to their
native Broadway, and Harry Warren, who created the music for the
Berkeley extravaganzas, was suddenly without work.  Yet, the changing international situation and the American entry into the war
abruptly changed this dismal outlook.  Musical comedies began to
appear in rapid profusion, and production reached an all-time high
of seventy-six films by 1944.

The conventional explanation for this surge of film musicals
was once again the desire for "escape."  War-time audiences, tired
of depressing news from the European front and rationing at home,
turned to the fantasy world of musical comedy for immediate relief.
Indeed, social and cultural historians of the period, such as Geoffrey Perrett and Richard P. Lingeman, use the increase in the number of Hollywood musicals as a measure of the public desire for
escape.[3]

Unfortunately, few of these historians appear to have seen the
majority of film musicals of this period.  The Wizard of Oz, Meet
Me In St. Louis, and Yolanda and the Thief, exercises in fantasy
or nostalgia, were the exception rather than the rule.  Actually,
most Hollywood musicals displayed patriotic motives and embraced
wartime themes.  As early as 1940, the stars of the previous decade
were already dressed in khaki in such musicals as Navy Blues or
You're in the Army Now, both produced by Warner Brothers.  Fred

Astaire abandoned his top hat and tails for the duration, and became a member of the RAF for The Story of Vernon and Irene Castle
(1939), a draftee for You'll Never Get Rich (1941), and a fighter
pilot for The Sky's the Limit (1943). Pure escapism was thus the
furthest thing from the film musicals' intentions.

While the producers, directors, stars, and screenwriters com-
mitted themselves to the winning of the war, the composers and lyricists of these new musicals appeared somewhat bewildered by the
swiftly changing events on the international scene. How could
their music help the war effort? President Roosevelt had given
music a lofty position in the mobilization for war:

> Music can help to inspire a fervor for the spiritual values
> of our way of life, and thus strengthen democracy against those
> forces which would subjugate and enthrall mankind.[4]

Despite the President's enthusiasm, songwriters remained at a loss
as government agencies harshly criticized their initial efforts at
wartime music.

Lyman Bryson, head of the Music Committee of the Office of War
Information, complained constantly about the latest popular tunes.
He found contemporary ballads too saccharine, noting that current
war songs "were just love songs with a once-over-lightly war background." Lyricists merely slipped a soldier into their songs, but
as Bryson explained, "it was still boy-meets-girl stuff." Bryson
also resisted the unbridled optimism of the first rash of war songs.
With such ditties as "We'll Meet Again," "The White Cliffs of Dov-
er," and "Blue Skies Are Just Around the Corner," he feared that
the listening audience would be lulled into a sense of security.[5]

Another OWI spokesman explained that the best war song thus

far had been "Der Fuher's Face," which gave Hitler a resounding Bronx cheer in a Donald Duck short. He explained: "Maybe this new ditty isn't exactly the suavest thing, but it's certainly right down to the ground. We want to give Hitler a more audible razzing than we've been doing. We've concentrated too much on hating the Japs when our number one menace is still Schickelgruber, the (Charlie) Chaplin of Berlin."[6]

The ultimate goal became the manufacture of "Freedom Songs." After an analysis of Goebbels' use of music for propaganda purposes, the OWI urged songwriters to "wave the flag and shout Hallelujah for all conquered and oppressed peoples."

If the goals of war music were so clearly marked, why the confusion and why the difficulty? Why were there not more songs of a martial nature during the first years of the war? The OWI again supplied the rationale: "The one-step and two-step of 1917 made possible a host of spirited martial songs such as "Over There," "K-K-K-Katy," "Hinky Dinky Parlez-Vous," "Howya Gonna Keep 'Em Down on the Farm," and a host of others." The major problem was that the 1940 audience preferred the fox-trot or swing.[7] Furthermore, the OWI argued, the active public of World War I had turned passive, since the radio partially supplanted the need to attend dances in order to hear the latest music.

The OWI seemed pressed for a solution to this dilemma. There was talk of asking "Fred Astaire or Arthur Murray to invent a fashionable new rip-snorting patriotic style of stepping that would span the bridge from 1918 to 1942. In this manner we must become more oompah and militaristic." The discussions with these dancing greats

never came to fruition, but the conversations of the OWI and memories of the glorious music of the past war seemed to prod songwriters into action.

In the first years of the war, movie musicals continually
looked back to the successful manner in which earlier songwriters
had tackled the mobilization of society in time of war. A cursory
glance at the musical films of the period might lead one to assume
that George M. Cohan was the most prolific film composer during
World War II, instead of Harold Arlen or Irving Berlin. Yankee
Doodle Dandy was merely the most prominent example. MGM bought the
Cohan play Little Nellie Kelly and refurbished it into a Judy Garland musical. Judy and Mickey Rooney portrayed Faye Templeton and
George M. Cohan in Babes on Broadway (1941), singing such Cohan hits
as "Yankee Doodle Dandy" and "Over There." "Over There" also graced
Four Jills and a Jeep (1944), and "Give My Regards To Broadway"
appeared in the Great American Broadcast (1941). Actually, Cohan,
who had just emerged from retirement to appear in Rodgers and Hart's
Broadway musical I'd Rather Be Right, had little to do with the revival of his songs. His musical numbers fulfilled two important
functions. First of all, they supplied the patriotic war songs
that Washington claimed were the utmost necessity. Secondly, the
use of old songs took the pressure off Hollywood studios to develop
a stable of composers and lyricists comparable to that of the 1930's
within a short period of time. Indeed, by 1939, when the musical
reached its nadir, Hollywood dismissed the popular songwriters of
the 1930's and was unable to fill the gap at such short notice.
Not until 1942 was a new generation of Hollywood composers operating

at full capacity.

Cohan was not alone in Hollywood's rummaging through composers' trunks from bygone days. Among the songs admired by the OWI, "K-K-K Katy" reappeared in Tin Pan Alley (1940). For Me And My Gal, the story of a vaudeville troupe during World War I, revived "How You Gonna Keep 'Em Down on the Farm," as well as "What Are You Going to Do to Help the Boys?" for the trio of Judy Garland, George Murphy, and Gene Kelly.

Perhaps the most fortuitous trunk rummaging was by Irving Berlin. He recalled his experience in the camp show Yip Yip Yaphank in 1917, and remembered that he had written a patriotic finale for the show. The song was so patriotic that Berlin felt that it might be a trifle excessive for the all-soldier show. The song remained unpublished until 1938. In that year Berlin returned from London after the Munich Pact and felt compelled to write a patriotic song, but he composed nothing that satisfied him. He remembered the old song that he had written and revised it slightly, giving it to Kate Smith to sing. "God Bless America" became one of the all-time successful songs of modern popular music. Berlin established a trust fund for the Boy and Girl Scouts of America from the royalties of the song. Within one year the Scouts received over $50,000. The Scouts were chosen as recipients because, as Herbert Bayard Swope explained, "their completely non-sectarian work was calculated to best promote unity of mind and patriotism, two sentiments that are inherent in the song itself." Even both the Democrats and the Republicans wanted to use the song for their convention theme in 1940.[8]

Other Irving Berlin World War I hits were also revived. He performed "Oh How I Hate to Get Up in the Morning," in both the stage and film version of This Is the Army (Warner Brothers, 1943), the World War II successor of Yip Yip Yaphank.[9] Rumor has it that an electrician overheard Berlin's rendition of the song and commented to a friend: "If the guy who wrote this song could hear the way this guy is singing it, he'd roll over in his grave." "Mandy," written in 1917, also found its way into the film version of This Is The Army, as did the classic "God Bless America."[10]

While most composers and lyricists looked to World War I for inspiration, others looked wherever they could find appropriate songs. Harold Arlen's "God's Country," a patriotic gem from a cynical Broadway musical Hooray For What? (1937), reappeared in Mickey Rooney and Judy Garland's Babes In Arms (1939). This hymn glorified the United States, where "smiles are broader and freedoms greater, and every man is his own director." On a contemporary note Mickey and Judy added: "All of you who think it's so much easier to give n; Count your blessings in this wondrous land we live in."

In this revival of past songs much of the original meaning was ost as lyrics had to be updated for present day audiences. Perhaps he most humorous incident concerned the patriotic sounding Gershwin une "Strike Up the Band." Despite the seemingly contemporary flavor f the song, it actually originated in a 1927 musical of the same ame which closed out of town. Morrie Ryskind softened the original eorge S. Kaufman libretto which was a vicious satire on international politics, the League of Nations, and war itself. This less cerbic version of Strike Up the Band reopened on Broadway in 1930.

At this time "Strike Up the Band" was an anti-military march:

> We fought in nineteen-seventeen,
> Rum-ta-ta tum-tum-tum!
> And drove the tyrant from the scene,
> Rum-ta-ta tum-tum-tum.
>
> We're in a bigger better war
> For your patriotic pastime.
> We don't know what we're fighting for--
> But we didn't know the last time!

By 1940, this viewpoint seemed highly impolitic for the film

version. Ira Gershwin revised the lyric for this pre-Pearl Harbor

musical to read:

> We hope there'll be no other war,
> But if we're forced into one--
> The flag that we'll be fighting for
> Is the Red and White and Blue one!

The finale of the 1940 film version of <u>Strike Up the Band</u> ends with

Mickey Rooney and Judy Garland superimposed against the flag for

which they would gladly fight.

The song underwent further revisions as the war progressed. A

1942 version assumed a more vehement tone:

> Again the Hun is at the gate
> For his customary pastime,
> Again he sings his Hymn of Hate--
> But we'll make this time the last time.

Recently Ira Gershwin voiced the hope that this later edition had

gone out of print.[11]

Despite a general acceptance of the World War I approach to

patriotic music in the first years of the war, this procedure even-

tually became self-defeating. After all, trunks have a bottom.

The <u>New York Times</u> began to criticize the "Proustian spirit that

has been brooding over the creative acres of Hollywood."[12] The

Music War Committee (MWC), an independent group of Broadway, Hollywood, and popular song composers and lyricists reached similar conclusions. The executive committee of the MWC argued: "Forget about 6/8 tempos and World War I. Today's songwriters should stop writing for the 1917 war. They sould adapt their patriotic and military ideas of the 1943 pattern of show business and showmanship."

The MWC's instructions to songwriters amounted to a complete reversal of the OWI approach to wartime melodies, which seemed opportune at a time when the OWI had been deprived of all domestic operations by the U. S. Congress. First of all, the MWC urged its members to assume a positive approach in their writing. "Forget the frustration of the 'Maybe I will lose my girl' or 'Is my girl back home two timing me' songs," they argued. Similarly, the MWC suggested that the songwriters not fret about the "lights going out all over Europe, but to sing of the victory to come." Oscar Hammerstein II earned harsh criticism on this point. The MWC believed that he should not have written "The Last Time I Saw Paris," the academy award winner from Lady Be Good in 1941. A more optimistic outlook would have led to "The Next Time I See Paris."[13]

Hopefully, this new approach to songwriting would produce successful World War II songs, instead of mere reprises of World War I ditties. Irving Berlin commented that the "Over Here" of World War II had yet to be written. "It will be written and when it comes you will know it. Maybe orchestra leaders don't like to play war tunes, but they'll play the big hit when they get it."[14]

In many respects, Irving Berlin was the leader in the search for relevant and contemporary songs. Although he revived his World War I song hits on many occasions, he also possessed a keen sensi-

tivity to current wartime events.  Although there are no classics
of a "God Bless America" caliber here, Berlin's songs for the American government revealed that music might play an important role
in the war effort.

Secretary of the Treasury Morgenthau asked Berlin to write a
song which would encourage the sale of war bonds.  The resultant
tune, "Any Bonds Today," was freed from all copyright or royalty
restrictions so that the "song may be used by anyone at anytime and
place" and thus increase bond sales.[15]  Even the Australian government adopted the song for use in their war austerity loan campaign.
Berlin followed soon after with "Angels of Mercy," the official Red
Cross song.[16]  Again at Morgenthau's request Berlin presented "I
Paid My Income Tax Today" to the U. S. government:

    I PAID MY INCOME TAX TODAY
    A thousand planes to bomb Berlin
    They'll all be paid for and I chipped in
    That cert'nly makes me feel okay
    Ten thousand more and that ain't hay!
    We must pay for the war somehow
    Uncle Sam was worried, but he isn't now.
    I PAID MY INCOME TAX TODAY.[17]

Berlin's first attempt to coordinate a patriotic song in a film
musical came with Holiday Inn (1942) directed by Mark Sandrich.
Bing Crosby's cozy little inn opened only on national holidays, and
July fourth provided an appropriate time for a song celebrating American virtues.  The "Freedom Song" was dedicated to ".all people
who strived to be free" and the song provided a musical listing of
all the freedoms proclaimed in the Bill of Rights.  While the lyrics
made no direct reference to the current war effort, the accompanying
visual montage supplied the necessary link.  A backdrop behind Bing
displayed the Statue of Liberty, planes and battleships, General

MacArthur, and FDR. The final image is that of the American flag. A star-spangled curtain is lowered and the song is ended.[18]

While the "Freedom Song" from Holiday Inn directly considers the war issue, "White Christmas" is mentioned more often as the ideal wartime song. One critic noted: "It was indeed a song in the wartime mood, a bit sad and yearning--an emotion with which both homesick soldiers and civilians could identify."[19] Ironically, Berlin never intended the song to have such a meaning: "It came out at a time when we were at war and it became a peace song in wartime, nothing I ever intended."[20]

While Berlin might compose a song as current as the daily newspaper, composers and lyricists of film musicals faced a certain difficulty. Songs composed for films might not reach a viewing audience for months, and, as a result, the topicality strived for in Berlin's government songs was usually impossible. Berlin himself hated this lag between composition and audience approval, and, for this reason, claimed that he preferred Broadway to Hollywood musicals. Despite this lack of immediacy, film musicals attempted to turn their attention from World War I to World War II, and, by 1943, try to explain the contemporary world situation to American film audiences.

While the Music War Committee urged its members to take an optimistic stance, events from Europe bouyed the spirits of composers and lyricists. By the end of 1943 Mussolini had fallen, Allied troops were on the attack in Europe, and the war in North Africa seemed over. At last there seemed to be a basis for hope. The songs of this latter period of the war reveal dreams of a brighter

day to come in the Hollywood musical. Harold Arlen converted from
"Blues in the Night" (1941) to the perky "Ac-cent-tchu-ate the Pos-
itive" for Here Come the Waves. Ira Gershwin and E. Y. Harburg
combined their lyrical talents to urge the world to "Make Way for
Tomorrow" in Cover Girl. Ethel Merman raised her ample voice in
Stage Door Canteen (1943) to sing a prophetic "Marching Through
Berlin," as though the war had already been won:

    We'll be singing Hallelujah
    Marching through Berlin
    The Devil put on a different face
    Came to plague the human race
    We'll put that old devil back in his place
    Sing Hallelujah!

Although the war had brought long separations and had disrupted
the romances of countless young men and women, even the tone of the
romantic ballads seemed to soften. In the early days of the war,
these songs expressed anxiety and concern, as soldiers worried
whether their women would wait for them, and the women worried about
their men returning alive. "Don't Sit Under the Apple Tree With
Anyone Else But Me" was appropriately one of the most popular songs
of 1942. A year later mooning hymns to a distant love seemed to
be taken less seriously. Perhaps the best example of this trend
was Ray Bolger's rendition of "The Girl I Love To Leave Behind" in
Stage Door Canteen. The Lorenz Hart lyric describes a young woman
who is "less refined than Lou Costello:"

    She has hair that she wears like Veronica Lake
    So that fifty per cent of her is blind.
    She is known to her daddy as "mother's mistake,"
    She's the girl I long to leave behind.

In keeping with this optimistic trend the army and the armed
forces experienced a glorification which has never been equalled.

Virtually every branch of the fighting forces received a song from noted songwriters which extolled their virtues. Berlin's This Is the Army praised the men on the ground and the men in the air ("American Eagles"), but then self-consciously added "How About a Cheer for the Navy?" as though he realized that he had forgotten something of great importance. Cole Porter also contributed "Glide, Glider, Glide" as well as "Sailors of the Sky." Musicals of the period claimed "It's a Swelluva Helluva Life in the Army" (Hey, Rookie). The hero of these military organizations was the American soldier, a very special breed of man, as Dennis Morgan explained in Hollywood Canteen:

> You can always tell a Yank,
> He's the kind of guy who's
> Always ready to drive a tank to save democracy
> And save the world from tyranny.

Interestingly, the aura of hope pervaded those songs which concerned events occuring away from the home front. However, as the songs approached subject matter closer to home, the optimism seemed to fade as if the daily sacrifices that each citizen made for the war effort seemed to stand in the way of the romantic ideals of the songwriters. Somehow "Co-operate with Your Air Raid Warden" (Priorities on Parade) or "He Loved Me Til the All-Clear Came" (Star Spangled Rhythm) lacked the glamor of the songs which preached optimism in the course of the war. Love no longer seemed as easy in the minds of lyricists as rationing, government bureaucratic hassles, shortages, and the black market pervaded the world of musical comedy films dealing with domestic life.

Betty Davis explained the difficulties of yet another curious shortage in Thank Your Lucky Stars. She wanders lonely through the

streets of a small town, and stares wistfully at a huge Victory
poster with pictures of virile representatives of the Army, Navy,
and Marines. She is alone now, because "there is no secret lover
that the draft board didn't discover." Now all the men "are either
too young or too old." The Arthur Schwartz-Frank Loesser song presents Bette with a strange alternative; she must date men below the
age of puberty, or men so old that she must carry them around the
dance floor.

Thus the songs of the wartime period provide a vivid tableau
of life on the home front. While songs of "escape" may have char-
acterized the first years of the war, musical comedy composers eventually turned their attention to the events at hand, and expressed
the contemporary situation in song. Thus, composers and lyricists
of the wartime musicals also displayed a definite commitment to the
wartime effort. As a result, the so-called "escapist" musical of
the early 1940's actually reflected changing wartime society and
encouraged patriotic support of the American soldier. Thus, in
song and in theme, the musical escaped its frivolous image in a time
of national emergency. When the war ended, the musical lost its
brief sense of commitment, and returned to its hitherto sanctioned
role as a relief for the tired businessman and an escape from contemporary life.

## III. THE MODERN MUSICAL

The Hollywood musical, like the rest of society, had to demobilize after World War II and adjust to post-war realities. The musical film had reached its peak during 1944, when more than seventy were released. However, with the end of the war, the popularity of the musical declined precipitously. By 1950 only twenty-two musicals were produced. As the 1960's and 1970's arrived, the number of musicals appearing each year could be counted on the fingers of one hand.

Part of the reason for the decline in the number of musicals produced by Hollywood can be attributed to their mounting expenses. Busby Berkeley extravaganzas would have been impossible in the 1950's and 1960's. Interestingly, whenever Berkeley directed a film after 1945, his films displayed an unusual intimate touch. Gone were the chorus girls of The Goldiggers series, as were the fabulous Warner Brothers sets.

The money problem led to continuing difficulties for the post-war musical. Occasionally, an expensive musical might triumph, as did The Sound of Music (1965) and West Side Story (1961). The critical and financial successes of these films would thus spawn other musical extravaganzas, such as Star (1968) and At Long Last Love (1975), which once again would close Hollywood pursestrings after critical pans and miniscule box office receipts. Thus, since 1950, the successful musical has been the exception rather than the rule, and no return to a musical film cycle comparable to the early depression years or the era of World War II, appears in sight.

The unwillingness to finance new musical films has also led

to a limitation of the experimentation that made the fledgling musical such a success. As a result, Hollywood producers have tended to play it safe in recent years by producing tested properties-- Broadway musicals. The musical created primarily for the screen has thus decreased in recent years, as adaptations of Broadway shows have come to dominate the musical film.

These Broadway shows have been adapted for the screen without substantial change. Usually the Broadway stars will be substituted by a hot Hollywood property in order to boost the film's chances for success. For this reason, Barbra Streisand replaced Carol Channing in Hello Dolly and Julie Andrews was passed over in favor of Audrey Hepburn in My Fair Lady. With the exception of personnel shifts, the musical is usually transfered to the screen unchanged. The songs remain the same, as does the choreography. The latter may present more dancers than the stage version, but the motions remain similar. Gene Kelly's Hello Dolly followed the Broadway original with utmost fidelity in these respects.

Thus, as Hollywood produces fewer and fewer original musicals, there are fewer chances for creative experimentation. Additionally, there is a question of the theme or format of these original musicals. Hollywood seemed to be unable to discover new directions for the musical in the post-war era. Ironically, while most American servicemen had returned home by 1945, the Hollywood musical continued with soldier and sailor themes for almost ten more years.

MGM produced On the Town in 1949, and presented Frank Sinatra, Gene Kelly, and Jules Munshin as sailors on leave in New York City. Interestingly, while the show had a topical quality when produced

on Broadway during the war, the film seemed anachronistic during
peacetime. Lloyd Bacon directed Call Me Mister for Twentieth-Cen-
tury Fox which presents Dan Dailey as a G. I. returning from Japan
after World War II. MGM was still demobilizing as late as 1955 with
It's Always Fair Weather, which begins with three army chums (Kelly,
Dailey, and Michael Kidd) returning from the European front.

The end of the war thus signalled a demise to a favorite theme
of the movie musical. The war could no longer be used as a major
element of the plot structure of the musical film. Some studios,
most notably MGM, sought new forms and themes for the musical during
the 1950's, while most studios relied on Broadway originals. Perhaps this accounts for the fond remembrance of the Arthur Freed
musicals during this decade. The Freed Unit produced excellent
musicals, to be sure, but compared to the output of other studios,
they looked even better. As a result, whenever the musical film
of the 1950's is discussed, it is often only the MGM films that are
seriously considered.

Arthur Freed began his producing career at MGM when the musical had reached its height. He co-produced The Wizard of Oz with
Mervyn LeRoy in 1939, and soon began producing Metro's most successful musical films--the Judy Garland - Mickey Rooney series, Cabin
in the Sky, Meet Me In St. Louis, The Ziegfeld Follies, and For Me
and My Gal. He resurrected the MGM musical by bringing talent from
without--the young Vincente Minnelli and Gene Kelly ·from Broadway,
Busby Berkeley from Warner Brothers, as well as developing a stable
of new composers and lyricists.

Unlike the majority of producers who packaged successful musi-

cals during the war, Freed continued his successful career throughout the 1950's. His films won countless Academy Awards during this
period and gave the MGM musical new life during the post-war period.
A list of these films includes the best produced in Hollywood: An
American in Paris, Gigi, Singin' in the Rain, The Band Wagon, Show-
boat, and The Harvey Girls. The success of these films can be attributed to Freed's encouragement of creativity and originality
among his stable of musical artists. By continually producing successful musicals, Freed remained untouched by the problems that
bothered other companies. However, as the money crunch eventually
affected MGM, Freed lost his independence by 1960. Until 1970,
when Freed finally left MGM, he was unable to produce a single film.
As a result, his creative department was dissolved, and the talent
drifted elsewhere. Although MGM dedicated That's Entertainment
(1974) to the memory of Arthur Freed, it had effectively given the
musical the death blow by the studio's refusal to allow him to con-
tinue his operations.[21]

Since 1960 there has been little experimentation within the
realm of the Hollywood musical. With such musicals as Star, Funny
Lady, Lady Sings the Blues, and At Long Last Love, Hollywood has
looked to the past for inspiration by providing backstage musicals
peppered with period melodies. A few musicals, however, have looked
to the present day for inspiration and have proved surprisingly popular. Whether adaptations of Broadway shows or original productions, such "rock musicals" as Jesus Christ Superstar, Godspell,
and Tommy have encorporated modern music, dance, and themes into
their format. However, at present it appears that this cycle has

also been laid to rest, and no future productions of this nature have been planned.

Thus the Hollywood musical remains in search of a form and a theme.  It is ironic that the popularity of That's Entertainment has led to a sequel, That's Entertainment Too!, another compendium of scenes from MGM musicals, but otherwise has not been channeled into a desire for new film musicals.  As of this writing, the Hollywood musical appears dead as no new films of this genre appear on production schedules.  The prohibitive cost, the decline of audience interest, and the lack of new and creative formats present formidable barriers to anyone wishing to produce a musical film today.  Hopefully, the pages of this book will rekindle an interest in Hollywood's unique genre--the musical film.

# NOTES

1. Mervyn LeRoy, interview, _Today Show_, March 22, 1974.

2. _New York Times_, October 29, 1939.

3. See: Richard R. Lingeman, _Don't You Know There's a War On?_ (New York, 1970), 218; Geoffrey Perrett, _Days of Sadness, Years of Triumph_ (Baltimore, 1974), 384. See also: Timothy E. Scheurer, "The Aesthetics of Form and Convention in the Movie Musical," _Journal of Popular Film_ (Fall, 1974), 307-324.

4. _New York Times_, June 19, 1941.

5. For discussions of the OWI, see: Sidney Weinberg, "What to Tell America: the Writers' Quarrel with the OWI," _Journal of American History_ (June, 1968); Gregory D. Black and Clayton R. Koppes, "OWI Goes to the Movies: The Bureau of Intelligence's Criticism of Hollywood, 1942-43," _Prologue_ (Spring, 1974), 44-59.

6. Variety, October 7, 1942, 2.

7. _Ibid._

8. _New York Times_, July 11, 14, 1940.

9. See: _Variety_, October 2, 1940 for the origin of _Yip, Yip, Yaphank_.

10. For the origins of this show, see: Max Wilk, _They're Playing Our Song_ (New York, 1973), 286-288.

11. Ira Gershwin, _Lyrics on Several Occasions_ (New York, 1973), 224-227; and, Robert Kimball and Alfred Simon, _The Gershwins_ (New York, 1973), 119.

12. Variety, May 5, 1940.

13. _Ibid._, May 26, 1943.

14. _New York Times Magazine_, June 6, 1943, 31.

15. _New York Times_, June 9, 1941.

16. _Ibid._, November 4, 1941.

17. _Ibid._, January 14, 1942.

18. For a discussion of _Holiday Inn_, see: Stanley Green and Burt Goldblatt, _Starring Fred Astaire_ (New York, 1973), 230-243.

19. Lingeman, _Don't You Know There's a War On?_, 214.

20. Michael Freedland, _Irving Berlin_ (New York, 1974), 148.

21. See: Hugh Fordin, _The World of Entertainment_ (New York, 1975).

THE SONGS

3

7

8

10

14

15

17

24

I'd Be Lost Without You, 613
I'd Do Anything, 734
I'd Do It Again, 380
I'd Do It For You, 861
I'd Know You Anywhere, 1178
I'd Leave My Happy Home For You, 704, 1008
I'd Like To Baby You, 1
I'd Like To Be A Bee In Your Boudoir, 857
I'd Like To Be A Happy Bride, 101
I'd Like To Make You Happy, 367
I'd Like To See Some Mo' Of Samoa, 277
I'd Like To Set You To Music, 429
I'd Like To Take You Out Dreaming, 268
I'd Love To Be A Talking Picture Queen, 713
I'd Love To Know You Better, 793
I'd Love To Make Love To You, 998
I'd Love To Play A Love Scene Opposite You, 605
I'd Love To Take Orders From You, 892
I'd Rather Be Blue, 313
I'd Rather Be Blue Over You Than Be Happy With Somebody Else, 695
I'd Rather Be Me, 754
I'd Rather Call You Baby, 605
I'd Rather Have A Pal Than A Gal,--Anytime, 339
I'd Rather Lead A Band, 293
I'd Rather Listen To Your Eyes, 892
Ida, 489, 260
If, 1151
If A Girl Isn't Pretty, 313
If A Were A Little Pond Lily, 673
If All The World Were Paper, 581
If Ever I Would Leave You, 139
If He Cared, 230
If He Walked Into My Life, 618
If I Could Be With You One Hour Tonight, 621
If I Could Go Back, 590
If I Could Learn To Love, 900

If I Didn't Have You, 709
If I Feel This Way Tomorrow Then It's Love, 993
If I Had A Dozen Hearts, 984
If I Had A Girl Like You, 166
If I Had A Million Dollars, 1100
If I Had A Talking Picture Of You, 70, 1005
If I Had My Druthers, 574
If I Had My Way, 474, 1002
If I Had You, 1176
If I Knew, 856
If I Knew You Better, 396
If I Love Again, 314
If I Love You A Mountain, 339
If I Loved You, 155
If I Only Had A Heart (A Brain), (The Nerve), 1164
If I Put My Heart In A Song, 671
If I Should Lose You, 852
If I Steal A Kiss, 540
If I Were A Bell, 376
If I Were A Rich Man, 273
If I Were A Traveling Salesman, 203
If I Were Adam And You Were Eve, 883
If I Were King, 1125
If I Were You, 736
If I'm Day Dreaming, Don't Wake Me Up Too Soon, 859
If I'm Lucky, 475
If It Isn't Pain Then It Isn't Love, 1021
If It's A Dream, 236
If It's A Dream, Don't Wake Me, 646
If It's All The Same To You, 579
If It's You, 79
If Love Remains, 1155
If Mama Was Married, 377
If Mother Could See Us Now, 341
If My Friends Could See Me Now, 1010
If Somebody Builds A Better Mousetrap, 284
If Something Doesn't Happen Soon, 247
If The Rain's Got To Fall, 378
If The Shoe Fits You Wear It, 510

31

43

Message From The Man In The
    Moon, A, 223
Mets Ton Joli Jupon, 917
Mexican Jumping Beat, 862
Mexicana, 653
Mi Vida, 153
Mia Cara, 78
Miami, 663
Midas Touch, The, 65
Midnight At The Masquerade, 691
Midsummer Madness, 191
Midsummer's Eve, 948
Milady, 675
Military Life, 137
Military Man, 786
Military Polka, 1147
Milkman Keep Those Bottles
    Quiet, 116
Million Dollars Worth Of Dreams,
    A, 84
Million Miles Away From The
    Door, 757
Million Miles From Manhattan, A,
    631
Mimi, 604
Mimi From Tahiti, 824
Mind If I Make Love To You, 417
Mine Alone, 465, 1030
Mine To Love, 1029
Minnie From Trinidad, 1185
Minnie The Moocher, 73
Minnie's In The Money, 319
Minstrel Days, 442
Minstrel Memories, 385
Minstrel Show, 40
Minuet In Boogie, 420
Miracle Of Miracles, 273
Miss Brown To You, 74
Miss Jemina Walks By, 235
Miss Julie July, 496
Miss Lindy Lou, 698
Miss Lulu From Louisville, 187
Miss Otis Regrets, 716
Miss Turnstiles, 742
Miss Wonderful, 769
Miss You, 992
Mississippi Dream Boat, 1019
Mississippi Siren, 298
Missouri Hayride, 247
Misstep, 1017
Mist Over The Moon, A, 550
Mister Deep Blue Sea, 541
Mister Hepster's Dictionary,
    872

Mister Pollyanna, 1103
Mister Snow, 155
Misto Christofo Columbo, 408
Moaning In The Moonlight, 535
Moke From Shamokin, A, 32
Molasses To Rum, 877
Molly O'Donohue, 1008
Mom, 886
Moments Like These, 659
Moments Like This, 184
Mon Ahan O Han, 543
Money Burns A Hole In My Pocket,
    587
Money In My Clothes, 991
Money Money Money, 127
Money To Burn, 378
Monkey Business, 247
Monkey Doodle-Doo, 178
Monkey Sat In The Cocoanut Tree,
    158
Monmart, 143
Monotonous, 710
Monsieur Baby, 60
Monsieur, 121
Montevideo, 96
Montparnasse, 1163
Moo Woo Woo, 414
Moody, 231
Moon And The Willow Tree, The,
    838
Moon Got In My Eyes, The, 244
Moon Kissed The Mississippi, The,
    510
Moon Over Las Vegas, 662
Moon Over Monte Carlo, 1100
Moon Over The Islands, 1140
Moon Shines Bright On Charlie
    Chaplin, 728
Moon Song, 400
Moon Struck, 181
Moonburn, 24
Moonface, 1047
Moonflowers, 833
Moonglow, 67
Moonlight And Pretzels, 665
Moonlight Bay, 1084
Moonlight Becomes You, 835
Moonlight Fiesta, 481
Moonlight In Havana, 666
Moonlight In Hawaii, 667
Moonlight On The Campus, 1129
Moonlight Over The Islands, 47,
    617
Moonlight Propaganda, 238

My Song Without Words, 198
My Strongest Weakness Is You, 933
My Sunny Tennessee, 1072
My Surpressed Desire, 318
My Sweet Bambino, 677
My Sweeter Than Sweet, 1018
My Swiss Hillbilly, 1058
My Walking Stick, 7
My Wife's A Wac, 861
My Wild Irish Rose, 968
My Wonderful One, Let's Dance, 1112
Mynah Bird, 226

'N Everything, 967
Nag Nag Nag, 983
Namely You, 574
Nancy's Goin' To Rio, 701
Nango, The, 1143
Nani Loa, 821
Nani Ona Pua, 1134
Natchez And The Robert E. Lee, The, 698
National Anthem, 628
Naughty Aloysius, 623
Naughty But Nice, 62
Naughty, Naughty I'm Surprised At You, 550
Navy Blues, 705
Navy Gets The Gravy And The Army Gets The Beans, The, 38
Navy Waltz, 922
Neapolitan Love Song, 370
Nearer And Dearer, 725
'Neath The Southern Moon, 703
'Neath The Yellow Moon In Old Tahiti, 824
Necessity, 278
Need I Say More, 197
Need I Speak, 1104
Nell Of New Rochelle, 994
Nellie Is A Darlin', 585
Nellie Kelly I Love You, 585
Nellie Martin, 1116
Nenita, 246
Neori Leong, 764
Nevada, 1150
Never, 365
Never Again, 956

Never Before, 374, 858
Never Give Up, 213
Never Go To Argentina, 1057
Never Gonna Dance, 1025
Never In A Million Years, 1137
Never Knew I Could Sing, 247
Never Look Back, 603
Never Mind Bo Peep, 41
Never Mind, 728
Never Say No, 978
Never So Beautiful, 404
Never Steal Anything Small, 708
Never Swat A Fly, 524
Never Trust A Jumping Bean, 274
Never Was There Such A Perfect Day, 266
Nevertheless, 1072
New Ashmolean Marching Society And Student's Conservatory Band, The, 1156
New Day, A, 403
New Faces, 709
New Generation, The, 346
New Love Is Old, A, 159
New Moon Is Over My Shoulder, 997
New O'leans, 1044
New Orleans, 494
New Sun In The Sky, A, 48, 214
New Year's Eve On Times Square, 124
New York, Let Me Sing, 1117
New York New York, 742
New York Town, 77
New York's A Nice Place To Visit, 135
Nice To Know You, 392
Nice Work If You Can Get It, 18, 208
Nickel's Worth Of Jive, A, 231
Night, 651
Night And Day, 321, 716
Night Is Filled With Music, 149
Night Is Young, The, 719
Night Of My Nights, 537
Night On Bear Mountain, 936
Night Over Shanghai, 916
Night Owl, 1033
Night Rock 'N' Roll Died, 865
Night They Invented Champagne, The, 333
Night They Raided Minsky's, The, 720
Night Time And You, 416

Oh I Can't Sit Down, 788
Oh I Didn't Know You'd Get That Way, 326
Oh It's A Lovely War, 728, 967
Oh Lady Be Good, 547
Oh Lawd I'm On My Way, 788
Oh Leo, It's Love, 1100
Oh Little Stars, 788
Oh Look At Me Now, 233
Oh Me Oh My, 1040
Oh Me, Oh My, Oh You, 991
Oh Mister Man Up In The Moon, 232
Oh Mother What Do I Do Now, 211
Oh My Goodness, 786
Oh Officer, 31
Oh Oh Oh, 1053
Oh Oh Oklahoma, 1182
Oh Say Do You See What I See, 1124
Oh Susanna, 462, 579, 1006
Oh That Mitzi, 747
Oh The Pity Of It All, 691
Oh Them Dudes, 562
Oh 'Tis Sweet To Think, 1095
Oh What A Beautiful Morning, 730
Oh What A Horse Was Charley, 358
Oh What A Lovely Dream, 681
Oh What I'll Do To That Wild Hungarian, 1048
Oh Why, 552
Oh You Beautiful Doll, 302, 729, 987, 1149
Oh You Beautiful Town, 889
Oh You Nasty Man, 325
Oh You Red Head, 1036
Ohio, 305
OK For TV, 1093
Okay Toots, 530
Oklahoma, 730
Oklahoma's One With Me, 662
Okolehao, 1134
Ol' Dan Patch, 932
Ol' Man River, 895, 896, 897, 1080
Ol' Spring Fever, 523
Old Black Joe, 1006
Old Calliope, The, 858
Old Demon Rum, 187
Old Devil Moon, 278
Old Dog Tray, 462
Old Fashioned Garden, 716

Old-Fashioned Tune Always Is New, An, 868
Old Flame Never Dies, An, 1131
Old Folks At Home, 462
Old Glory, 975
Old Home Guard, The, 59
Old Kilarney Fair, 930
Old King Cole, 1129
Old Love Is A True Love, A, 912
Old Man, 1157
Old Man Blues, 164
Old Man Rhythm, 733
Old Man Rip, 615
Old Music Master, 1103
Old Sad Eyes, 721
Old School Bell, The, 184
Old Square Dance Is Back Again, The, 774
Old Straw Hat, An, 810
Oldest Established Permanent Floating Crap Game, 376
Olive Tree, The, 537
Oliver, 734
On A Clear Day, 735
On A Desert Island With You, 188
On A Holiday In My Playroom, 943
On A Little Island By A Sunlit Sea, 145
On A Little Two Seat Tandem, 669
On A Rainy Night In Rio, 1083
On A Sunny Afternoon, 113, 704
On An Island With You, 736
On How To Be Lovely, 312
On Moonlight Bay, 737
On San Francisco Bay, 937
On The Atchison Topeka And The Santa Fe, 391
On The Beam, 1177
On The Boardwalk At Atlantic City, 1070
On The Bumpy Road To Love, 577
On The Erie Canal, 271
On The Gay White Way, 691, 1163
On The Mississippi, 242
On The Riviera, 740
On The Sentimental Side, 240
On The Street Where You Live, 687
On The Sunny Side Of The Street, 322, 398, 495, 741, 1108
On The Swing Shift, 975

54

Sugar Plum, 1044
Sultan's Daughter, The, 998
Sultan's Palace, 1088
Summer Holidays, 678
Summer In Heidelberg, 996
Summer Night, 908
Summer Serenade, 1015
Summertime, 788, 819
Sun Never Sets On Swing, The, 266
Sun Showers, 114, 1110
Sunbonnet Sue, 1002
Sunday, 286
Sunday Jumps, 855
Sunday Mornin', 365
Sunday, Monday And Always, 235
Sunflower Song, 528
Sunny, 588, 1003, 1004, 1080
Sunny Side Of Things, The, 99
Sunny Side Up, 70
Sunrise Sunset, 273
Sunshine Cake, 828
Supercalifragilisticexpiali-docious, 630
Superstar, 508
Sur Le Plage, 97
Sure Thing, 195, 828
Surrey With The Fringe On Top, 730
Susannah I'm Betting On You, 678
Swami Song, 177
Swan, The, 313
Swanee, 513, 514, 819, 969
Swanee River, 1006
Swanee Shuffle, 379
Sweater Girl, 1007
Sweater, A Sarong, And A Peek-aboo Bang, A, 975
Swedish Pastorale, 552
Sweep It, 862
Sweeping The Clouds Away, 766
Sweet And Lovely, 1111
Sweet And Low, 110, 1028
Sweet And Simple, 325
Sweet As A Song, 860
Sweet Charity, 1010
Sweet Cider Time, 401
Sweet Dreams Sweetheart, 438, 1071
Sweet Genevieve, 489
Sweet Georgia Brown, 107
Sweet Heartache, 422
Sweet Irish Sweetheart Of Mine,

A, 755
Sweet Is The Word For You, 1134
Sweet Jennie Lee, 609
Sweet Leilani, 1134
Sweet Lips (Kiss My Blues Away), 639
Sweet Little Alice Blue Gown, 493
Sweet Lucy Brown, 163
Sweet Melody Of Night, 347
Sweet Music, 1011
Sweet Nothings Of Love, 453
Sweet Packard, 893
Sweet Potato Piper, 838
Sweet Rhyming Minstrel, The, 986
Sweet Someone, 597
Sweet Sue, 824
Sweet Sunday, 944
Sweet Varsity Sue, 571
Sweet Vermosa Brown, 493
Sweeter Than You, 1097
Sweetest Kid I've Ever Known, 999
Sweetest Music This Side Of Heaven, The, 626
Sweetheart Of School, 460
Sweetheart Of The Blues, 613
Sweetheart Time, 1076
Sweetheart Waltz, The, 181
Sweetheart We Need Each Other, 829
Sweethearts, 1015
Sweethearts Forever, 199
Sweethearts Of America, 791
Sweethearts On Parade, 1017
Sweetie Pie, 613
Swing Chariot Swing, 726
Swing Concerto, 867
Swing High Swing Low, 1021
Swing In Line, 1104
Swing Is Here To Sway, 8
Swing It Mother Goose, 517
Swing Low Sweet Lariat, 257
Swing Low Sweet Rhythm, 423
Swing Me An Old Fashioned Song, 581
Swing Mr. Mendelssohn Swing, 266
Swing Tap, The, 1068
Swing That Cheer, 310
Swing Trot, 50
Swing Your Lady, 1026
Swing Your Partner, 1027

Swing Your Partner Round And Round, 391
Swing Your Sweetheart 'Round The Fire, 144
Swing Your Way Through College, 141
Swingali, 37, 222
Swinging Down The Lane, 479
Swinging In The Corn, 301, 800
Swinging On A Star, 357
Swinging The Blues, 291
Swinging The Jinx Away, 93, 461
Swingy Little Things, 878
Sympathy, 170, 279, 281

T. S. U. Alma Mater, 780
Tableaux Of Jewels, 442
Tahiti, 756
Tahiti Honey, 641
Tahm Boom Bah, 424
T'Ain't Nobody's Bizness If I Do, 551
Tait College Song, 367, 368
Take A Chance, 410
Take A Flower, 712
Take A Lesson From The Lark, 894
Take A Little One Step, 723
Take A Number From One To Ten, 183
Take A Tip From A Gypsy, 808
Take A Tip From The Tulip, 800
Take Back Your Gold, 1066
Take Back Your Mink, 376
Take It And Git, 457
Take It Away, 870, 1051
Take It Big, 1034
Take It Easy, 44, 265
Take It From There, 187
Take It On The Chin, 433
Take Me In Your Arms, 411, 738
Take Me Out To The Ball Game, 889
Take Me To Broadway, 928
Take Me To The Fair, 139
Take Me To Town, 1036
Take Ten Terrific Girls, 720
Take The Door To The Left, 7
Take The World Off Your Shoulders, 709

Take This Ring, 1013
Take Your Place In The Sun, 14
Takin' A Slow Burn, 563
Taking A Chance On Love, 128, 461, 478
Taking Care Of You, 678, 973
Taking Miss Mary To The Ball, 736
Tale Of Love, 818
Tale Of The Tailors, 46
Tale Of Vermilion O'Toole, The, 1036
Talented Shoes, 1088
Tales Of The Vienna Woods, 371
Talk To The Animals, 239
Talking To Myself, 332
Tallahassee, 1128
Taming Of The Shrew, 157
Tampico, 890
Tanda Wanda Hoy, 38
Tangerine, 284
Tango, 879
Tango Del Rio, 1165
Tanya, 46
Tap Happy, 1013
Tap Your Feet, 1068
Tapioca, The, 105, 1065
Tar Heels, 3
Tattle Tale Eyes, 797
Tea Cup, 492
Tea For Two, 723, 1040, 1163
Teamwork, 834
Tear, A Kiss, A Smile, A, 234
Teen Canteen, 520
Telephone Hour, 126
Tell Me It's You, 374
Tell Me While We're Dancing, 86
Tell Me Why My Nights Are Lonely, 495
Tell Me Why The Nights Are Lonely, 737
Tell Me With Your Eyes, 725
Tell Us Which One You Do Love, 727
Telling My Troubles To A Mule, 99
Temple, The, 508
Temporarily, 1175
Temporarily Blue, 625
Temptation, 356
Tempus Fugit, 124
Ten Cents A Dance, 603
Ten Days With Baby, 1009
Ten Easy Lessons, 177

63

65

70

72

Wish I May, 68
Wish You Were Here, 123
Wishes Come True, 426
Wishful Thinking, 1037
Wishing, 327
Wishing And Waiting For Love,
    108, 217
Wishing Waltz, 1012
With A Flair, 59
With A Little Bit Of Luck, 687
With A Song In My Heart, 758,
    958, 1062, 1163, 1168
With A Twist Of The Wrist, 820
With Every Breath I Take, 409
With My Banjo On My Knee, 49
With My Eyes Wide Open I'm
    Dreaming, 894, 982
With My Guitar And You, 1020
With Plenty Of Money And You,
    363, 888
With The Warm Sun Upon Me, 271
With You, 798
With You Gone, 372
With You On My Mind, 989
With You, With Me, 1038
Without A Word Of Warning, 1109
Without Imagination, 348
Without Love, 70, 901
Without You, 687
Without You I'm Just Drifting,
    5
Without Your Love, 131
Wo Ho, 718
Woman Behind The Man Behind The
    Gun, The, 647
Woman In Love, 376
Woman In The Shoe, The, 589
Woman Is A Sometime Thing, A,
    788
Woman Needs Something Like That,
    A, 604
Woman's Kiss, A, 279
Woman's Touch, 134
Won't Dance, 1075
Wonder Bar, 1165
Wonder Why, 825
Wonderful Copenhagen, 382
Wonderful Home Sweet Home, 1163
Wonderful Wonderful Day, 873
Wonderful World Of The Brothers
    Grimm, 1166
Wonderful Wasn't It?, 806
Wondrin' When, 496
Woodchopper's Ball, 1151

Wooden Indian, 3
Wooden Shoes, 1015
Wooden Woman, 459
Word A Day, A, 1093
Words Are In My Heart, The, 362
Work While You May, 771
Workshop Song, The, 42
World Is A Circle, The, 590
World Is My Apple, The, 809
World's Most Beautiful Girl, 29
Worry About Tomorrow, Tomorrow,
    124
Worry Bird, The, 1117
Worry Song, The, 19
Worthy Of You, 493
Would There Be Love, 981
Would You?, 839, 863, 913
Would You Believe Me?, 599
Wouldn't It Be Funny?, 675
Wouldn't It Be Loverly, 687
Wouldn't It Be Nice, 938
Wouldn't It Be Wonderful, 494
Wrap Your Troubles In Dreams
    (And Dream Your Troubles
    Away), 806
Wrong Thing At The Right Time,
    44
Wrong To Dream, 948
Wunderbar, 538


Ya Comin' Up Tonight--Huh?, 318
Ya Got Class, 404
Ya Gotta Give The People Hoke,
    25
Yaaka Hula Hickey Dula, 26
Yacht Club Boys, The, 965
Yam, The, 149
Yama Yama Man, 987
Yankee Doodle Band, 573
Yankee Doodle Blues, 478, 819
Yankee Doodle Boy, 580
Yankee Doodle Dandy, 876, 1169
Yankee Doodle Hayride, 782
Yawning Song, 1088
Yearning Just For You, 1017
Years Before Us, The, 1156
Yellow Dog Blues, 962
Yes Indeed, 1035
Yes M'Lord, 270
Yes Or No, 837

76

THE SHOWS

AARON SLICK FROM PUNKIN CRICK   (1952)
STARS:   Alan Young, Dinah Shore
DIR:      Claude Binyon
SONGS:   Jay Livingston - Ray Evans
Life Is A Beautiful Thing; Why Should I Believe In Love; Still
Water; Marshmallow Moon; Purt 'Nigh But Not Plumb; I'd Like To
Baby You; Saturday Night In Punkin Crick; Will You Be At Home
In Heaven?; Chores; The General Store; The Spider And The Fly;
Step Right Up; Soda Shop.
RCA LPM-3006

ABBOTT AND COSTELLO IN HOLLYWOOD   (1945)
STARS:   Abbott, Costello
DIR:      S. Sylvan Simon
SONGS:   Hugh Martin - Ralph Blane

ABOUT FACE   (1952)
STARS:   Aileen Stanley Jr., Gordon MacRae
DIR:      Roy Del Ruth
SONGS:   Peter De Rose - Charles Tobias
Piano, Bass and Drums; No Other Girl For Me; I'm Nobody; Spring
Has Sprung; Wooden Indian; Reveille; S. M. I. March; Tar Heels;
They Haven't Lost A Father Yet

ADORABLE   (1933)
STARS:   Janet Gaynor, Henry Garat
DIR:      William Dieterle
SONGS:   Richard Whiting - George Marion Jr.

AFTER THE DANCE   (1935)
STARS:   Nancy Carroll, George Murphy
DIR:      Lee Bulgakov

AIN'T MISBEHAVIN'   (1955)
STARS:   Rory Calhoun, Piper Laurie
DIR:      Edward Buzzell
Ain't Misbehavin'; A Little Love Can Go A Long Way (Sammy Fain -
Paul Francis Webster); The Dixie Mambo (Sammy Burke - Charles
Henderson): I Love That Rickey Tickey Tickey (Johnnie Scott -
Sammy Cahn).

ALEXANDER'S RAGTIME BAND   (1938)
STARS:   Tyrone Power, Alice Faye
DIR:      Henry King
SONGS:   Irving Berlin
Alexander's Ragtime Band; Easter Parade; Remeber; Everybody's
Doing It; Blue Skies; My Walking Stick; Everybody Step; A Pretty
Girl Is Like A Melody; When The Midnight Choo-Choo Leaves For
Alabam; Heat Wave; We're On Our Way To France; All Alone; Say It
With Music; What'll I do?; International Rag; Ragtime Violin; Go
To The Devil; This Is The Life; Oh How I Hate To Get Up In The
Morning; Now It Can Be Told; I Can Always Find A Little Sunshine
In The YMCA.
Merman In The Movies:   1930 - 38   Encore ST-101

8. ALI BABA GOES TO TOWN   (1937)
   STARS:   Eddie Cantor, Tony Martin
   DIR:     David Butler

9. ALL ASHORE   (1953)
   STARS:   Mickey Rooney, Dick Haymes
   DIR:     Richard Quine
   SONGS:   Robert Wells - Fred Karger
   You're A Buddy; Heave Ho, My Hearties; Boy Meets Girl; I Love
   No One But You

10. ALL THE KING'S HORSES   (1935)
    STARS:   Carl Brisson, Mary Ellis
    DIR:     Frank Tuttle
    SONGS:   Sam Coslow

11. ALL-AMERICAN CO-ED   (1941)
    STARS:   Frances Langford, Johnny Downs
    DIR:     Le Roy Prinz

12. ALL-AMERICAN SWEETHEART   (1938)
    STARS:   Patricia Farr, Scott Colton
    DIR:     Lambert Hillyer
    SONGS:   Ben Oakland - Milton Drake

13. ALLERGIC TO LOVE   (1944)
    STARS:   Noah Beery Jr., Martha O'Driscoll
    DIR:     Edward Lilley

14. ALMOST MARRIED   (1942)
    STARS:   Jane Frazee, Robert Paige
    DIR:     Charles Lamont

15. ALONG CAME YOUTH   (1931)
    STARS:   Charles "Buddy" Rogers, Frances Dee
    DIR:     Lloyd Corrigan, Norman McLeod

16. ALWAYS A BRIDESMAID   (1943)
    STARS:   The Andrews Sisters, Patrick Knowles
    DIR:     Erle C. Kenton

17. ALWAYS LEAVE THEM LAUGHING   (1949)
    STARS:   Milton Berle, Virginia Mayo
    DIR:     Roy Del Ruth

18. AMERICAN IN PARIS, AN   (1951)
    STARS:   Gene Kelly, Leslie Caron
    DIR:     Vincente Minnelli
    SONGS:   George and Ira Gershwin
    I Got Rhythm; Embraceable You; 'S Wonderful; Nice Work If You
    Can Get It; By Strauss; Tra-La-La; Our Love Is Here To Stay;
    I'll Build A Stairway To Paradise (lyrics by E. Ray Goetz and
    B. G. De Sylva); Concerto In F; An American In Paris
    Metro 552

9.   ANCHORS AWEIGH   (1945)
     STARS:  Frank Sinatra, Kathryn Grayson
     DIR:    George Sidney
     We Hate To Leave; What Makes The Sun Set?; The Charm Of You; I
     Begged Her; I Fall In Love Too Easily (Jule Styne - Sammy Cahn);
     The Worry Song (Sammy Fain - Ralph Freed); (All Of A Sudden) My
     Heart Sings (Herpin - Harold Rome)
     Curtain Calls CC 100/17

0.   AND THE ANGELS SING   (1944)
     STARS:  Dorothy Lamour, Betty Hutton
     DIR:    Claude Binyon
     SONGS:  Jimmy VanHeusen - Johnny Burke

1.   ANGELS WITH BROKEN WINGS   (1941)
     STARS:  Binnie Barnes, Gilbert Roland
     DIR:    Donald Vorhaus
     SONGS:  Jule Styne - Eddie Cherkose

2.   ANIMAL CRACKERS   (1930)
     STARS:  Marx Brothers, Lillian Roth
     DIR:    Victor Heerman

3.   ANNIE GET YOUR GUN   (1950)
     STARS:  Betty Hutton, Howard Keel
     DIR:    George Sidney
     SONGS:  Irving Berlin
     Colonel Buffalo Bill; Doin' What Comes Naturally; The Girl That
     I Marry; There's No Business Like Show Business; You Can't Get
     A Man With A Gun; My Defenses Are Down; I'm An Indian Too; I
     Got The Sun In The Morning; Anything You Can Do; They Say It's
     Wonderful
     MGM-2-SES-42-ST

4.   ANYTHING GOES   (1936)
     STARS:  Bing Crosby, Ethel Merman
     DIR:    Lewis Milestone
     You're The Top; Anything Goes; All Through The Night; I
     Get A Kick Out Of You; Blow Gabriel Blow; There'll Always Be A
     Lady Fair (Cole Porter); Moonburn (Hoagy Carmichael - Edward
     Heyman); Sailor Beware (Richard Whiting - Leo Robin); My Heart
     And I; Shanghi-De-Ho; Am I Awake?; Hopelessly In Love (Frederick
     Hollander - Leo Robin);
     Decca DL-4251

5.   ANYTHING GOES   (1956)
     STARS:  Bing Crosby, Mitzi Gaynor
     DIR:    Robert Lewis
     SONGS:  Cole Porter
     I Get A Kick Out Of You; Anything Goes; You're The Top; Blow,
     Gabriel, Blow; It's Delovely; All Through The Night; Second
     Hand Turban And A Crystal Ball; And, Ya Gotta Give The People
     Hoke; You Can Bounce Right Back (Jimmy Van Heusen - Sammy Cahn)
     Decca DL-8318

26. APPLAUSE  (1929)
    STARS:  Helen Morgan, Joan Peters
    DIR:    Rouben Mamoulian

27. APRIL IN PARIS  (1952)
    STARS:  Doris Day, Ray Bolger
    DIR:    David Butler
    SONGS:  Vernon Duke - Sammy Cahn
    Give Me Your Lips; I Know A Place; I'm Gonna Ring The Bell To-
    Night; That's What Makes Paris Paree; Isn't It Wonderful?;
    April In Paris (Lyric - E. Y. Harburg)

28. APRIL LOVE  (1957)
    STARS:  Pat Boone, Shirley Jones
    DIR:    Henry Levin
    SONGS:  Sammy Fain - Paul Francis Webster
    April Love; Do It Yourself; The Bentonville Fair; Clover In The
    Meadow; Give Me A Gentle Girl
    Dot 9000

29. APRIL SHOWERS  (1948)
    STARS:  Ann Sheridan, Jack Carson
    DIR:    James V. Kern

30. ARE YOU WITH IT?  (1948)
    STARS:  Donald O'Connor, Olga San Juan
    DIR:    Jack Hively
    SONGS:  Sidney Miller - Inez James

31. ARGENTINE NIGHTS  (1940)
    STARS:  Ritz Brothers, Constance Moore
    DIR:    Albert S. Rogell

32. AROUND THE WORLD  (1943)
    STARS:  Kay Kyser, Mischa Auer
    DIR:    Allan Dwan
    SONGS:  Jimmy McHugh - Harold Adamson

33. ARTISTS AND MODELS  (1937)
    STARS:  Jack Benny, Ida Lupino
    DIR:    Raoul Walsh

34. ARTISTS AND MODELS  (1955)
    STARS:  Dean Martin, Jerry Lewis
    DIR:    Frank Tashlin
    SONGS:  Harry Warren - Jack Brooks
    Artists And Models; Inamorata; When You Pretend; You Look So
    Familiar; The Lucky Song; Bat Lady

35. ARTISTS AND MODELS ABROAD  (1938)
    STARS:  Jack Benny, Joan Bennett
    DIR:    Mitchell Leisen

36. AT LONG LAST LOVE  (1975)

STARS:    Cybill Shepherd, Burt Reynolds
DIR:      Peter Bogdanovich
SONGS:    Cole Porter
Which; Poor Young Millionaire; You're The Top; Friendship; Find
Me A Primitive Man; But In The Morning, No; At Long Last Love;
Well, Did You Evah?; From Alpha To Omega; Let's Misbehave; Just
One Of Those Things; I Get A Kick Out Of You; I Loved Him; Most
Gentlemen Don't Like Love; A Picture Of Me Without You
RCA ABL2-0967

37.  AT THE CIRCUS  (1939)
     STARS:   Marx Brothers
     DIR:     Edward Buzzell
     SONGS:   Harold Arlen - E. Y. Harburg

38.  AT WAR WITH THE ARMY  (1950)
     STARS:   Dean Martin, Jerry Lewis
     DIR:     Hal Walker
     SONGS:   Jerry Livingston - Mack David
     You And Your Beautiful Eyes; Tanda Wanda Hoy; The Navy Gets The
     Gravy And The Army Gets The Beans

39.  ATHENA  (1954)
     STARS:   Jane Powell, Debbie Reynolds
     DIR:     Richard Thorpe
     SONGS:   Hugh Martin - Ralph Blane
     Athena; Your Beautiful Eyes; Girl Next Door; Vocalize; I Never
     Felt Better; Love Can Change The Stars; Venezia; Imagine
     Mercury MG 25202(10")

40.  BABES IN ARMS  (1939)
     STARS:   Judy Garland, Mickey Rooney
     DIR:     Busby Berkeley
     Where Or When; The Lady Is A Tramp; Babes In Arms (Richard
     Rogers - Lorenz Hart); I Cried For You (Abe Lyman - Gus Arn-
     heim - Arthur Freed); God's Country (Harold Arlen - E.Y. Har-
     burg); Good Morning; You Are My Lucky Star (Nacio Herb Brown-
     Arthur Freed); Minstrel Show; Opera vs. Jazz (arranged: Roger
     Edens)
     Curtain Calls 100/6-7

41.  BABES IN TOYLAND  (1934)
     STARS:   Laurel and Hardy
     DIR:     Gus Meins and Charles Rogers

42.  BABES IN TOYLAND  (1961)
     STARS:   Ray Bolger, Tommy Sands
     DIR:     Jack Donohue
     SONGS:   Victor Herbert - Glen MacDonough
     I Can't Do The Sum; Just A Toy; Floretta; Castle In Spain; We
     Won't Be Happy Till We Get It; Lemonade; Just A Whisper Away;
     March Of The Toys; Toyland; The Workshop Song; The Forest Of
     No Return; Slowly He Sank Into The Sea (George Bruns - Mel
     Leven)
     Buena Vista STER-4022

43. BABES ON BROADWAY (1941)
    STARS: Judy Garland, Mickey Rooney
    DIR:    Busby Berkeley
    (I Like New York In June) How About You?; Babes On Broadway;
    Blackout Over Broadway (Burton Lane - Ralph Freed); Anything
    Can Happen In New York; Chin Up, Cheerio, Carry On (Burton
    Lane - E. Y. Harburg); Hoe Down (Roger Edens - Ralph Freed);
    Bombshell From Brazil (Roger Edens); F. D. R. Jones (Harold
    Rome); Mama Yo Quiero (I Want My Mama) (Vincente Paiva -
    Jararaca - Al Stillman)
    Curtain Calls 100/6-7

44. BABES ON SWING STREET (1944)
    STARS: Ann Blyth, Peggy Ryan
    DIR:    Edward Lilley

45. BACHELOR OF ARTS (1934)
    STARS: Tom Brown, Anita Louise
    DIR:    Louis King

46. BALALAIKA (1939)
    STARS: Nelson Eddy, Ilona Massey
    DIR:    Reinhold Schunzel

47. BAMBOO BLONDE (1946)
    STARS: Frances Langford, Ralph Edwards
    DIR:    Anthony Mann
    SONGS: Lew Pollack - Mort Greene

48. THE BAND WAGON (1953)
    STARS: Fred Astaire, Cyd Charisse
    DIR:    Vincente Minelli
    SONGS: Arthur Schwartz - Howard Dietz
    A Shine On Your Shoes; By Myself; Dancing In The Dark; I Guess
    I'll Have To Change My Plan; A New Sun In The Sky; Louisiana
    Hayride; That's Entertainment; I Love Louisa; Girl Hunt Ballet
    MGM 2-SES-44-ST

49. BANJO ON MY KNEE (1936)
    STARS: Walter Brennan, Joel McCrea
    DIR:    John Cromwell
    SONGS: Jimmy McHugh - Harold Adamson

50. BARKLEYS OF BROADWAY, THE (1949)
    STARS: Ginger Rogers, Fred Astaire
    DIR:    Charles Walters
    You'd Be Hard To Replace; Week-end In The Country; Manhattan
    Downbeat; Shoes With Wings On; Swing Trot; My One And Only
    Highland Flying (Harry Warren - Ira Gershwin); They Can't Take
    That Away From Me (George and Ira Gershwin)
    MGM-2-SES-51ST

51. BARNYARD FOLLIES (1940)
    STARS: Mary Lee, Rufe Davis
    DIR:    Frank McDonald

52. BATHING BEAUTY   (1944)
    STARS:   Red Skelton, Esther Williams
    DIR:     George Sidney
    SONGS:   Johnny Green - Harold Adamson

53. BATTLE OF PARIS   (1929)
    STARS:   Gertrude Lawrence, Charles Ruggles
    DIR:     Robert Flory

54. BE YOURSELF   (1930)
    STARS:   Fanny Brice, Harry Green
    DIR:     Thornton Freeland

55. BEAT THE BAND   (1947)
    STARS:   Frances Langford, Ralph Edwards
    DIR:     John Auer
    SONGS:   Leigh Harline - Mort Greene

56. BEAUTIFUL BLONDE FROM BASHFUL BEND   (1949)
    STARS:   Betty Grable, Cesar Romero
    DIR:     Preston Sturges

57. BEAUTIFUL BUT BROKE   (1944)
    STARS:   Joan Davis, John Hubbard
    DIR:     Charles Barton

58. BECAUSE YOU'RE MINE   (1952)
    STARS:   Mario Lanza, Doretta Morrow
    DIR:     Alexander Hall
    Because You're Mine (Nicholas Brodszky - Sammy Cahn); Lee-Ah-Loo
    (Ray Sinatra - John Leeman); The Song Angels Sing (Irving Aaron-
    son - Paul Francis Webster); You Do Something To Me; All The
    Things You Are (Cole Porter); The Lord's Prayer (Albert Hay
    Malotte); Granada (Augustin Lara)
    RCA LM-7015

59. BEDKNOBS AND BROOMSTICKS   (1971)
    STARS:   Angela Lansbury, David Tomlinson
    DIR:     Robert Stevenson
    SONGS:   Richard M. and Robert B. Sherman
    The Old Home Guard; The Age Of Not Believing; With A Flair; A
    Step In The Right Direction; Eglantine, Don't Let Me Down; The
    Beautiful Briny; Portobello Road; Substitutiary Locomotion
    Buena Vista S-5003

60. BEDTIME STORY, A   (1933)
    STARS:   Maurice Chevalier, Helen Twelvetrees
    DIR:     Norman Taurog
    SONGS:   Ralph Rainger - Leo Robin

61. BEHIND THE EIGHT BALL   (1942)
    STARS:   Ritz Brothers, Carol Bruce
    DIR:     William Morgan
    SONGS:   Gene DePaul - Don Raye

62. BELLE OF NEW YORK, THE   (1952)
    STARS:  Fred Astaire, Vera-Ellen
    DIR:    Charles Walters
    When I'm Out With The Belle Of New York;  Oops; Naughty But
    Nice; Baby Doll; Seeing's Believing; Bachelor's Dinner Song;
    Thank You Mr. Currier, Thank You Mr. Ives; I Love To Beat A Big
    Bass Drum (Harry Warren - Johnny Mercer); I Wanna Be A Dancing
    Man (Burton Lane - Alan Jay Lerner); Let A Little Love Come In
    (Roger Edens)
    MGM E-108   (10")

63. BELLE OF THE NINETIES   (1934)
    STARS:  Mae West, Roger Pryor
    DIR:    Leo McCarey
    SONGS:  Arthur Johnston - Sam Coslow

64. BELLE OF THE YUKON   (1944)
    STARS:  Randolph Scott, Gypsy Rose Lee
    DIR:    William A. Seiter
    SONGS:  Jimmy Van Heusen - Johnny Burke

64. BELLS ARE RINGING   (1960)
    STARS:  Judy Holliday, Dean Martin
    DIR:    Vincente Minnelli
    SONGS:  Jule Styne - Betty Comden - Adolph Green
    Bells Are Ringing; It's A Perfect Relationship; Is It A Crime?;
    It's A Simple Little System; Do It Yourself; It's Better Than
    A Dream; Hello, Hello There; Mu Cha Cha; Just In Time; Drop
    That Name; Long Before I Knew You; The Midas Touch; I'm Goin'
    Back
    Capitol SW-1435

66. BELLS OF ST. MARY'S   (1945)
    STARS:  Bing Crosby, Ingrid Bergman
    DIR:    Leo McCarey
    In The Land Of Beginning Again (George Meyer - Grant Clarke);
    Aren't You Glad You're You (Jimmy Van Heusen - Johnny Burke);
    The Bells Of St. Mary's (A. E. Adams - Douglas Furber)
    Decca DL-5052

67. BENNY GOODMAN STORY   (1956)
    STARS:  Steve Allen, Donna Reed
    DIR:    Valentine Davies
    Let's Dance; Down South Camp Meetin'; King Porter Stomp; Bugle
    Call Rag; It's Been So Long; Roll 'Em; Don't Be That Way; You
    Turned The Tables On Me; Goody, Goody; Slipped Disk; Stompin'
    At The Savoy; One O'Clock Jump; Memories Of You; China Boy;
    Moonglow; Avalon; And The Angels Sing; Jersey Bounce; Sometimes
    I'm Happy; Shine; Sing, Sing, Sing
    Decca 78252/3

68. BEST FOOT FORWARD   (1943)
    STARS:  Lucille Ball, William Gaxton
    DIR:    Eddie Buzzell
    SONGS:  Ralph Blane - Hugh Martin

69. BEST OF ENEMIES   (1933)
    STARS:  Charles "Buddy" Rogers, Marian Nixon
    DIR:    Rian James
    SONGS:  Will Jason - Val Burton

70. BEST THINGS IN LIFE ARE FREE, THE   (1956)
    STARS:  Gordon MacRae, Dan Dailey
    DIR:    Michael Curtiz
    SONGS:  Buddy DeSylva - Lew Brown - Ray Henderson
    The Best Things In Life Are Free; You Try Somebody Else; Sonny
    Boy; Without Love; Button Up Your Overcoat; Black Bottom; This
    Is The Mrs.; This Is My Lucky Day; One More Time; Sunny Side
    Up; Together; Good News; Just A Memory; It All Depends On You;
    Broken Hearted; If I Had A Talking Picture Of You; Don't Hold
    Everything; Birth Of The Blues;
    Liberty LRP-3017

71. BETTY CO-ED   (1946)
    STARS:  Jean Porter, Shirley Mills
    DIR:    Arthur Dreifuss

72. BIG BOY   (1930)
    STARS:  Al Jolson, Claudia Dell
    DIR:    Alan Crosland

73. BIG BROADCAST OF 1932, THE   (1932)
    STARS:  Bing Crosby, Burns and Allen
    DIR:    Frank Tuttle

74. BIG BROADCAST OF 1936   (1935)
    STARS:  Jack Oakie, Burns and Allen
    DIR:    Norman Taurog

75. BIG BROADCAST OF 1937   (1936)
    STARS:  Burns and Allen, Jack Benny
    DIR:    Mitchell Leisen
    SONGS:  Ralph Rainger - Leo Robin

76. BIG BROADCAST OF 1938   (1938)
    STARS:  W. C. Fields, Martha Raye
    DIR:    Mitchell Leisen

77. BIG CITY BLUES   (1932)
    STARS:  Joan Blondell, Eric Linden
    DIR:    Mervyn LeRoy

78. BIG POND, THE   (1930)
    STARS:  Maurice Chevalier, Claudette Colbert
    DIR:    Hobart Henley

79. BIG STORE, THE   (1941)
    STARS:  Marx Brothers, Tony Martin
    DIR:    Charles Reisner

80. THE BIRDS AND THE BEES   (1956)

91

STARS:   George Gobel, Mitzi Gaynor
DIR:     Norman Taurog
SONGS:   Harry Warren - Mack David
The Same Thing Happens With The Birds And The Bees; Each Time
I Dream; La Parisienne; Little Miss Tippy-Toes (Harold Adamson)

81.  BIRTH OF THE BLUES   (1941)
     STARS:   Bing Crosby, Mary Martin
     DIR:     Victor Schertzinger
     The Waiter And The Porter And The Upstairs Maid (Johnny Mercer)
     Gotta Go To The Jail House (Harry Tugend - Robert E. Dolan); St
     Louis Blues; Memphis Blues (W. C. Handy); By The Light Of The
     Silvery Moon (Gus Edwards - Edward Madden); Tiger Rag (Original
     Dixieland Jazz Band); Waiting At The Church (F. W. Leigh -
     Henry Pether); Cuddle Up A Little Closer (Karl Hoschna - Otto
     Harbach); Wait Till The Sun Shines Nellie (Harry Von Tilzer -
     Andrew Sterling); That's Why They Call Me Shine (Ford Dabney -
     Cecil Mack - Lew Brown); Melancholy Baby (Ernie Burnett -
     George Norton); St. James Infirmary (Joe Primrose); Birth Of Th
     Blues (Ray Henderson - Lew Brown - B. G. DeSylva)
     Decca DL-4255

82.  BITTER SWEET   (1940)
     STARS:   Jeanette MacDonald, Nelson Eddy
     DIR:     W. S. Van Dyke
     SONGS:   Noel Coward

83.  BLONDE CRAZY   (1931)
     STARS:   James Cagney, Joan Blondell
     DIR:     Roy Del Ruth

84.  BLONDE RANSOM   (1945)
     STARS:   Donald Cook, Virginia Grey
     DIR:     William Beaudine
     SONGS:   Jack Brooks

85.  BLONDIE GOES LATIN   (1941)
     STARS:   Penny Singleton, Arthur Lake
     DIR:     Frank R. Strayer
     SONGS:   Bob Wright - Chet Forrest

86.  BLONDIE OF THE FOLLIES   (1932)
     STARS:   Marion Davies, Robert Montgomery
     DIR:     Edmund Goulding

87.  BLOSSOMS ON BROADWAY   (1937)
     STARS:   Edward Arnold, Shirley Ross
     DIR:     Richard Wallace

88.  THE BLUE ANGEL   (1959)
     STARS:   Curt Jurgens, Mae Britt
     DIR:     Edward Dmytryk
     Falling In Love Again (Frederick Hollander); Lola Lola (Jay
     Livingston - Ray Evans); I Yi Yi (Harry Warren - Mack Gordon)

89. BLUE SKIES   (1929)
    STARS:   Helen Twelvetrees, Frank Albertson
    DIR:     Alfred E. Werker
    SONGS:   Lew Pollack - Walter Bullock

90. BLUE SKIES   (1946)
    STARS:   Bing Crosby, Fred Astaire
    DIR:     Stuart Heisler
    SONGS:   Irving Berlin
    All By Myself; Heat Wave; Getting Nowhere; You Keep Coming Back
    Like A Song; I've Got My Captain Working For Me Now; Serenade
    To An Old-Fashioned Girl; Russian Lullaby; I'll See You In
    C-U-B-A; A Pretty Girl Is Like A Melody; Not For All The Rice
    In China; How Deep Is The Ocean; Everybody Step; A Couple of
    Song And Dance Men; Puttin' On The Ritz; The Little Things In
    Life; You'd Be Surprised; Always
    Decca DL-4259

91. BLUEBIRD, THE   (1940)
    STARS:   Shirley Temple, Spring Byington
    DIR:     Walter Lang
    SONGS:   Alfred Newman - Walter Bullock

92. BLUES IN THE NIGHT   (1941)
    STARS:   Pricilla Lane, Richard Whorf
    DIR:     Anatole Litvak
    SONGS:   Harold Arlen - Johnny Mercer

93. BORN TO DANCE   (1936)
    STARS:   Eleanor Powell, James Stewart
    DIR:     Roy Del Ruth
    SONGS:   Cole Porter
    I've Got You Under My Skin; Easy To Love; I'm Nuts About You;
    Rap-Tap On Wood; Swinging The Jinx Away; Rolling Home; Love Me
    Love My Pekinese; Hey, Babe, Hey
    C.I. F. 3001

94. BORN TO SING   (1942)
    STARS:   Virginia Weidler, Ray McDonald
    DIR:     Edward Ludwig

95. BOTTOMS UP   (1934)
    STARS:   Spencer Tracy, John Boles
    DIR:     David Butler

96. BOWERY TO BROADWAY   (1944)
    STARS:   Jack Oakie, Donald Cook
    DIR:     Charles Lamont

97. THE BOY FRIEND   (1971)
    STARS:   Twiggy, Christopher Gable
    DIR:     Ken Russell
    SONGS:   Sandy Willson
    Perfect Young Ladies; The Boy Friend; I Could Be Happy With

You; Fancy Forgetting; Sur Le Plage; The You-Don't-Want-To-Play
With-Me Blues; A Room In Bloomsbury; It's Never Too Late To Fa
In Love; Safety In Numbers; Poor Little Pierrette; The Riviera
All I Do Is Dream Of You; You Are My Lucky Star (Nacio Herb
Brown - Arthur Freed)
MGM - 1SE - 32ST

98.  BOYS FROM SYRACUSE   (1940)
     STARS:  Joe Penner, Allan Jones
     DIR:    A. Edward Sutherland
     SONGS:  Richard Rogers - Lorenz Hart

99.  BREAKING THE ICE   (1938)
     STARS:  Bobby Breen, Dolores Costello
     DIR:    Edward F. Cline
     LYRICS: Paul Francis Webster

100. BREWSTER'S MILLIONS   (1935)
     STARS:  Jack Buchanan, Lili Damiti
     DIR:    Thornton Freeland
     SONGS:  Ray Noble - Douglas Furber

101. BRIDE OF THE REGIMENT   (1930)
     STARS:  Vivienne Segal, Roger Pryor
     DIR:    John Francis Dillon
     SONGS:  Ed Ward - Al Bryan

102. BRIGADOON   (1954)
     STARS:  Gene Kelly, Van Johnson
     DIR:    Vincente Minnelli
     SONGS:  Frederick Loewe - Alan Jay Lerner
     Brigadoon; Almost Like Being In Love; Waiting For My Dearie;
     I'll Go Home With Bonnie Jean; Once In The Highlands; There But
     For You Go I; Down On McConachy Square; The Heather On The Hil
     MGM 2-SES-50-ST

103. BRIGHT LIGHTS   (1931)
     STARS:  Dorothy MacKaill, Frank Fay
     DIR:    Michael Curtiz

104. BRIGHT LIGHTS   (1935)
     STARS:  Joe E. Brown, Ann Dvorak
     DIR:    Busby Berkeley

105. BRING ON THE GIRLS   (1945)
     STARS:  Veronica Lake, Sonny Tufts
     DIR:    Sidney Lanfield
     SONGS:  Jimmy McHugh - Harold Adamson

106. BROADWAY   (1929)
     STARS:  Glenn Tryon, Merna Kennedy
     DIR:    Paul Fejos
     SONGS:  Con Conrad - Archie Gottler - Sidney Mitchell

107. BROADWAY (1942)
    STARS: George Raft, Pat O'Brien
    DIR:   William A. Seiter

108. BROADWAY BABIES (1929)
    STARS: Alice White, Sally Eilers
    DIR:   Mervyn LeRoy

109. BROADWAY BAD (1933)
    STARS: Joan Blondell, Ricardo Cortez
    DIR:   Sidney Lanfield
    SONGS: Harry Akst - Sidney Mitchell

110. BROADWAY GONDOLIER (1935)
    STARS: Joan Blondell, Dick Powell
    DIR:   Lloyd Bacon
    SONGS: Harry Warren - Al Dubin

111. BROADWAY HOSTESS (1935)
    STARS: Winnie Shaw, Genevieve Toblin
    DIR:   Frank McDonald

112. BROADWAY MELODY (1929)
    STARS: Bessie Love, Anita Paige
    DIR:   Harry Beaumont
    Give My Regards To Broadway (George M. Cohan); The Wedding Of
    The Painted Doll; Broadway Melody; Love Boat; Boy Friend; You
    Were Meant For Me (Nacio Herb Brown - Arthur Freed); Truthful
    Deacon Brown (William Robinson)
    Raviola 69

113. BROADWAY MELODY OF 1936 (1935)
    STARS: Jack Benny, Eleanor Powell
    DIR:   Roy Del Ruth
    SONGS: Nacio Herb Brown - Arthur Freed

114. BROADWAY MELODY OF 1937 (1937)
    STARS: Eleanor Powell, Robert Taylor
    DIR:   Roy Del Ruth
    SONGS: Nacio Herb Brown - Arthur Freed

115. BROADWAY MELODY (1940)
    STARS: Fred Astaire, Eleanor Powell
    DIR:   Norman Taurog
    SONGS: Cole Porter
    I Concentrate On You; Between You And Me; I've Got My Eyes On
    You; Begin The Beguine; Please Don't Monkey With Broadway; and
    I Am The Captain (anon.)
    C.I.F. 3002

116. BROADWAY RHYTHM (1944)
    STARS: George Murphy, Ginny Simms
    DIR:   Roy Del Ruth

117. BROADWAY SCANDALS  (1929)
    STARS:  Sally O'Neil, Jack Egan
    DIR:    George Archainbaud
    SONGS:  James F. Hanley

118. BROADWAY SERENADE  (1939)
    STARS:  Jeanette MacDonald
    DIR:    Robert Z. Leonard
    LYRICS: Gus Kahn

119. BROADWAY THROUGH A KEYHOLE  (1933)
    STARS:  Constance Cummings, Paul Kelly
    DIR:    Lowell Sherman
    SONGS:  Harry Revel - Mack Gordon

120. BROADWAY TO HOLLYWOOD  (1933)
    STARS:  Alice Brady, Frank Morgan
    DIR:    Walter Mack

121. BUCCANEER'S GIRL  (1950)
    STARS:  Yvonne De Carlo, Philip Friend
    DIR:    Frederick De Cordova
    SONGS:  Walter Scharf - Jack Brooks
    Here's To The Ladies; Monsieur; Because You're In Love; A
    Sailor Sails The Seven Seas

122. BUCK BENNY RIDES AGAIN  (1940)
    STARS:  Jack Benny, Eddie "Rochester" Anderson
    DIR:    Mark Sandrich
    SONGS:  Jimmy McHugh - Frank Loesser

123. BUCK PRIVATES  (1941)
    STARS:  Lee Bowman, Al Curtis
    DIR:    Arthur Lubin
    SONGS:  Hughie Prince - Don Raye

124. BUNDLE OF JOY  (1956)
    STARS:  Eddie Fisher, Debbie Reynolds
    DIR:    Norman Taurog
    SONGS:  Josef Myrow - Mack Gordon
    I Never Felt This Way Before; Lullaby In Blue; Worry About
    Tomorrow, Tomorrow; All About Love; Some Day Soon; Bundle Of
    Joy; What's So Good About Good Morning; New Year's Eve On Times
    Square; Tempus Fugit
    RCA LPM-1399

125. BY THE LIGHT OF THE SILVERY MOON  (1953)
    STARS:  Doris Day, Gordon MacRae
    DIR:    David Butler
    My Home Town Is A One Horse Town; Just One Girl (Lyn Udall -
    Karl Kennett); I'll Forget You (Ernest R. Ball - Annelu Burns);
    By The Light Of The Silvery Moon (Gus Edwards - Edward Madden);
    Be My Little Bumble Bee (Stanley Murphy - Henry Marshall); King

Chanticleer (A Seymour Brown - Nat D. Ayer); If You Were The
Only Girl In The World (Nat D. Ayer - Clifford Grey); Ain't We
Got Fun (Richard Whiting - Gus Kahn - Raymond Egan); Your Eyes
Have Told Me So (Walter Blaufuss - Egbert Van Alstyne - Gus
Kahn)
Capitol H-422

126. BYE BYE BIRDIE   (1963)
     STARS:   Dick Van Dyke, Janet Leigh
     DIR:     George Sidney
     SONGS:   Charles Strouse - Lee Adams
     Bye Bye Birdie; Telephone Hour; How Lovely To Be A Woman; Put
     On A Happy Face; One Boy; Honestly Sincere; Hymn For A Sunday
     Evening; One Last Kiss; A Lot Of Living To Do; Kids; Rosie;
     Shriner's Ballet
     RCA LSO-1081

127. CABARET   (1972)
     STARS:   Liza Minnelli, Joel Grey
     DIR:     Bob Fosse
     SONGS:   John Kander - Fred Ebb
     Willkomen; Mein Herr; Two Ladies; Maybe This Time I'll Be
     Lucky; Tiller Girls; Money, Money, Money; Married; If You
     Could See Her Through My Eyes; Tomorrow; Caberet
     ABC DS-752

128. CABIN IN THE SKY   (1943)
     STARS:   Ethel Waters, Eddie Anderson
     DIR:     Vincente Minnelli
     Cabin In The Sky; Honey In The Honeycomb; Love Me Tomorrow;
     In My Old Virginia Home (Vernon Duke - John LaTouche); Taking
     A Chance On Love (Duke - LaTouche - Ted Fetter); Happiness Is
     Just A Thing Called Joe; That Old Debbil Consequence; Li'l
     Black Sheep; Some Folk Work (Harold Arlen - E. Y. Harburg);
     Going Up (Duke Ellington); Shine (Cecil Mack - Ford Dabney -
     Lew Brown); Things Ain't What They Used To Be (Mercer Elling-
     ton)
     Col. CCL-2792

129. CADDY, THE   (1953)
     STARS:   Dean Martin, Jerry Lewis
     DIR:     Norman Taurog
     SONGS:   Harry Warren - Jack Brooks
     What Would You Do Without Me?; You're The Right One; It Takes
     A Lot Of Little Likes To Make One Big Love; Gay Continental;
     That's Amore; It's A Whistlin' Kind Of Morning

130. CADET GIRL   (1941)
     STARS:   Carole Landis, George Montgomery
     DIR:     Ray McCarey
     SONGS:   Ralph Rainger - Leo Robin

131. CAFE SOCIETY   (1939)

```
        STARS:   Madeline Carroll, Fred MacMurray
        DIR:     Edward H. Gifford
```

132.  CAIN AND MABEL   (1936)
```
        STARS:   Marion Davies, Clark Gable
        DIR:     Lloyd Bacon
        SONGS:   Harry Warren - Al Dubin
```

133.  CAIRO   (1942)
```
        STARS:   Jeanette MacDonald, Robert Young
        DIR:     W. S. VanDyke
        SONGS:   Arthur Schwartz - E. Y. Harburg
```

134.  CALAMITY JANE   (1953)
```
        STARS:   Doris Day, Howard Keel
        DIR:     David Butler
        SONGS:   Sammy Fain - Paul Francis Webster
```
Secret Love; Deadwood Stage; I Can Do Without You; Black Hills
Of Dakota; Just Blew In From The Windy City; Woman's Touch;
Higher Than A Hawk; 'Tis Harry I'm Plannin' To Marry;
Col. CL-6273

135.  CALENDAR GIRL   (1947)
```
        STARS:   Jane Frazee, William Marshall
        DIR:     Allan Dwan
        SONGS:   Jimmy McHugh - Harold Adamson
```

136.  CALL ME MADAM   (1953)
```
        STARS:   Ethel Merman, Donald O'Connor
        DIR:     Walter Lang
        SONGS:   Irving Berlin
```
Hostess With The Mostes' On The Ball; Ocarina; Marrying For
Love; It's A Lovely Day Today; You're Just In Love; Can You
Use Any Money Today; International Rag; Something To Dance
About; Best Thing For You
Decca DL-5465

137.  CALL ME MISTER   (1951)
```
        STARS:   Betty Grable, Dan Dailey
        DIR:     Lloyd Bacon
```
Japanese Girl Like American Boy; I Just Can't Do Enough For
You Baby; Love Is Back In Business; Whistle And Walk Away
(Sammy Fain - Mack Gordon); It's A Man's World (Josef Myrow -
Mack Gordon); Lament To Pots And Pans (Earl K. Brent - Jerry
Seelen); Call Me Mister; The Going-Home Train; Military Life
(Harold Rome)

138.  CALL OUT THE MARINES   (1942)
```
        STARS:   Victor MacLaglen, Edmund Lowe
        DIR:     Frank Ryan and William Hamilton
        SONGS:   Harry Revel - Mort Greene
```

139.  CAMELOT   (1967)
```
        STARS:   Richard Harris, Vanessa Redgrave
```

SONGS:  Frederick Loewe - Alan Jay Lerner
I Wonder What The King Is Doing Tonight; Simple Joys of Maiden-
hood; C'est Moi; Camelot; The Lusty Month Of May; Follow Me;
How To Handle A Woman; Take Me To The Fair; If Ever I Would
Leave You; What Do The Simple Folk Do?; I Loved You Once In
Silence; Guenevere
Warner Bros. SB-1712

140. CAMPUS HONEYMOON  (1948)
     STARS:  Lyn Wilde, Lee Wilde
     DIR:    Will Jason
     SONGS:  Richard Sale

141. CAMPUS RHYTHM  (1943)
     STARS:  Johnny Downs, Gale Storm
     DIR:    Arthur Dreifuss

142. CAN THIS BE DIXIE?  (1936)
     STARS:  Jane Withers, Slim Summerville
     DIR:    George Marshall
     SONGS:  Harry Akst - Sidney Clare

143. CAN-CAN  (1960)
     STARS:  Frank Sinatra, Shirley MacLaine
     DIR:    Walter Lang
     SONGS:  Cole Porter
     Monmart'; Maidens Typical Of France; C'est Magnifique; Live
     And Let Live; It's All Right With Me; Let's Do It; Just One
     Of Those Things; You Do Something To Me; I Love Paris
     Capitol SW-1301

144. CAN'T HELP SINGING  (1944)
     STARS:  Deanna Durbin, Robert Paige
     DIR:    Frank Ryan
     SONGS:  Jerome Kern - E. Y. Harburg

145. CAPTAIN CAUTION  (1940)
     STARS:  Victor Mature, Louise Platt
     DIR:    Richard Wallace
     SONGS:  Phil Ohman - Foster G. Carling

146. CAPTAIN JANUARY  (1936)
     STARS:  Shirley Temple, Guy Kibbe
     DIR:    David Butler
     SONGS:  Lew Pollack - Jack Yellen
     Early Bird; At The Codfish Ball; The Right Somebody To Love
     20th Century Fox T-906e.

147. CAPTAIN OF THE GUARD  (1930)
     STARS:  Laura LaPlante, John Boles
     DIR:    John S. Robinson
     SONGS:  Heinz Roemheld - William F. Dugan

148. CAREER GIRL  (1943)

STARS:  Frances Langford, Edward Norris
DIR:    Wallace W. Fox

149.  CAREFREE  (1938)
      STARS:  Ginger Rogers, Fred Astaire
      DIR:    Mark Sandrich
      SONGS:  Irving Berlin
      Change Partners, I Used To Be Color Blind; The Yam; The Night
      Is Filled With Music; Since They Turned 'Loch Lomond' Into
      Swing
      Col. SG-32472

150.  CARELESS LADY  (1932)
      STARS:  Joan Bennett, John Boles
      DIR:    Kenneth McKenna

151.  CARMEN JONES  (1954)
      STARS:  Dorothy Dandridge, Harry Belafonte
      DIR:    Otto Preminger
      SONGS:  Georges Bizet - Oscar Hammerstein II
      Haberna; You Talk Just Like My Maw; Card Scene; Dere's A Cafe
      On De Corner; Flower Song; My Joe; Beat Out Dat Rhythm On A
      Drum; Stan' Up And Fight; Whizzin' Away Along De Track
      RCA LM-1881

152.  CARNEGIE HALL  (1947)
      STARS:  William Prince, Marsha Hunt
      DIR:    Edgar G. Ulmer

153.  CARNIVAL IN COSTA RICA  (1947)
      STARS:  Dick Haymes, Vera-Ellen
      DIR:    Gregory Ratoff

154.  CAROLINA BLUES  (1944)
      STARS:  Kay Kyser and his orchestra, Ann Miller
      DIR:    Leigh Jason
      SONGS:  Jule Styne - Sammy Cahn

155.  CAROUSEL  (1956)
      STARS:  Gordon MacRae, Shirley Jones
      DIR:    Henry King
      SONGS:  Richard Rodgers- Oscar Hammerstein II
      Carousel Waltz; You're A Queer One, Julie Jordan; Mister Snow;
      If I Loved You; When The Children Are Asleep; June Is Bustin'
      Out All Over; Blow High, Blow Low; Stonecutters Cut It On
      Stone; What's The Use Of Wondrin'; A Real Nice Clambake; You'll
      Never Walk Alone
      Capitol SW-694

156.  CASA MANANA  (1951)
      STARS:  Robert Clarke, Virginia Welles
      DIR:    Jean Yarbrough
      Fifty Games Of Solitaire On Saturday Night (Louis and Robert
      Herscher); I Hear A Rhapsody (George Fragos - Jack Baker);

Cielito Lindo; Bounce (Jay Livingston - Ray Evans - Olsen and Johnson); People Like You (Harold Cooke - Otis Bigelow); Madame Will Drop Her Shawl (Herb Pine - Sam Brown)

157. CASANOVA IN BURLESQUE (1944)
     STARS:  Joe E. Brown, June Havoc
     DIR:    Leslie Goodwins
     SONGS:  Walter Kent - Kim Gannon

158. CASBAH  (1948)
     STARS:  Yvonne DeCarlo, Tony Martin
     DIR:    John Berry
     SONGS:  Harold Arlen - Leo Robin

159. CAT AND THE FIDDLE, THE  (1934)
     STARS:  Ramon Novarro, Jeannette MacDonald
     DIR:    William K. Howard
     SONGS:  Jerome Kern - Otto Harbach

160. CENTENNIAL SUMMER  (1946)
     STARS:  Jeanne Crain, Linda Darnell
     DIR:    Otto Preminger
     SONGS:  Jerome Kern - Oscar Hammerstein II - Leo Robin

161. CHAMPAGNE WALTZ, THE  (1937)
     STARS:  Gladys Swarthout, Fred MacMurray
     DIR:    Edward Sutherland

162. CHASING RAINBOWS  (1930)
     STARS:  Bessie Love, Charles King
     DIR:    Charles F. Reisner

163. CHATTERBOX  (1943)
     STARS:  Joe E. Brown, Judy Canova
     DIR:    Joseph Santley

164. CHECK AND DOUBLE CHECK  (1930)
     STARS:  Freeman F. Cosden, Charles F. Correll (Amos 'n' Andy)
     DIR:    Melville Brown

165. CHEER UP AND SMILE  (1930)
     STARS:  Arthur Lake, Dixie Lee
     DIR:    Sidney Lanfield
     SONGS:  Jesse Greer - Ray Klages

166. CHILDREN OF DREAMS  (1931)
     STARS:  Margaret Schilling, Paul Gregory
     DIR:    Alan Crosland
     SONGS:  Sigmund Romberg - Oscar Hammerstein II

167. CHILDREN OF PLEASURE  (1930)
     STARS:  Lawrence Gray, Wynne Gibson
     DIR:    Harry Beaumont
     SONGS:  Fred Fisher - Andy Rice

168. CHIP OFF THE OLD BLOCK   (1944)
     STARS:   Donald O'Connor, Peggy Ann Blyth
     DIR:     Charles Lamont

169. CHITTY CHITTY BANG BANG   (1968)
     STARS:   Dick Van Dyke, Sally Ann Howes
     DIR:     Ken Hughes
     SONGS:   Richard M. and Robert B. Sherman
     You Two; Toot Sweets; Hushabye Mountain; Me Ol'Mam Boo; Truly
     Scrumptious; Chitty Chitty Bang Bang; Lovely, Lonely Man; The
     Roses Of Success; Chu-Chi Face; Doll On A Music Box
     United Artists  UAS-5188

170. CHOCOLATE SOLDIER, THE   (1941)
     STARS:   Rise Stevens, Nelson Eddy
     DIR:     Roy Del Ruth

171. CIGARETTE GIRL   (1947)
     STARS:   Leslie Brooks, Jimmy Lloyd
     DIR:     Gunther V. Fritsch
     SONGS:   Allan Roberts - Doris Fisher

172. CINDERELLA JONES   (1946)
     STARS:   Joan Leslie, Robert Alda
     DIR:     Busby Berkeley
     SONGS:   Jule Styne - Sammy Cahn

173. CINDERFELLA   (1960)
     STARS:   Jerry Lewis, Anna Maria Alberghetti
     DIR:     Frank Tashlin
     SONGS:   Harry Warren - Jack Brooks
     Somebody; Princess Waltz; Let Me Be A People
     Dot 38001

174. CLOSE HARMONY   (1929)
     STARS:   Nancy Carroll, Charles "Buddy" Rogers
     DIR:     John Cromwell and Edward Sutherland
     SONGS:   Richard J. Whiting - Leo Robin

175. COCKEYED CAVALIERS   (1934)
     STARS:   Bert Wheeler, Robert Woolsey
     DIR:     Mark Sandrich

176. COCKEYED WORLD, THE   (1929)
     STARS:   Victor McLaglen, Edmund Lowe
     DIR:     Raoul Walsh

177. COCOANUT GROVE   (1938)
     STARS:   Fred MacMurray, Harriet Hilliard
     DIR:     Alfred Santell

178. COCOANUTS   (1929)
     STARS:   The Marx Brothers
     DIR:     Joseph Santley, Robert Florey

SONGS: Irving Berlin

179. COLLEEN (1936)
     STARS: Ruby Keeler, Dick Powell
     DIR:   Alfred E. Green
     SONGS: Harry Warren - Al Dubin

180. COLLEGE COACH (1933)
     STARS: Dick Powell, Ann Dvorak
     DIR:   William A. Wellman

181. COLLEGE HOLIDAY (1936)
     STARS: Jack Benny, Burns and Allen
     DIR:   Frank Tuttle

182. COLLEGE HUMOR (1933)
     STARS: Bing Crosby, Jack Oakie
     DIR:   Wesley Ruggles
     SONGS: Arthur Johnston - Sam Coslow
     Learn To Croon; Down The Old Ox Road; Moon Struck; Alma Mater;
     Colleen Of Killarney; Classroom Number; Play Ball; I'm A Bach-
     elor Of The Art Of Ha-Cha-Cha
     Col. C2L-43

183. COLLEGE RHYTHM (1934)
     STARS: Jack Oakie, Joe Penner
     DIR:   Norman Taurog
     SONGS: Harry Revel - Mack Gordon

184. COLLEGE SWING (1938)
     STARS: Bob Hope, George Burns and Gracie Allen
     DIR:   Raoul Walsh
     LYRICS: Frank Loesser

185. COLLEGIATE (1936)
     STARS: Joe Penner, Jack Oakie
     DIR:   Ralph Murphy
     SONGS: Harry Revel - Mack Gordon

186. COMIN' ROUND THE MOUNTAIN (1951)
     STARS: Abbott and Costello
     DIR:   Charles T. Lamont
     Agnes Clung (Dorothy Shay - Hessie Smith); You Broke Your Prom-
     ise (Eddie Pola - Irving Taylor - George Wyle); Sagebrush Sadie
     (Britt Wood); Why Don't Someone Marry Mary Ann? (Britt Wood -
     Wilbur Beatty); There'll Never Be Another Notch On Father's
     Shotgun.

187. CONEY ISLAND (1943)
     STARS: Betty Grable, George Montgomery
     DIR:   Walter Lang
     SONGS: Ralph Rainger - Leo Robin

188. CONNECTICUT YANKEE, A (1931)

103

STARS:   Will Rogers, Maureen O'Sullivan
DIR:     David Butler
SONGS:   Richard Rodgers - Lorenz Hart

189.  CONNECTICUT YANKEE, A   (1949)
STARS:   Bing Crosby, Rhonda Fleming
DIR:     Tay Garnett
SONGS:   Jimmy Van Heusen - Johnny Burke
Once And For Always; If You Stub Your Toe On The Moon; When
Is Sometime?; Busy Doing Nothing; Twixt Myself And Me.
Decca DL-4261

190.  COPACABANA   (1947)
STARS:   Groucho Marx, Carmen Miranda
DIR:     Alfred W. Green
SONGS:   Sam Coslow

191.  CORONADO   (1935)
STARS:   Johnny Downs, Betty Burgess
DIR:     Norman McLeod

192.  COUNTESS OF MONTE CRISTO, THE   (1948)
STARS:   Sonja Henie, Olga San Juan
DIR:     Frederick De Cordova
SONGS:   Saul Chaplin - Jack Brooks

193.  THE COUNTRY GIRL   (1954)
STARS:   Bing Crosby, Grace Kelly
DIR:     George Seaton
SONGS:   Harold Arlen - Ira Gershwin
Dissertation On The State Of Bliss; The Search Is Through; The
Land Around Us; It's Mine, It's Yours.
Decca DL-4264

194.  COURT JESTER   (1956)
STARS:   Danny Kaye, Glynis Johns
DIR:     Norman Panama, Melvin Frank
SONGS:   Sylvia Fine - Sammy Cahn
Life Could No Better Be; They'll Never Outfox The Fox; Baby,
Let Me Take You Dreaming; My Heart Knows A Lovely Song; I Live
To Love; Willow Waley; Pass The Basket; Where Walks My True
Love; Maladjusted Jester.
Decca DL-8212

195.  COVER GIRL   (1944)
STARS:   Rita Hayworth, Gene Kelly
DIR:     Charles Vidor
SONGS:   Jerome Kern - Ira Gershwin

196.  COWBOY FROM BROOKLYN   (1938)
STARS:   Dick Powell, Pat O'Brien
DIR:     Lloyd Bacon
LYRICS:  Johnny Mercer

197. COWBOY IN MANHATTAN  (1943)
     STARS:  Frances Langford, Robert Paige
     DIR:    Frank Woodruff
     SONGS:  Milton Rosen - Everett Carter

198. CRAZY HOUSE  (1943)
     STARS:  Olsen and Johnson
     DIR:    Edward Cline

199. CROONER, THE  (1932)
     STARS:  David Manners, Ann Dvorak
     DIR:    Lloyd Bacon

200. CROSS MY HEART  (1946)
     STARS:  Betty Hutton, Sonny Tufts
     DIR:    John Berry

201. CUBAN LOVE SONG  (1931)
     STARS:  Lawrence Tibbett, Lupe Velez
     DIR:    W. S. Van Dyke
     SONGS:  Jimmy McHugh - Dorothy Fields - Herbert Stothart

202. CUBAN PETE  (1946)
     STARS:  Desi Arnaz, Ethel Smith
     DIR:    Jean Yarbrough

203. CUCKOOS, THE  (1930)
     STARS:  Bert Wheeler, Robert Woolsey
     DIR:    Paul Sloane

204. CURLY TOP  (1935)
     STARS:  Shirley Temple, John Boles
     DIR:    Irving Cummings
     SONGS:  Ray Henderson - Irving Caesar - Ted Koehler

205. DADDY LONG LEGS  (1955)
     STARS:  Fred Astaire, Leslie Caron
     DIR:    Jean Negulesco
     SONGS:  Johnny Mercer
     Something's Gotta Give; Sluefoot; Dream; Thunderbird; How I
     Made The Team; C-a-t Spells Cat; Welcome Egghead; History Of
     The Beat; Daddy Long Legs.

206. DAMES  (1934)
     STARS:  Joan Blondell, Dick Powell
     DIR:    Ray Enright

207. DAMN YANKEES  (1958)
     STARS:  Tab Hunter, Gwen Verdon
     DIR:    George Abbott, Stanley Domen
     SONGS:  Richard Adler - Jerry Ross
     Whatever Lola Wants; Shoeless Joe From Hannibal, Mo.; There's
     Something About An Empty Chair; Two Lost Souls; A Little
     Brains, A Little Talent; Goodbye Old Girl; Who's Got The Pain;

105

Six Months Out Of Every Year; Heart; Those Were The Good Old
Days.
RCA   LSO-1047

208.   DAMSEL IN DISTRESS   (1937)
       STARS:   Fred Astaire, Joan Fontaine
       DIR:     George Stevens
       SONGS:   George and Ira Gershwin
       Foggy Day; Things Are Looking Up; I Can't Be Bothered Now;
       Nice Work If You Can Get It; The Jolly Tar And The Milkmaid;
       Stiff Upper Lip; Put Me To The Test; Sing Of Spring.
       Curtain Calls CC 100/19

209.   DANCE, FOOLS, DANCE   (1931)
       STARS:   Joan Crawford, Lester Vail
       DIR:     Harry Beaumont

210.   DANCE, GIRL, DANCE   (1933)
       STARS:   Alan Dinehart, Evelyn Knapp
       DIR:     Frank Strayer

211.   DANCE, GIRL, DANCE   (1940)
       STARS:   Maureen O'Hara, Louis Hayward
       DIR:     Dorothy Arzner
       SONGS:   Bob Wright - Chet Forrest

212.   DANCE OF LIFE   (1929)
       STARS:   Hal Skelly, Nancy Carroll
       DIR:     John Cromwell, Edward Sutherland
       SONGS:   Richard Whiting - Leo Robin - Sam Coslow

213.   DANCING FEET   (1936)
       STARS:   Ben Lyon, Joan Marsh
       DIR:     Joseph Santley
       SONGS:   Sammy Stept - Sidney Mitchell

214.   DANCING IN THE DARK   (1949)
       STARS:   William Powell, Mark Stevens
       DIR:     Irving Reis
       SONGS:   Arthur Schwartz - Howard Dietz

215.   DANCING LADY   (1933)
       STARS:   Joan Crawford, Clark Gable
       DIR:     Robert Z. Leonard

216.   DANCING ON A DIME   (1941)
       STARS:   Grace McDonald, Robert Paige
       DIR:     Joseph Santley

217.   DANCING SWEETIES   (1930)
       STARS:   Grant Withers, Sue Carol
       DIR:     Ray Enright

218. DANGEROUS NAN McGREW  (1930)
     STARS:  Helen Kane, Victor Moore
     DIR:    Malcolm St. Clair

219. DANGEROUS WHEN WET  (1953)
     STARS:  Esther Williams, Fernando Lamas
     DIR:    Charles Walters
     SONGS:  Arthur Schwartz - Johnny Mercer
     In My Wildest Dreams; I Like Men; Ain't Nature Grand; I Got
     Out Of Bed On The Right Side; Liquapep.

220. DARLING LILI  (1970)
     STARS:  Julie Andrews, Rock Hudson
     DIR:    Blake Edwards
     SONGS:  Henry Mancini - Johnny Mercer
     Whistling Away In The Dark; Little Birds; Girl In No Man's
     Land; Gypsy Violin; I'll Give You Three Guesses; Darling Lili;
     Smile Away Each Rainy Day; Can-Can Cafe; Skal; Your Good-Will
     Ambassador.
     RCA  LSPX-1000

221. DATE WITH JUDY, A  (1948)
     STARS:  Wallace Beery, Jane Powell
     DIR:    Richard Thorpe

222. DAY AT THE CIRCUS, A  (1939)
     STARS:  The Marx Brothers, Kenny Baker
     DIR:    Mervyn Le Roy
     SONGS:  Harold Arlen - E. Y. Harburg

223. DAY AT THE RACES, A  (1937)
     STARS:  The Marx Brothers, Allan Jones
     DIR:    Sam Wood
     SONGS:  Bronislaw Kaper - Walter Jurmann - Gus Kahn

224. DEEP IN MY HEART  (1954)
     STARS:  Jose Ferrer, Merle Oberon
     DIR:    Stanley Donen
     MUSIC:  Sigmund Romberg  (Lyricist follows in parentheses)
     Stout Hearted Men; The Desert Song; One Kiss; You Will Remember
     Vienna; Softly As In A Morning Sunrise; It; Lover Come Back To
     Me; When I Grow Too Old To Dream (Oscar Hammerstein II); Deep
     In My Heart; Serenade; Your Land And My Land (Dorothy Donnelly);
     Leg Of Mutton (Roger Edens); Mr. And Mrs. (Cyrus Wood); I Love
     To Go Swimmin' With Wimmin (Ballard MacDonald); Auf Wiedersehn
     (Herbert Reynolds); Road To Paradise; Will You Remember (Sweet-
     heart)? (Rida Johnson Young).
     MGM  2-SES-54ST

225. DELICIOUS  (1931)
     STARS:  Janet Gaynor, Charles Farrell
     DIR:    David Butler
     SONGS:  George and Ira Gershwin

226. DELIGHTFULLY DANGEROUS  (1945)
     STARS:  Jane Powell, Ralph Bellamy
     DIR:    Arthur Lubin
     SONGS:  Morton Gould - Edward Heyman

227. DESERT SONG, THE  (1929)
     STARS:  John Boles, Carlotta King
     DIR:    Roy Del Ruth
     SONGS:  Sigmund Romberg - Oscar Hammerstein II

228. DESERT SONG, THE  (1943)
     STARS:  Dennis Morgan, Irene Manning
     DIR:    Robert Florey

229. DESERT SONG  (1953)
     STARS:  Kathryn Grayson, Gordon MacRae
     DIR:    Bruce Humberstone
     SONGS:  Sigmund Romberg - Oscar Hammerstein II - Otto Harbach
     The Desert Song; Long Live The Night; The Riff Song; Romance;
     Eastern Dance; One Alone; One Flower; Gay Parisienne (Serge
     Walters - Jack Scholl).
     Capitol SW-1842

230. DEVIL MAY CARE  (1929)
     STARS:  Ramon Novarro, Marion Harris
     DIR:    Sidney Franklin
     SONGS:  Herb Stothart - Clifford Grey

231. DIAMOND HORSESHOE  (1945)
     STARS:  Betty Grable, Dick Haymes
     DIR:    George Seaton
     SONGS:  Harry Warren - Mack Gordon

232. DIMPLES  (1936)
     STARS:  Shirley Temple, Frank Morgan
     DIR:    William A. Seiter
     SONGS:  Jimmy McHugh - Ted Koehler
     What Did The Bluebird Say?; He Was A Dandy; Picture Me Without
     You; Oh Mister Man Up In The Moon.
     20th Century Fox T-906e

233. DISC JOCKEY  (1951)
     STARS:  Ginny Simms, Tom Drake
     DIR:    Will Jason
     Show Me You Love Me; Let's Meander Through The Meadow (Roz
     Gordon - S. Steuben); After Hours; Nobody Wants Me (Roz Gor-
     don); Disc Jockey; In My Heart (Dick Hazard - Herb Jeffries);
     Peaceful Country (Foy Willing); Brain Wave (George Shearing);
     Oh Look At Me Now (Joe Bushkin - John DeVries); The Roving Kind
     (Arnold Stanton - Jessie Cavanaugh); Go Tell Aunt Rhody (Tra-
     ditional).

234. DIXIANA  (1930)

STARS:   Bebe Daniels, Everett Marshall
DIR:     Luther Reed
SONGS:   Harry Tierney - Anne Caldwell

235. DIXIE  (1943)
STARS:   Bing Crosby, Dorothy Lamour
DIR:     A. Edward Sutherland
SONGS:   Jimmy Van Heusen - Johnny Burke

236. DIXIE JAMBOREE  (1944)
STARS:   Frances Langford, Guy Kibbe
DIR:     Christy Cabanne
SONGS:   Michael Breen - Sam Neuman

237. DIZZY DAMES  (1936)
STARS:   Marjorie Rambeau, Florine McKinney
DIR:     William Nigh

238. DO YOU LOVE ME?  (1946)
STARS:   Maureen O'Hara, Dick Haymes
DIR:     Gregory Ratoff

239. DOCTOR DOLITTLE  (1967)
STARS:   Rex Harrison, Anthony Newley
DIR:     Richard Fleischer
SONGS:   Leslie Bricusse
My Friend The Doctor; The Vegetarian; Talk To The Animals; At
The Crossroads; I've Never Seen Anything Like It; When I Look
In Your Eyes; Like Animals; After Today; Fabulous Places; I
Think I Like You; Doctor Dolittle; Something In Your Smile.
20th Cent. Fox   DTCS 5101

240. DOCTOR RHYTHM  (1938)
STARS:   Bing Crosby, Mary Carlisle
DIR:     Frank Tuttle
SONGS:   Jimmy Monaco - Johnny Burke
My Heart Is Taking Lessons; This Is My Night To Dream; On The
Sentimental Side; Doctor Rhythm; Only A Gypsy Knows; P. S. 43;
Trumpet Player's Lament.
Decca   DL-4253

241. DOLL FACE  (1945)
STARS:   Vivian Blaine, Dennis O'Keefe
DIR:     Lewis Seiler
SONGS:   Jimmy McHugh - Harold Adamson

242. DOLLY SISTERS, THE  (1945)
STARS:   Betty Grable, June Haver
DIR:     Irving Cummings

243. DON'T GET PERSONAL  (1942)
STARS:   Hugh Herbert, Mischa Auer
DIR:     Charles Lamont
SONGS:   Norman Behens - Jack Brooks

244. DOUBLE OR NOTHING  (1937)
    STARS:  Bing Crosby, Martha Raye
    DIR:    Theodore Reed

245. DOWN AMONG THE SHELTERING PALMS  (1953)
    STARS:  William Lundigan, Gloria DeHaven
    DIR:    Edmund Goulding
    SONGS:  Harold Arlen - Ralph Blane
    I'm A Ruler Of A South Sea Island; Who Will It Be When The
    Time Comes; What Make De Difference; Down Among The Sheltering
    Palms; All Of Me.

246. DOWN ARGENTINE WAY  (1940)
    STARS:  Don Ameche, Betty Grable
    DIR:    Robert Cummings

247. DOWN MISSOURI WAY  (1946)
    STARS:  Martha O'Driscoll, John Carradine
    DIR:    Josef Berne
    SONGS:  Walter Kent - Kim Gannon

248. DOWN TO EARTH  (1947)
    STARS:  Rita Hayworth, Larry Parks
    DIR:    Alexander Hall
    SONGS:  Allan Roberts - Doris Fisher

249. DOWN TO THEIR LAST YACHT  (1934)
    STARS:  Mary Boland, Polly Moran
    DIR:    Paul Sloane

250. DuBARRY WAS A LADY  (1943)
    STARS:  Red Skelton, Lucille Ball
    DIR:    Roy Del Ruth

251. DUCHESS OF IDAHO  (1950)
    STARS:  Esther Williams, Van Johnson
    DIR:    Robert Z. Leonard
    Of All Things; Or Was It Spring?; Warm Hands, Cold Heart; You
    Can't Do Wrong Doin' Right; Let's Choo Choo Choo To Idaho
    (Floyd Huddlestone - Al Rinker); Singlefoot Serenade (M. Beel-
    by - G. M. Beilenson); Baby Come Out Of The Clouds (Harry Nemo
    Lee Pearl); You Won't Forget Me (Fred Spielman - Kermit Goell).

252. DUCK SOUP  (1933)
    STARS:  The Marx Brothers
    DIR:    Leo McCarey
    SONGS:  Harry Ruby - Bert Kalmar

253. EARL CARROLL SKETCH BOOK  (1946)
    STARS:  Constance Moore, William Marshall
    DIR:    Albert S. Rogell
    SONGS:  Jule Styne - Sammy Cahn

254. EARL CARROLL'S VANITIES (1945)
     STARS:  Dennis O'Keefe, Constance Moore
     DIR:    Joseph Stanley

255. EAST SIDE OF HEAVEN (1939)
     STARS:  Bing Crosby, Joan Blondell
     DIR:    David Butler
     SONGS:  Jimmy Monaco - Johnny Burke
     Hang Your Clothes On A Hickory Limb; That Sly Old Gentleman
     From Featherbed Lane; Sing A Song Of Moonbeams; East Side Of
     Heaven.
     Decca  DL-4253

256. EASTER PARADE (1948)
     STARS:  Judy Garland, Fred Astaire
     DIR:    Charles Walters
     SONGS:  Irving Berlin
     Happy Easter; Drum Crazy; It Only Happens When I Dance With
     You; Everybody's Doing It Now; I Want To Go Back To Michigan;
     A Fella With An Umbrella; I Love A Piano; Snooky Ookums; Rag-
     time Violin; When The Midnight Choo-Choo Leaves For Alabam';
     Shaking The Blues Away; Stepping Out With My Baby; A Couple Of
     Swells; Beautiful Faces; The Girl On The Magazine Cover; Better
     Luck Next Time; Easter Parade.
     MGM - 2 - SES - 40ST

257. EASY TO LOOK AT (1945)
     STARS:  Gloria Jean, Kirby Grand
     DIR:    Ford Beebe
     SONGS:  Arthur Altman - Charles Newman

258. EASY TO LOVE (1953)
     STARS:  Esther Williams, Van Johnson
     DIR:    Charles Walters
     SONGS:  Vic Mizzy - Mann Curtis
     Look Out! I'm Romantic; That's What A Rainy Day Is For; Didja
     Ever.

259. EASY TO WED (1946)
     STARS:  Esther Williams, Van Johnson
     DIR:    Eddie Buzzell

260. EDDIE CANTOR STORY (1953)
     STARS:  Keefe Brasselle
     DIR:    Alfred E. Green
     Ida, Sweet As Apple Cider; Now's The Time To Fall In Love; How
     'Ya Gonna Keep 'Em Down On The Farm; When I'm The President;
     Row, Row, Row; One Hour With You; Josephine, Please No; Lean
     On The Bell; Pretty Baby; Yes, Sir, That's My Baby; Ma, He's
     Making Eyes At Me; Makin' Whoopee.

261. EMBARRASSING MOMENTS (1934)
     STARS:  Chester Morris, Marian Nixon
     DIR:    Edward Laemmle

262. EMPEROR WALTZ, THE (1948)
    STARS: Bing Crosby, Joan Fontaine
    DIR:    Billy Wilder
    Get Yourself A Phonograph (Jimmy Van Heusen - Johnny Burke);
    Friendly Mountains (lyrics by Johnny Burke); A Kiss In Your
    Eyes (Johnny Burke - Richard Heuberger); I Kiss Your Hand Ma-
    dame (Fritz Rotter - Ralph Erwin); Whistler And His Dog (Arthur
    Pryor); The Emperor Waltz (Johann Strauss - Johnny Burke).
    Decca DL-4260

263. EVER SINCE EVE (1944)
    STARS: Ina Ray Hutton, Hugh Herbert
    DIR:    Arthur Dreifuss

264. EVERY DAY'S A HOLIDAY (1937)
    STARS: Mae West, Edmund Lowe
    DIR:    A. Edward Sutherland

265. EVERY NIGHT AT EIGHT (1935)
    STARS: George Raft, Alice Faye
    DIR:    Raoul Walsh

266. EVERYBODY SING (1938)
    STARS: Allan Jones, Fanny Brice
    DIR:    Edwin L. Marin

267. EVERYTHING I HAVE IS YOURS (1952)
    STARS: Marge and Gower Champion
    DIR:    Robert Z. Leonard
    Derry Down Dilly (Johnny Green - Johnny Mercer); Serenade To A
    New Baby (Johnny Green); Casablanca (Richard Priborsky); Seven-
    teen Thousand Telephone Poles (Saul Chaplin); Like Monday Fol-
    lows Sunday (Douglas Furber - Rex Newman - Clifford Grey -
    Johnny Green); My Heart Skips A Beat (Walter Donaldson - Chet
    Forrest - Bob Wright); General Hiram Johnson Jefferson Brown
    (Walter Donaldson - Gus Kahn); Everything I Have Is Yours (Bur-
    ton Lane - Harold Adamson).
    MGM 2-SES-52ST

268. EXCUSE MY DUST (1951)
    STARS: Red Skelton, Monica Lewis
    DIR:    Roy Rowland
    SONGS: Arthur Schwartz - Dorothy Fields
    Get A Horse; Spring Has Sprung; That's For Children; Lorelei
    Brown; Goin' Steady; I'd Like To Take You Out Dreaming; It
    Couldn't Happen To Two Nicer People; Where Can I Run From?

269. FABULOUS DORSEYS, THE (1947)
    STARS: Tommy and Jimmy Dorsey
    DIR:    Alfred W. Green

270. FANCY PANTS (1950)
    STARS: Bob Hope, Lucille Ball
    DIR:    George Marshall

SONGS:  Jay Livingston - Ray Evans
Home Cookin'; Fancy Pants; Yes M'Lord.

71.  THE FARMER TAKES A WIFE  (1953)
     STARS:  Betty Grable, Dale Robertson
     DIR:    Henry Levin
     SONGS:  Harold Arlen - Dorothy Fields
     Somethin' Real Special; We're In Business; With The Warm Sun
     Upon Me; Today I Love Ev'rybody; On The Erie Canal; Can You
     Spell Schenectady?; We're Doin' It For The Natives In Jamaica;
     When I Close My Door; I Could Cook; Look Who's Been Dreaming.

72.  FEUDIN', FUSSIN' AND A-FIGHTIN'  (1948)
     STARS:  Donald O'Connor, Marjorie Main
     DIR:    George Sherman

73.  FIDDLER ON THE ROOF  (1971)
     STARS:  Topol, Molly Picon
     DIR:    Norman Jewison
     SONGS:  Jerry Bock - Sheldon Harnick
     Tradition; Matchmaker, Matchmaker; If I Were A Rich Man; Sabbath
     Prayer; To Life; Miracle Of Miracles; Tevye's Dream; Sunrise,
     Sunset; Bottle Dance; Do You Love Me?; Far From The Home I
     Love; Anatevka.
     United Artists  2-UA-10900

74.  FIESTA  (1941)
     STARS:  Anne Ayars, George Negrete
     DIR:    Le Roy Prinz

75.  FIESTA  (1947)
     STARS:  Esther Williams, Akim Tamiroff
     DIR:    Richard Thorpe

76.  FIFTY MILLION FRENCHMEN  (1931)
     STARS:  Olsen and Johnson
     DIR:    Lloyd Bacon

77.  FIFTY-SECOND STREET  (1937)
     STARS:  Ian Hunter, Leo Carrillo
     DIR:    Harold Young
     SONGS:  Harold Spina - Walter Bullock

78.  FINIAN'S RAINBOW  (1968)
     STARS:  Fred Astaire, Petula Clark
     DIR:    Francis Ford Coppola
     SONGS:  Burton Lane - E. Y. Harburg
     This Time Of Year; How Are Things In Glocca Morra?; Look To
     The Rainbow; If This Isn't Love; Something Sort Of Grandish;
     That Great Come-And-Get-It Day; Old Devil Moon; When The Idle
     Poor Become The Idle Rich; When I'm Not Near The Girl I Love;
     Necessity; The Begat.
     Warner Bros.  SB-2550

113

279. FIREFLY, THE    (1937)
     STARS:   Jeanette MacDonald, Allan Jones
     DIR:     Robert A. Leonard

280. FIRST BABY, THE    (1936)
     STARS:   Johnny Downs, Shirley Dean
     DIR:     Lewis Seiler

281. FIRST LOVE    (1939)
     STARS:   Deanna Durbin, Robert Stack
     DIR:     Henry Koster

282. FIVE PENNIES, THE    (1959)
     STARS:   Danny Kaye, Barbara Bel Geddes
     DIR:     Melville Shavelson
     NEW SONGS:  Sylvia Fine
     The Five Pennies; Lullaby In Ragtime; Goodnight - Sleep Tight;
     Follow The Leader; When The Saints Come Marching In; Schnit-
     zelbank (new lyrics).
     Dot  29500

283. 5000 FINGERS OF DR. T    (1953)
     STARS:   Peter Lind Hayes, Mary Healy
     DIR:     Roy Rowland
     SONGS:   Frederick Hollander - Dr. Seuss (Tehdore Geisel);
     The Kid's Song; Ten Happy Fingers; Get Together Weather; Dream
     Stuff; The Dressing Song; Dungeon Elevator; Victorious; Hyp-
     notic Duel.

284. FLEET'S IN, THE    (1942)
     STARS:   Dorothy Lamour, William Holden
     DIR:     Victor Schertzinger

285. FLIRTATION WALK    (1934)
     STARS:   Dick Powell, Ruby Keeler
     DIR:     Frank Borzage
     SONGS:   Allie Wrubel - Mort Dixon

286. FLOWER DRUM SONG    (1961)
     STARS:   Nancy Kwan, Miyoshi Umeki
     DIR:     Henry Koster
     SONGS:   Richard Rodgers - Oscar Hammerstein II
     You Are Beautiful; 100 Million Miracles; I Enjoy Being A Girl;
     I Am Going To Like It Here; Chop Suey; Don't Marry Me; Grant
     Avenue; Love, Look Away; Fan Tan Fanny; Gliding Through My
     Memoree; The Other Generation; Sunday.
     Decca  DL-79098

287. FLYING DOWN TO RIO    (1933)
     STARS:   Dolores Del Rio, Fred Astaire
     DIR:     Thornton Freeland
     SONGS:   Vincent Youmans - Edward Eliscu - Gus Kahn

288. FLYING HIGH    (1931)

STARS:   Charlotte Greenwood, Bert Lahr
DIR:     Charles F. Reisner
SONGS:   Jimmy McHugh - Dorothy Fields

89. FOLIES BERGERE   (1935)
STARS:   Maurice Chevalier, Merle Oberon
DIR:     Roy Del Ruth

90. FOLLIES' GIRL   (1943)
STARS:   Wendy Barrie, Doris Nolan
DIR:     William Rowland

91. FOLLOW THE BAND   (1943)
STARS:   Leon Erroll, Eddie Quillan
DIR:     Jean Yarbrough

92. FOLLOW THE BOYS   (1944)
STARS:   George Raft, Vera Zorina
DIR:     Edward Sutherland

93. FOLLOW THE FLEET   (1936)
STARS:   Ginger Rogers, Fred Astaire
DIR:     Mark Sandrich
SONGS:   Irving Berlin
I'm Putting All My Eggs In One Basket; We Saw The Sea; Let's
Face The Music And Dance; Let Yourself Go; But Where Are You?;
I'd Rather Lead A Band; Get Thee Behind Me Satan.
Col. SG-32472

94. FOLLOW THE LEADER   (1930)
STARS:   Ed Wynn, Ginger Rogers
DIR:     Norman Taurog

95. FOLLOW THROUGH   (1930)
STARS:   Charles "Buddy" Rogers, Nancy Carroll
DIR:     Laurance Schwab and Lloyd Corrigan

96. FOLLOW YOUR HEART   (1936)
STARS:   Marion Talley, Michael Bartlett
DIR:     Aubrey Scotto
SONGS:   Victor Schertzinger - Walter Bullock - Sidney Mitchell

97. FOOLS FOR SCANDAL   (1938)
STARS:   Carole Lombard, Fernand Gravet
DIR:     Mervyn LeRoy
SONGS:   Richard Rodgers - Lorenz Hart

98. FOOTLIGHT GLAMOUR   (1943)
STARS:   Penny Singleton, Arthur Lake
DIR:     Frank Strayer

99. FOOTLIGHT PARADE   (1933)
STARS:   James Cagney, Joan Blondell
DIR:     Lloyd Bacon

300. FOOTLIGHT SERENADE   (1942)
     STARS:   John Payne, Betty Gravel
     DIR:     Gregory Ratoff

301. FOOTLIGHT VARIETIES   (1951)
     STARS:   Leon Errol, The Sportsmen
     DIR:     Hal Yates
     Hi Time (John Rarig - Marty Sperzel); The Show Must Go On (Gor-
     don Jenkins - Tom Adair); You Only Want It 'Cause You Haven't
     Got It (Basil Thomas - Barbara Gordon - Harry Parr Davies);
     Swinging In The Corn (Allie Wrubel - Herb Magidson); Liberace
     Boogie (Liberace).

302. FOR ME AND MY GAL   (1942)
     STARS:   Judy Garland, Gene Kelly
     DIR:     Busby Berkeley

303. FORTY-SECOND STREET   (1933)
     STARS:   Warner Baxter, Bebe Daniels
     DIR:     Lloyd Bacon
     SONGS:   Harry Warren - Al Dubin

304. FOUR JACKS AND A JILL   (1941)
     STARS:   Ray Bolger, Anne Shirley
     DIR:     Jack Hively
     SONGS:   Harry Revel - Mort Greene

305. FOUR JILLS IN A JEEP   (1944)
     STARS:   Kay Francis, Carole Landis
     DIR:     William A. Seiter

306. FOX MOVIETONE FOLLIES   (1929)
     STARS:   Sue Carol, Lola Lane
     DIR:     David Butler
     SONGS:   Con Conrad - Archie Gottler - Sidney Mitchell

307. FRANKIE AND JOHNNY   (1935)
     STARS:   Helen Morgan, Chester Morris
     DIR:     John H. Auer

308. FREDDIE STEPS OUT   (1946)
     STARS:   Freddie Stewart, June Preisser
     DIR:     Arthur Dreifuss

309. FREE AND EASY   (1930)
     STARS:   Buster Keaton, Anita Paige
     DIR:     Edward Sedgwick

310. FRESHMAN YEAR, THE   (1938)
     STARS:   Constance Moore, William Lundigan
     DIR:     Frank McDonald

311. FUN AND FANCY FREE   (1947)
     STARS:   Dinah Shore, Edgar Bergen
     DIR:     William Morgan

312. FUNNY FACE (1957)
    STARS:  Fred Astaire, Audrey Hepburn
    DIR:    Stanley Donen
    SONGS:  George and Ira Gershwin
    Funny Face; How Long Has This Been Going On?; Clap Yo' Hands;
    He Loves And She Loves; 'S Wonderful; Lt's Kiss And Make Up,
    Also: Think Pink; Bonjour Paris; On How To Be Lovely (Roger
    Edens - Leonard Gershe).
    Verve 15001

313. FUNNY GIRL  (1968)
    STARS:  Barbra Streisand, Omar Sharif
    DIR:    William Wyler
    SONGS:  Jule Styne - Bob Merrill
    I'm The Greatest Star; If A Girl Isn't Pretty; Roller Skate
    Rag; His Love Makes Me Beautiful; People; You Are Woman, I Am
    Man; Don't Rain On My Parade; Sadie, Sadie; The Swan; Funny
    Girl.  Also: I'd Rather Be Blue (Fred Fisher - Billy Rose);
    Second Hand Rose (James Hanley - Grant Clark); My Man (Maurice
    Yvain - Channing Pollack).
    Col.  OS-3220

314. FUNNY LADY  (1975)
    STARS:  Barbra Streisand, James Caan
    DIR:    Herbert Ross
    How Lucky Can You Get; So Long Honey Lamb; Isn't It Better?; I
    Like Him/I Like Her; Blind Date; Let's Hear It For Me (John
    Kander - Fred Ebb).  Lyrics by Billy Rose: I Found A Million
    Dollar Baby (Harry Warren); Me And My Shadow (Al Jolsen, Dave
    Dreyer); I Got A Code In My Nose (Arthur Fields - Fred Hall);
    It's Only A Paper Moon (Harold Arlen - E. Y. Harburg); More
    Than You Know; Great Day (Vincent Youmans - Edward Eliscu);
    Clap Hands, Here Comes Charley (Joseph Meyer - Ballard MacDon-
    ald).  Also: If I Love Again (Ben Oakland - J. P. Murray); Am
    I Blue? (Harry Akst - Grant Clarke).
    Arista - AL9004

315. FUNNY THING HAPPENED ON THE WAY TO THE FORUM, A  (1966)
    STARS:  Zero Mostel, Jack Gilford
    DIR:    Richard Lester
    SONGS:  Stephen Sondheim
    Comedy Tonight; Free; Lovely; Everybody Ought To Have A Maid;
    Bring Me My Bride.
    United Artists  UAS-5144

316. GAIETY GIRLS  (1938)
    STARS:  Jack Hulbert, Patricia Ellis
    DIR:    Thronton Freeland
    SONGS:  Mischa Spoliansky - William Kernell

317. GALS, INC.  (1943)
    STARS:  Leon Errol, Harriet Hilliard
    DIR:    Leslie Goodwins
    SONGS:  Milton Rosen - Everett Carter

318. GANG WAR   (1928)
     STARS:   Olive Borden, Jack Pickford

319. GANG'S ALL HERE, THE   (1943)
     STARS:   Alice Faye, Carmen Miranda
     DIR:     Busby Berkeley
     SONGS:   Harry Warren - Leo Robin

320. GARDEN OF THE MOON   (1938)
     STARS:   Pat O'Brien, Margaret Lindsay
     DIR:     Busby Berkeley
     SONGS:   Harry Warren - Al Dubin - Johnny Mercer

321. GAY DIVORCEE, THE   (1934)
     STARS:   Fred Astaire, Ginger Rogers
     DIR:     Mark Sandrich
     Looking For A Needle In A Haystack; The Continental (Con Con-
     rad - Herb Magidson); Don't Let It Bother You; Let's K-nock
     K-nees (Harry Revel - Mack Gordon); Night And Day (Cole Por-
     ter).
     EMI EMTC-101

322. GENE KRUPA STORY   (1959)
     STARS:   Sal Mineo, Susan Kohner
     DIR:     Don Weis
     Exactly Like You; On The Sunny Side Of The Street (Jimmy Mc-
     Hugh - Dorothy Fields); Battle Of The Saxes (Leith Stevens);
     Cherokee (Ray Noble); I Love My Baby (Harry Warren - Bud Green)
     In The Mood (Joe Garland - Andy Razaf); Memories Of You (Eubie
     Blake - Andy Razaf); Royal Garden Blues (Spencer and Clarence
     Williams); Oahu Dance (Leith Stevens - Ray Noble); Let There
     Be Love (Lionel Rand - Ian Grant).
     Verve 15010

323. GENTLEMEN MARRY BRUNETTES   (1955)
     STARS:   Jane Russell, Jeanne Crain
     DIR:     Richard Sale
     Have You Met Miss Jones?; My Funny Valentine; I've Got Five Dol-
     lars (Richard Rodgers - Lorenz Hart); You're Driving Me Crazy;
     Gentlemen Marry Brunettes (Herbert Spencer - Earle Hagan - Rich
     ard Sale); I Wanna Be Loved By You (Harry Ruby - Herbert Stot-
     hart - Bert Kalmar); Daddy (Bob Troup); Ain't Misbehavin' (Fats
     Waller - Harry Brooks - Andy Razaf).
     Coral 57013

324. GENTLEMEN PREFER BLONDES   (1953)
     STARS:   Jane Russell, Marilyn Monroe
     DIR:     Howard Hawks
     SONGS:   Jule Styne - Leo Robin
     Bye Bye Baby; A Little Girl From Little Rock; Diamonds Are A
     Girl's Best Friend; and, Ain't There Anyone Here For Love?;
     When Love Goes Wrong (Harry Carmichael - Harold Adamson).
     MGM 2353-067 (Import)

25. GEORGE WHITE'S SCANDALS (1934)
    STARS:  Rudy Vallee, Jimmy Durante
    DIR:    George White
    SONGS:  Ray Henderson - Irving Caesar - Jack Yellen

26. GEORGE WHITE'S SCANDALS (1935)
    STARS:  Alice Faye, James Dunn
    DIR:    George White

27. GEORGE WHITE'S SCANDALS OF 1945 (1945)
    STARS:  Joan Davis, Jack Haley
    DIR:    Felix E. Feist

28. GERALDINE (1953)
    STARS:  John Carroll, Stan Freberg
    DIR:    R. G. Springsteen
    Geraldine (Victor Young - Sidney Clare); Wintertime Of Love
    (Young - Edward Heyman); Flaming Lips (Freberg); Rat Now (Fuzzy
    Knight); Also: Black Is The Color; Along The Colorado Trail;
    The Foggy Dew (lyrics: Irwin Coster).

29. GET HEP TO LOVE (1942)
    STARS:  Gloria Jean, Donald O'Connor
    DIR:    Charles Lamont

30. GHOST CATCHERS (1944)
    STARS:  Olsen and Johnson
    DIR:    Edward L. Cline

31. G. I. JANE (1951)
    STARS:  Jean Porter, Tom Neal
    DIR:    Reginald La Borg
    Gee I Love My G. I. Jane; I Love Girls (Jimmy Dodd); Baby I
    Can't Wait (Johnny Clark - Diane Manners); What's To Be Is Gon-
    na Be (Teepee Mitchell - Johnny Anz).

32. GIFT OF GAB, THE (1934)
    STARS:  Edmund Lowe, Gloria Stuart
    DIR:    Karl Freund

33. GIGI (1958)
    STARS:  Leslie Caron, Maurice Chevalier
    DIR:    Vincente Minnelli
    SONGS:  Frederick Loewe - Alan Jay Lerner
    Gigi; Thank Heaven For Little Girls; It's A Bore; The Parisians;
    She Is Not Thinking Of Me; The Night They Invented Champagne;
    I Remember It Well; Say A Prayer For Me Tonight; I'm Glad I'm
    Not Young Anymore.
    MGM E3641 ST

34. GIRL CRAZY (1932)
    STARS:  Bert Wheeler, Robert Woolsey
    DIR:    William A. Seiter
    SONGS:  George and Ira Gershwin

119

335. GIRL CRAZY  (1943)
    STARS:  Judy Garland, Mickey Rooney
    DIR:    Norman Taurog
    SONGS:  George and Ira Gershwin
    Treat Me Rough; Sam And Delilah; Bidin' My Time; Embraceable
    You; Fascinating Rhythm; I Got Rhythm; But Not For Me; Cactus
    Time In Arizona; Barbary Coast.
    Curtain Calls  CC100/9-10

336. GIRL FRIEND, THE  (1935)
    STARS:  Ann Sothern, Jack Haley
    DIR:    Eddie Buzzell
    SONGS:  Arthur Johnston - Gus Kahn

337. GIRL FROM MISSOURI  (1934)
    STARS:  Jean Harlow, Franchot Tone
    DIR:    Jack Conway

338. THE GIRL MOST LIKELY  (1958)
    STARS:  Jane Powell, Cliff Robertson
    DIR:    Mitchell Leisen
    SONGS:  Hugh Martin - Ralph Blane
    I Don't Know What I Want; We Gotta Keep Up With The Joneses;
    Travelogue; Balboa; Crazy Horse; All The Colors Of The Rain-
    bow; The Girl Most Likely (Nelson Riddle - Bob Russell).

339. THE GIRL NEXT DOOR  (1953)
    STARS:  Dan Daily, June Haver
    DIR:    Richard Sale
    SONGS:  Josef Myrow - Mack Gordon
    If I Love You A Mountain; Girl Next Door; You Nowhere Guy; I'd
    Rather Have A Pal Than A Gal--Anytime.

340. GIRL OF THE GOLDEN WEST  (1938)
    STARS:  Nelson Eddy, Jeanette MacDonald
    DIR:    Robert Z. Leonard

341. GIRL RUSH  (1944)
    STARS:  Wally Brown, Alan Carney
    DIR:    Gordon Douglas
    SONGS:  Lew Pollack - Harry Harris

342. GIRL RUSH  (1955)
    STARS:  Rosalind Russell, Fernando Lamas
    DIR:    Robert Pirosh
    SONGS:  Hugh Martin - Ralph Blane
    If You'll Only Take A Chance; Occasional Man; At Last We're
    Alone; Champagne; Birmin'ham; Out Of Doors; Homesick Hillbilly;
    Chose Your Partner; Girl Rush.

343. GIRL WITHOUT A ROOM  (1933)
    STARS:  Charles Farrell, Charles Ruggles
    DIR:    Ralph Murphy
    SONGS:  Will Jason - Val Burton

344. GIVE A GIRL A BREAK   (1953)
     STARS:   Debbie Reynolds, Marge and Gower Champion
     DIR:     Stanley Donen
     SONGS:   Burton Lane - Ira Gershwin
     Give A Girl A Break; In Our United State; It Happens Every
     Time; Nothing Is Impossible; Applause, Applause.
     Ben Bagley's Ira Gershwin Revisited   PS-1353

345. GIVE ME A SAILOR   (1938)
     STARS:   Bob Hope, Martha Raye
     DIR:     Elliot Nugent
     SONGS:   Ralph Rainger - Leo Robin

346. GIVE OUT SISTERS   (1942)
     STARS:   The Andrews Sisters, Grace MacDonald
     DIR:     Edward F. Cline

347. GIVE US THIS NIGHT   (1936)
     STARS:   Gladys Swarthout, Jan Kiepura
     DIR:     Alexander Hall
     SONGS:   Erich Korngold - Oscar Hammerstein II

348. GLAMOUR GIRL   (1948)
     STARS:   Susan Reed, Virginia Grey
     DIR:     Arthur Dreifuss

349. GLENN MILLER STORY   (1954)
     STARS:   James Stewart, June Allyson
     DIR:     Anthony Mann
     Moonlight Serenade; Tuxedo Junction; Little Brown Jug; String
     of Pearls; In The Mood; Pennsylvania 6-5000; St. Louis Blues
     March; American Patrol; Basin Street Blues; Love Theme.
     MCA   2036

350. GLORIFYING THE AMERICAN GIRL   (1929)
     STARS:   Mary Eaton, Dan Healy
     DIR:     Millard Webb

351. GO INTO YOUR DANCE   (1935)
     STARS:   Al Jolson, Ruby Keeler
     DIR:     Archie Mayo
     SONGS:   Harry Warren - Al Dubin

352. GO WEST   (1940)
     STARS:   The Marx Brothers
     DIR:     Eddie Buzzell

353. GO WEST YOUNG LADY   (1941)
     STARS:   Penny Singleton, Glenn Ford
     DIR:     Frank B. Strayer
     SONGS:   Saul Chaplin - Sammy Cahn

354. GODSPELL   (1973)
     STARS:   Victor Garber, David Haskell

DIR:     John-Michael Tebelak
SONGS:   Stephen Schwartz
Day By Day; Save The People; By My Side; We Beseech Thee; All
For The Best; Prepare Ye The Way Of The Lord; Learn Your Les-
sons; Bless The Lord; All Good Gifts; Light Of The World; On
The Willows; Turn Back, O Man; Alas For You; Beautiful City.
Bell 1118

355.   GOIN' TO TOWN   (1935)
       STARS:   Mae West, Paul Cavanaugh
       DIR:     Alexander Hall
       SONGS:   Sammy Fain - Sam Coslow - Irving Kahal

356.   GOING HOLLYWOOD   (1933)
       STARS:   Marion Davies, Bing Crosby
       DIR:     Raoul Walsh
       SONGS:   Nacio Herb Brown - Arthur Freed
       Going Hollywood, Our Big Love Scene; Make Hay While The Sun
       Shines; Cinderella's Fella; After Sundown; Temptation;
       Beautiful Girl.
       Col. C2L-43

357.   GOING MY WAY   (1944)
       STARS:   Bing Crosby, Rise Stevens
       DIR:     Leo McCarey
       Swinging On A Star; Day After Forever; Going My Way (Jimmy
       Van Heusen - Johnny Burke); Too-Ra-Lo-Too-Roo-La (J. R. Shan-
       non.
       Decca  DL-4257

358.   GOING PLACES   (1938)
       STARS:   Dick Powell, Anita Louise
       DIR:     Ray Enright
       SONGS:   Harry Warren - Johnny Mercer

359.   GOLD DIGGERS IN PARIS   (1938)
       STARS:   Rudy Vallee, Rosemary Lane
       DIR:     Ray Enright
       MUSIC:   Harry Warren

360.   GOLD DIGGERS OF BROADWAY   (1929)
       STARS:   Nancy Welford, Conway Tearle
       DIR:     Roy Del Ruth
       SONGS:   Joe Burke - Al Dubin

361.   GOLD DIGGERS OF 1933   (1933)
       STARS:   Warren William, Joan Blondell
       DIR:     Mervyn LeRoy
       SONGS:   Harry Warren - Al Dubin

362.   GOLD DIGGERS OF 1935   (1935)
       STARS:   Dick Powell, Gloria Stuart
       DIR:     Busby Berkeley
       SONGS:   Harry Warren - Al Dubin

363. GOLD DIGGERS OF 1937  (1936)
STARS:  Dick Powell, Joan Blondell
DIR:    Lloyd Bacon

364. GOLDEN DAWN  (1930)
STARS:  Vivienne Segal, Walter Woold
DIR:    Ray Enright

365. GOLDEN GIRL  (1951)
STARS:  Mitzi Gaynor, Dale Robertson
DIR:    Lloyd Bacon
California Moon (Joe Cooper - Sam Lerner - George Jessel); Sun-
Day Mornin' (Ken Darby - Eliot Daniel); Never (Lionel Newman -
Eliot Daniel); Kiss Me Quick And Go (Eliot Daniel).

366. GOLDWYN FOLLIES  (1938)
STARS:  Adolphe Menjou, The Ritz Brothers
DIR:    George Marshall

367. GOOD NEWS  (1930)
STARS:  Bessie Love, Mary Lawlor
DIR:    Nick Grinde and Edgar J. McGregor

368. GOOD NEWS  (1947)
STARS:  June Allyson, Peter Lawford
DIR:    Charles Walters
Good News (Tait College); He's A Lady's Man; Lucky In Love;
The Best Things In Life Are Free; Just Imagine; Varsity Drag
(Ray Henderson - Lew Brown - B. G. DeSylva); The French Les-
son (Roger Edens - Adolph Green - Betty Comden); Pass That
Peace Pipe (Hugh Martin - Ralph Blane).
MGM 2-SES-49ST

369. GREAT AMERICAN BROADCAST  (1941)
STARS:  Alice Faye, John Payne
DIR:    Archie Mayo
SONGS:  Harry Warren - Mack Gordon

370. GREAT VICTOR HERBERT, THE  (1939)
STARS:  Walter Connolly, Mary Martin
DIR:    Andrew L. Stone
MUSIC:  Victor Herbert

371. GREAT WALTZ, THE  (1938)
STARS:  Luise Rainer, Fernand Gravet
DIR:    Julien Duvivier
SONGS:  Oscar Hammerstein II

372. GREAT WALTZ, THE  (1972)
STARS:  Horst Bucholz, Mary Costa
DIR:    Andrew L. Stone
SONGS:  Johann Strauss - Robert Wright, George Forrest
Crystal and Gold; Nightfall, Warm; Wine, Women, And Song; Love
Is Music; Louder And Faster; With You Gone; Through Jetty's

123

Eyes; Say Yes; Six Drinks; Who Are You?; The Great Waltz In
Boston; Indigo (Adapted By Roland Shaw).
MGM - 1SE - 39ST

373.  GREAT ZIEGFELD, THE   (1936)
      STARS:  William Powell, Myrna Loy
      DIR:    Robert Z. Leonard

374.  GREENWICH VILLAGE   (1944)
      STARS:  Carmen Miranda, Don Ameche
      DIR:    Walter Lang
      SONGS:  Nacio Herb Brown - Leo Robin

375.  GULLIVER'S TRAVELS   (1939)
      STARS:  Jessica Dragonette, Lanny Ross
      DIR:    Dave Fleisher

376.  GUYS AND DOLLS   (1955)
      STARS:  Marlon Brando, Jean Simmons
      DIR:    Joseph L. Mankiewicz
      SONGS:  Frank Loesser
      Adelaide; Woman In Love; Pet Me, Poppa; Sit Down, You're Rockin
      The Boat; I'll Know; Luck Be A Lady; Guys And Dolls; Fugue For
      Tinhorns; Oldest Established Permanent Floating Crap Game; A
      Bushel And A Peck; Adelaide's Lament; If I Were A Bell; I've
      Never Been In Love Before; Take Back Your Mink; Sue Me.

377.  GYPSY   (1962)
      STARS:  Rosaline Russell, Natalie Wood
      DIR:    Mervyn LeRoy
      SONGS:  Jule Styne - Stephen Sondheim
      Let Me Entertain You; Some People; Small World; Baby June And
      Her Newsboys; Mr. Goldstone; Little Lamb; You'll Never Get
      Away From Me; If Mama Was Married; All I Need Is The Girl;
      Everything's Coming Up Roses; Together Wherever We Go; Rose's
      Turn; You Gotta Have A Gimmick.
      Warner Bros.  BS-1480

378.  HALF A SIXPENCE   (1968)
      STARS:  Tommy Steele, Cyril Ritchard
      DIR:    George Sidney
      SONGS:  David Heneker
      All In The Cause Of Economy; Half A Sixpence; Money To Burn;
      I Don't Believe A Word Of It; I'm Not Talking To You; She's
      Too Far Above Me; A Proper Gentleman; If The Rain's Got To
      Fall; The Race Is On; Flash, Bang, Wallop; I Know What I Am;
      This Is My World.
      RCA LSO-1146

379.  HALLELUJAH   (1929)
      STARS:  Daniel L. Haymes, Mae McKinney
      DIR:    King Vidor
      SONGS:  Irving Berlin

380. HALLELUJAH, I'M A BUM  (1933)
    STARS:  Al Jolson, Harry Langdon
    DIR:    Lewis Milestone
    SONGS:  Richard Rodgers - Lorenz Hart

381. HANGOVER SQUARE  (1945)
    STARS:  Laird Cregar, Linda Darnell
    DIR:    John Brahm

382. HANS CHRISTIAN ANDERSEN  (1952)
    STARS:  Danny Kaye, Farley Granger
    DIR:    Charles Vidor
    SONGS:  Frank Loesser
    I'm Hans Christian Andersen; The King's New Clothes; Inch-worm;
    Wonderful Copenhagen; Thumbelina; Anywhere I Wander; No Two
    People; Ugly Duckling.
    Decca DL 8479

383. THE HAPPIEST MILLIONAIRE  (1967)
    STARS:  Tommy Steele, Fred MacMurray
    DIR:    Norman Tokar
    SONGS:  Richard M. and Robert B. Sherman
    I'll Always Be Irish; Detroit; Fortuosity; It Won't Be Long
    'Till Christmas; What's Wrong With That; Watch Your Footwork;
    Bye-Yum Pum Pum; Are We Dancing?; There Are Those; Let's Have
    A Drink On It; Valentine Candy; Strengthen The Dwelling.
    Buena Vista STER-5001

384. HAPPINESS AHEAD  (1934)
    STARS:  Dick Powell, Josephine Hutchinson
    DIR:    Mervyn LeRoy

385. HAPPY DAYS  (1930)
    STARS:  Frank Albertson, Warner Baxter
    DIR:    Benjamin Stoloff

386. HAPPY GO LUCKY  (1943)
    STARS:  Mary Martin, Dick Powell
    DIR:    Curtis Bernhardt
    SONGS:  Jimmy McHugh - Frank Loesser

387. HAPPY LANDING  (1938)
    STARS:  Sonja Henie, Don Ameche
    DIR:    Roy Del Ruth

388. HARD WAY, THE  (1942)
    STARS:  Ida Lupino, Dennis Morgan
    DIR:    Vincent Sherman

389. HAROLD TEEN  (1934)
    STARS:  Hal LeRoy, Rochelle Hudson
    DIR:    Murray Roth
    SONGS:  Sammy Fain - Irving Kahal

390. HARVEST MELODY  (1943)
     STARS:   Rosemary Lane, Johnny Downs
     DIR:     Sam Newfield

391. HARVEY GIRLS, THE  (1946)
     STARS:   Judy Garland, John Hodiak
     DIR:     George Sidney
     SONGS:   Harry Warren - Johnny Mercer
     On The Atcheson, Topeka And The Santa Fe; In The Valley When
     The Evening Sun Goes Down; Wait And See; Swing Your Partner
     Round And Round; The Wild, Wild West; It's A Great Big World.
     MCA MCFM-2588  (import)

392. HAT CHECK HONEY  (1944)
     STARS:   Grace McDonald, Leon Errol
     DIR:     Edward F. Cline

393. HATS OFF  (1936)
     STARS:   Mae Clarke, John Payne
     DIR:     Boris Petroff
     SONGS:   Ben Oakland - Herb Magidson

394. HAVING A WONDERFUL TIME  (1938)
     STARS:   Ginger Rogers, Douglas Fairbanks Jr.
     DIR:     Alfred Santell

395. HAWAIIAN NIGHTS  (1939)
     STARS:   Mary Carlisle, Constance Moore
     DIR:     Albert Rogell
     SONGS:   Matt Malneck - Frank Loesser

396. HEADS UP  (1930)
     STARS:   Charles "Buddy" Rogers, Helen Kane
     DIR:     Victor Schertzinger

397. HEAT'S ON, THE  (1943)
     STARS:   Mae West, Victor Moore
     DIR:     Gregory Ratoff

398. HELEN MORGAN STORY  (1957)
     STARS:   Ann Blyth, Paul Newman
     DIR:     Michael Curtiz
     Bill; Why Was I Born?; Can't Help Lovin' That Man; Don't Ever
     Leave Me (Jerome Kern - Oscar Hammerstein II); I Can't Give
     You Anything But Love, Baby; On The Sunny Side Of The Street
     (Jimmy McHugh - Dorothy Fields); Do, Do, Do; Someone To Watch
     Over Me; The Man I Love; I've Got A Crush On You (George and
     Ira Gershwin); If You Were The Only Girl In The World (Nat
     Ayer - Clifford Grey); Avalon (Vincent Rose - Al Jolson - B. G.
     DeSylva); Breezin' Along With The Breeze (Richard Whiting -
     Haven Gillespie - Seymour Simons); Body And Soul (Johnny Green
     Ed Heyman - Robert Sauer - Frank Eyton); April In Paris (Ver-
     non Duke - E. Y. Harburg); Just A Memory (Ray Henderson - B. G.
     DeSylva - Lew Brown); Deep Night (Charles Henderson - Rudy Val-

lee); My Melancholy Baby (Ernie Burnett - George Norton).
RCA LOC-1030

399. HELLO DOLLY  (1969)
STARS:  Barbra Streisand, Walter Matthau
DIR:  Gene Kelly
SONGS:  Jerry Herman
Hello Dolly; Put On Your Sunday Clothes; Dancing; So Long Dear-
ie; It Takes A Woman; Ribbons Down My Back; Before The Parade
Passes By; Elegance; Love Is Only Love; It Only Takes A Moment.
20th Cent. 102

400. HELLO EVERYBODY  (1933)
STARS:  Kate Smith, Randolph Scott
DIR:  William Seiter
SONGS:  Arthur Johnston - Sam Coslow

401. HELLO FRISCO HELLO  (1943)
STARS:  Alice Faye, John Payne
DIR:  H. Bruce Humberstone

402. HELLZAPOPPIN'  (1941)
STARS:  Olsen and Johnson, Martha Raye
DIR:  Henry C. Potter
SONGS:  Don Raye - Gene DePaul

403. HERE COME THE CO-EDS  (1945)
STARS:  Abbott and Costello, Peggy Ryan
DIR:  Edgar Fairchild
SONGS:  Edgar Fairchild - Jack Brooks

404. HERE COME THE GIRLS  (1953)
STARS:  Bob Hope, Tony Martin
DIR:  Claude Binyon
SONGS:  Jay Livingston - Ray Evans
Heavenly Days; Never So Beautiful; When You Love Someone; Ya
Got Class; Girls; It's Torment; See The Circus; Ali Baba.

405. HERE COME THE WAVES  (1944)
STARS:  Bing Crosby, Betty Hutton
DIR:  Mark Sandrich
SONGS:  Harold Arlen - Johnny Mercer
I Promise You; There's A Fellow Waiting In Poughkeepsie; My
Mama Thinks I'm A Star; Let's Take The Long Way Home; Here Come
The Waves; Ac-Cent-Tchu-Ate The Positive.
Decca  DL-4258

406. HERE COMES ELMER  (1943)
STARS:  Al Pearce, Dale Evans
DIR:  Joseph Santley

407. HERE COMES THE BAND  (1934)
STARS:  Ted Lewis, Virginia Bruce
DIR:  Paul Sloane

408. HERE COMES THE GROOM   (1951)
     STARS:   Bing Crosby, Jane Wyman
     DIR:     Frank Capra
     Misto Christofo Columbo; Bonne Nuit; Your Own Little House
     (Jay Livingston - Ray Evans); In The Cool, Cool, Cool Of The
     Evening (Hoagy Carmichael - Johnny Mercer).
     Decca  DL-4262

409. HERE IS MY HEART   (1934)
     STARS:   Bing Crosby, Kitty Carlisle
     DIR:     Frank Tuttle
     LYRICS: Leo Robin (Composer follows in parentheses)
     June In January; You Can't Make A Monkey Of The Moon; Here Is
     My Heart; With Every Breath I Take (Ralph Rainger); Love is
     Just Around The Corner (Lewis Gensler).
     Decca  DL-4250

410. HEY, ROOKIE   (1944)
     STARS:   Joe Besser, Ann Miller
     DIR:     Charles Barton

411. HI, BUDDY   (1943)
     STARS:   Harriet Hilliard, Dick Foran
     DIR:     Harold Young

412. HI GAUCHO   (1936)
     STARS:   Steffi Duna, John Carroll
     DIR:     Tommy Atkins
     SONGS:   Albert Hay Malotte

413. HI, GOOD LOOKIN'   (1944)
     STARS:   Harriet Hilliard, Kirby Grant
     DIR:     Edward Lilley

414. HI NEIGHBOR   (1942)
     STARS:   Jean Parker, John Archer
     DIR:     Charles Lamont

415. HIDEAWAY GIRL   (1937)
     STARS:   Shirley Ross, Robert Cummings
     DIR:     George Archinbaud

416. HIGH SCHOOL HERO   (1946)
     STARS:   Freddie Stewart, June Preisser
     DIR:     Arthur Dreifuss

417. HIGH SOCIETY   (1956)
     STARS:   Bing Crosby, Grace Kelly
     DIR:     Charles Walters
     SONGS:   Cole Porter
     Little One; Who Wants To Be A Millionaire?; True Love; You're
     Sensational; I Love You Samantha; Now You Has Jazz; Well Did
     You Evah; Mind If I Make Love To You; High Society Calypso.
     Capitol  SW-750

418. HIGH SOCIETY BLUES  (1930)
    STARS:  Janet Gaynor, Charles Farrell
    DIR:    David Butler
    SONGS:  James Hanley - Joe McCarthy

419. HIGH, WIDE AND HANDSOME  (1937)
    STARS:  Irene Dunne, Randolph Scott
    DIR:    Rouben Mamoulian
    SONGS:  Jerome Kern - Oscar Hammerstein II
    Can I Forget You?; Allegheny Al; Folks Who Live On The Hill;
    High, Wide And Handsome; He Wore A Star; The Things I Want;
    Can You Marry Me Tomorrow Maria?
    Jerome Kern In Hollywood, 1934 - 1938  JJA 19747D

420. HIGHER AND HIGHER  (1943)
    STARS:  Michele Morgan, Jack Haley
    DIR:    Tim Whelan
    SONGS:  Jimmy McHugh - Harold Adamson

421. HIPS, HIPS, HOORAY  (1934)
    STARS:  Bert Wheeler, Robert Woolsey
    DIR:    Mark Sandrich
    SONGS:  Harry Ruby - Bert Kalmar

422. HIT PARADE  (1937)
    STARS:  Frances Langford, Phil Regan
    DIR:    Gus Meins

423. HIT PARADE OF 1941  (1940)
    STARS:  Kenny Baker, Frances Langford
    DIR:    John H. Auer
    SONGS:  Jule Styne - Walter Bullock

424. HIT PARADE OF 1943  (1943)
    STARS:  John Carroll, Susan Hayward
    DIR:    Albert S. Rogell
    SONGS:  Jule Styne - Harold Adamson

425. HIT PARADE OF 1947  (1947)
    STARS:  Joan Edwards, Eddie Albert
    DIR:    Frank McDonald

426. HIT PARADE OF 1951  (1950)
    STARS:  John Carroll, Marie McDonald
    DIR:    John H. Auer
    You're So Nice; How Would I Know?; Wishes Come True; You Don't
    Know The Other Side Of Me; A Very Happy Character Am I (Floyd
    Huddleston - Al Rinker); Square Dance Samba And Boca Chica
    (Buddy Garrett - Sy Miller).

427. HIT THE DECK  (1930)
    STARS:  Polly Walker, Jack Oakie
    DIR:    Luther Reed
    MUSIC:  Vincent Youmans

428. HIT THE DECK   (1955)
     STARS:   Jane Powell, Tony Martin
     DIR:     Roy Rowland
     SONGS:   Vincent Youmans - Leo Robin - Clifford Grey - Irving
     Caesar   -   Sidney Clare
     More Than You Know; Keepin' Myself For You; Sometimes I'm Hap-
     py; A Kiss Or Two; Lucky Bird; Join The Navy; Loo-Loo; Why Oh
     Why; I Know That You Know; The Lady From The Bayou; Hallelujah;
     and Ciribiribin (H. Johnson - Pestalazza).
     MGM 2-SES-43ST

429. HIT THE ICE   (1943)
     STARS:   Abbott and Costello
     DIR:     Charles Lamont
     SONGS:   Harry Revel - Paul Francis Webster

430. HITTING A NEW HIGH   (1937)
     STARS:   Lili Pons, Edward Everett Horton
     DIR:     Raoul Walsh
     SONGS:   Jimmy McHugh - Harold Adamson

431. HI'YA CHUM   (1943)
     STARS:   The Ritz Brothers, Jane Frazee
     DIR:     Harold Young
     SONGS:   Gene DePaul - Don Raye

432. HI'YA SAILOR   (1943)
     STARS:   Donald Woods, Elyse Knox
     DIR:     Jean Yarbrough

433. HOLD EVERYTHING   (1930)
     STARS:   Winnie Lightner, Joe E. Brown
     Dir:     Roy Del Ruth
     SONGS:   Joe Burke - Al Dubin

434. HOLD THAT CO-ED   (1938)
     STARS:   John Barrymore, George Murphy
     DIR:     George Marshall

435. HOLIDAY IN HAVANA   (1949)
     STARS:   Desi Arnaz, Mary Hatcher
     DIR:     Jean Yarbrough

436. HOLIDAY IN MEXICO   (1946)
     STARS:   Walter Pidgeon, Jose Iturbi
     DIR:     George Sidney

437. HOLIDAY INN   (1942)
     STARS:   Bing Crosby, Fred Astaire
     DIR:     Mark Sandrich
     SONGS:   Irving Berlin
     Come To Holiday Inn; Happy Holiday; I'll Capture Your Heart
     Singing; Abraham; Lazy; White Christmas; Easter Parade, I've
     Got Plenty To Be Thankful For; Be Careful, It's My Heart; Let's

Start The New Year Right; I Can't Tell A Lie; You're Easy To
Dance With; Song Of Freedom; Say It With Firecrackers.
Decca DL-4256

438. HOLLYWOOD CANTEEN   (1944)
STARS:   Jack Benny, Eddie Cantor
DIR:     Delmer Daves
Don't Fence Me In (Cole Porter); You Can Always Tell A Yank
(Burton Lane - E. Y. Harburg); What Are You Doing The Rest Of
Your Life? (Burton Lane - Ted Koehler); I'm Getting Corns For
My Country (Dick Charles - Jean Barry); We're Having A Baby
(My Baby And Me) (Vernon Duke - Harold Adamson); Sweet Dreams
Sweetheart (M. K. Jerome - Ted Koehler); Voodoo Moon (Obdulio
Morales - Julio Blanco - Marian Sunshine); The General Jumped
At Dawn (Jimmy Mundy - Larry Neal); Tumblin' Tumbleweeds (Bob
Nolan); Ballet In Jive (Ray Heindorf); Hollywood Canteen (M. K.
Jerome - Ray Heindorf - Ted Koehler).
Curtain Calls CC 100/11-12

439. HOLLYWOOD HOTEL   (1937)
STARS:   Dick Powell, Rosemary and Lola Lane
DIR:     Busby Berkeley
SONGS:   Richard Whiting - Johnny Mercer
I'm Like A Fish Out Of Water; I've Hitched My Wagon To A Star;
Let That Be A Lesson To You; Silhouetted In The Moonlight;
Hooray For Hollywood; Can't Teach My Heart New Tricks; Sing
You Son Of A Gun.
EOH 99601

440. HOLLYWOOD OR BUST   (1956)
STARS:   Dean Martin - Jerry Lewis
DIR:     Frank Tashlin
SONGS:   Sammy Fain - Paul Francis Webster
Hollywood Or Bust; A Day In The Country; It Looks Like Love;
Let's Be Friendly; The Wild And Wooly West.

441. HOLLYWOOD PARTY   (1934)
STARS:   Jimmy Durante, Lupe Velez
DIR:     Roy Rowland
SONGS:   Richard Rodgers - Lorenz Hart

442. HOLLYWOOD REVUE   (1929)
STARS:   Marion Davies, Norma Shearer
DIR:     C. Reisner

443. HOLY TERROR   (1931)
STARS:   George O'Brien, Sally Eilers
DIR:     Irving Cummings

444. HOLY TERROR, THE   (1937)
STARS:   Jane Withers, Tony Martin
DIR:     James Tinling
SONGS:   Harry Akst - Sidney Clare

445. HONEY   (1930)
    STARS:  Nancy Carroll, Skeets Gallagher
    DIR:    Wesley Ruggles
    SONGS:  W. Franke Harling - Sam Coslow

446. HONEYCHILE   (1951)
    STARS:  Judy Canova, Eddie Foy, Jr.
    DIR:    R. J. Springsteen
    Honeychile (Harold Spina - Jack Elliott); More Than I Care To
    Remember (Matt Terry - Ted Johnson); Rag Mop (Deacon Anderson -
    Johnny Lee Wills); Tutti Fruiti (Ann Canova - Jack Elliott).

447. HONEYMOON AHEAD   (1945)
    STARS:  Allan Jones, Grace McDonald
    DIR:    Reginald LeBorg
    SONGS:  Milton Rosen - Everett Carter

448. HONEYMOON LANE   (1931)
    STARS:  Eddie Dowling, June Collyer
    DIR:    William J. Craft
    SONGS:  James Hanley - Eddie Dowling

449. HONEYMOON LODGE   (1943)
    STARS:  David Bruce, June Vincent
    DIR:    Edward Lilley

450. HONKY TONK   (1929)
    STARS:  Sophie Tucker, Lila Lee
    DIR:    Lloyd Bacon
    SONGS:  Milton Ager - Jack Yellen

451. HONOLULU   (1939)
    STARS:  Eleanor Powell, Robert Young
    DIR:    Eddie Buzzell
    SONGS:  Harry Warren - Gus Kahn

452. HOORAY FOR LOVE   (1935)
    STARS:  Ann Sothern, Gene Raymond
    DIR:    Walter Lang
    SONGS:  Jimmy McHugh - Dorothy Fields

453. HOT FOR PARIS   (1929)
    STARS:  Victor McLaglen, Fifi D'Orsay
    DIR:    Raoul Walsh
    SONGS:  Walter Donaldson - Edgar Leslie

454. HOT HEIRESS   (1931)
    STARS:  Ona Munson, Ben Lyon
    DIR:    Clarence Badger
    SONGS:  Richard Rodgers - Lorenz Hart

455. HOW THE WEST WAS WON   (1963)
    STARS:  Spencer Tracy, Carroll Baker
    DIR:    Henry Hathaway, John Ford and George Marshall

SONGS: Alfred Newman (lyricists follow in parentheses)
How The West Was Won (Ken Darby); Home In The Meadow (Sammy
Cohn); and Raise A Ruckus; Wait For The Hoedown; What Was Your
Name In The States? (Johnny Mercer).
MGM S-1ES-ST

456. HOW TO SUCCEED IN BUSINESS WITHOUT REALLY TRYING (1967)
STARS: Robert Morse, Michele Lee
DIR: David Swift
SONGS: Frank Loesser
How To; The Company Way; A Secretary Is Not A Toy; Been A Long
Day; I Believe In You; Grand Old Ivy; Rosemary; Gotta Stop
That Man; Brotherhood Of Man.
United Artists: UAS-5151

457. HOW'S ABOUT IT? (1943)
STARS: The Andrews Sisters, Robert Paige
DIR: Eric C. Fenton

458. HUCKLEBERRY FINN (1974)
STARS: Jeff East, Harvey Korman
DIR: J. Lee Thompson
SONGS: Richard M. and Robert B. Sherman
Freedom; Huckleberry Finn; Someday, Honey Darlin'; Rose In A
Bible; Cairo, Illinois; Royalty; Royal Nonesuch; What's Right,
What's Wrong; Rotten Luck.
United Artists LA-229-F

459. I AM SUZANNE (1934)
STARS: Lilian Harvey, Gene Raymond
DIR: Rowland V. Lee
SONGS: Frederick Hollander

460. I CAN'T GIVE YOU ANYTHING BUT LOVE BABY (1940)
STARS: Broderick Crawford, Peggy Moran
DIR: Albert S. Rogell

461. I DOOD IT (1943)
STARS: Red Skelton, Lena Horne
DIR: Vincente Minnelli

462. I DREAM OF JEANIE (1952)
STARS: Ray Middleton, Bill Shirley
DIR: Allan Dwan
My Old Kentucky Home; Old Folks At Home; Oh Suzanna; Old Dog
Tray; Ring De Banjo; Camptown Races; Jeanie; Come Where My
Love Lies Dreaming (Stephen Foster); A Ribbon In Your Hair; I
See Her Still In My Dreams; Head Over Heels (Stephen Foster -
Allan Dwan); On Wings Of Song (Mendelssohn); Lo Hear The Gen-
tle Lark.

463. I DREAM TOO MUCH (1935)
STARS: Lily Pons, Henry Fonda
SONGS: Jerome Kern - Dorothy Fields

464. I LIKE IT THAT WAY  (1934)
     STARS:  Gloria Stuart, Roger Pryor
     DIR:    Harry Lachman

465. I LIVE FOR LOVE  (1935)
     STARS:  Dolores Del Rio, Everett Marshall
     DIR:    Busby Berkeley
     SONGS:  Allie Wrubel - Mort Dixon

466. I LOVE MELVIN  (1953)
     STARS:  Donald O'Connor, Debbie Reynolds
     DIR:    Don Weis
     SONGS:  Josef Myrow - Mack Gordon
     And There You Are; I Wanna Wander; Lady Love; Life Has Its
     Funny Little Ups And Downs; Saturday Afternoon Before The Game;
     We Never Met As Yet; Where Did You Learn To Dance?
     MGM  2-SES-52ST

467. I LOVED YOU WEDNESDAY  (1933)
     STARS:  Warner Baxter, Elissa Landi
     DIR:    Henry King

468. I MARRIED AN ANGEL  (1942)
     STARS:  Jeanette MacDonald, Nelson Eddy
     DIR:    W. S. Van Dyke

469. I SURRENDER DEAR  (1948)
     STARS:  Gloria Jean, David Street
     DIR:    Arthur Dreifuss

470. I WONDER WHO'S KISSING HER NOW  (1947)
     STARS:  June Haver, Mark Stevens
     DIR:    Lloyd Bacon
     SONGS:  Joe Howard - Will Hough - Frank Adams

471. ICE-CAPADE REVUE  (1942)
     STARS:  Ellen Drew, Richard Denning
     DIR:    Bernard Vorhaus

472. ICE FOLLIES OF 1939  (1939)
     STARS:  Joan Crawford, James Stewart
     DIR:    Reinhold Schunzel

473. ICELAND  (1942)
     STARS:  Sonja Henie, John Payne
     DIR:    H. Bruce Humberstone
     SONGS:  Harry Warren - Mack Gordon

474. IF I HAD MY WAY  (1940)
     STARS:  Bing Crosby, Gloria Jean
     DIR:    David Butler

475. IF I'M LUCKY  (1946)
     STARS:  Perry Como, Vivian Blaine

DIR:    Lewis Seiler
SONGS:  Joseph Myrow - Edgar DeLange

476.  IF YOU KNEW SUSIE   (1948)
      STARS:  Eddie Cantor, Joan Davis
      DIR:    Gordon M. Douglas
      SONGS:  Jimmy McHugh - Harold Adamson

477.  I'LL BE YOURS   (1947)
      STARS:  Deanna Durbin, Tom Drake
      DIR:    William A. Seiter

478.  I'LL GET BY   (1950)
      STARS:  June Haver - William Lundigan
      DIR:    Richard Sale
      Taking A Chance On Love (Vernon Duke - Ted Fetter - John La-
      Touche); Once In A While (Michael Edwards - Bud Green); Fifth
      Avenue; There Will Never Be Another You (Harry Warren - Mack
      Gordon); I've Got The World On A String (Harold Arlen - Ted
      Koehler); You Make Me Feel So Young (Josef Myrow - Mack Gor-
      don); Yankee Doodle Blues (George Gershwin - Irving Caesar -
      B. G. DeSylva); It's Been A Long, Long Time (Jule Styne - Sam-
      my Cahn); I'll Get By (As Long As I Have You) (Fred Ahlert -
      Roy Turk); McNamara's Band (J. J. Stamford - Shamus O'Connor).

479.  I'LL SEE YOU IN MY DREAMS   (1951)
      STARS:  Danny Thomas, Doris Day
      DIR:    Michael Curtiz
      LYRICS: Gus Kahn (Composer follows in parentheses)
      My Buddy; Carolina In The Morning; Makin' Whoopee; Yes Sir,
      That's My Baby; Love Me Or Leave Me (Walter Donaldson); It Had
      To Be You; Swinging Down The Lane; I'll See You In My Dreams;
      The One I Love Belongs To Somebody Else (Isham Jones); Ain't
      We Got Fun; Ukelele Lady (Richard Whiting); I Wish I Had A
      Girl (G. L. Kahn); Memories (Egbert Van Alstyne); Pretty Baby
      (Van Alstyne - Tony Jackson); Nobody's Sweetheart (Billy Mey-
      ers - Elmer Schoebel - Ernie Erdman); Your Eyes Have Told Me
      So (Walter Blaufuss - Van Alstyne); I Never Knew (Ted Fiorito);
      Toot Toot Tootsie Goodbye (Al Jolson - E. Erdman) No, No, Nora
      (T. Fiorito - E. Erdman).
      Col.   CL-6198

480.  I'LL TAKE ROMANCE   (1937)
      STARS:  Grace Moore, Melvyn Douglas
      DIR:    Edward H. Griffith

481.  I'LL TELL THE WORLD   (1945)
      STARS:  Lee Tracy, Brenda Joyce
      DIR:    Leslie Goodwins

482.  I'M NO ANGEL   (1933)
      STARS:  Mae West, Cary Grant
      DIR:    Wesley Ruggles
      SONGS:  Ben Ellison - Gladys DuBois - Harvey Brooks

No One Loves Me Like That Dallas Man Of Mine; They Call Me
Sister Honky Tonk; I Want You, I Need You; I've Found A New
Way To Go To Town; I'm No Angel.
Col. CL-2751

483.  I'M NOBODY'S SWEETHEART NOW  (1940)
      STARS:  Dennis O'Keefe, Constance Moore
      DIR:    Arthur Lubin

484.  IN CALIENTE  (1935)
      STARS:  Dolores Del Rio, Pat O'Brien
      DIR:    Lloyd Bacon

485.  IN PERSON  (1935)
      STARS:  Ginger Rogers, George Brent
      DIR:    William A. Seiter
      SONGS:  Oscar Levant - Dorothy Fields

486.  IN SOCIETY  (1944)
      STARS:  Abbott and Costello
      DIR:    Jean Yarbrough

487.  IN THE GOOD OLD SUMMERTIME  (1949)
      STARS:  Judy Garland, Van Johnson
      DIR:    Robert Z. Leonard
      Merry Christmas (Fred Spielman - Janice Torre); Meet Me Tonight
      In Dreamland (Lee Friedman - Beth Slater Whitson); Put Your
      Arms Around Me Honey (Harry Von Tilzer - Junie McCree); Play
      That Barber Shop Chord (Lewis Muir - William Tracey - Ballard
      MacDonald); I Don't Care (Harry Sutton - Jean Lenox); Last
      Night When We Were Young (Harold Arlen - E. Y. Harburg).
      MGM - 2 - SES - 49ST

488.  IN THE NAVY  (1941)
      STARS:  Abbott and Costello
      DIR:    Arthur Lubin
      SONGS:  Don Raye - Gene DePaul

489.  INCENDIARY BLONDE  (1945)
      STARS:  Betty Hutton, Arturo de Cordova
      DIR:    George Marshall

490.  INNOCENTS OF PARIS  (1929)
      STARS:  Maurice Chevalier, Sylvia Breecher
      DIR:    Richard Wallace
      SONGS:  Richard Whiting - Leo Robin

491.  INSPECTOR GENERAL, THE  (1949)
      STARS:  Danny Kaye, Walter Slezac
      DIR:    Henry Koster
      SONGS:  Sylvia Fine

492.  INTERNATIONAL HOUSE  (1933)

136

```
        STARS:  Peggy Hopkins Joyce, W. C. Fields
        DIR:    Edward Sutherland
        SONGS:  Ralph Rainger - Leo Robin

493.    IRENE  (1940)
        STARS:  Anna Neagle, Ray Milland
        DIR:    Herbert Wilcox
        SONGS:  Harry Tierney - Joseph McCarthy

494.    IS EVERYBODY HAPPY?  (1929)
        STARS:  Ted Lewis, Ann Pennington
        DIR:    Archie Mayo

495.    IS EVERYBODY HAPPY?  (1943)
        STARS:  Ted Lewis, Nan Wynn
        DIR:    Charles Barton

496.    ISN'T IT ROMANTIC?  (1948)
        STARS:  Veronica Lake, Mary Hatcher
        DIR:    Norman Z. McLeod
        SONGS:  Jay Livingston - Ray Evans

497.    IT HAPPENED IN BROOKLYN  (1947)
        STARS:  Frank Sinatra, Peter Lawford
        DIR:    Richard Whorf
        SONGS:  Jule Styne - Sammy Cahn
        It's The Same Old Dream; Time After Time; I Believe; Whose Baby
        Are You?; Brooklyn Bridge; Song's Gotta Come From The Heart.
        Col.  CL-2913

498.    IT HAPPENED ON FIFTH AVENUE  (1947)
        STARS:  Don DeFore, Ann Harding
        DIR:    Roy Del Ruth
        SONGS:  Harry Revel - Paul Francis Webster

499.    IT'S A DATE  (1940)
        STARS:  Deanna Durbin, Kay Francis
        DIR:    William A. Seiter

500.    IT'S A GREAT FEELING  (1949)
        STARS:  Dennis Morgan, Doris Day
        DIR:    David Butler
        SONGS:  Jule Styne - Sammy Cahn

501.    IT'S A GREAT LIFE  (1929)
        STARS:  Rosetta and Vivian Duncan
        DIR:    Sam Wood

502.    IT'S ALWAYS FAIR WEATHER  (1955)
        STARS:  Gene Kelly, Dan Dailey
        DIR:    Stanley Donen and Gene Kelly
        SONGS:  Andre Previn - Betty Comden - Adolph Green
        Music Is Better Than Words; March, March; I Like Myself; Once
        Upon A Time; Thanks A Lot But No Thanks; The Time For Parting;
```

Situation-wise; Why Are We Here?; Stillman's Gym; Baby You
Knock Me Out; Sleeper Phones; Blue Danube.
MGM 2353-036 (Import)

503. IT'S GREAT TO BE ALIVE   (1933)
STARS:   Gloria Stuart, Raul Roulien
DIR:     Alfred Werker
SONGS:   William Kernell

504. JACK AND THE BEANSTALK   (1952)
STARS:   Abbott and Costello
DIR:     Jean Yarbrough
SONGS:   Bob Russell - Lester Lee
Dreamer's Cloth; Jack And The Beanstalk; He Never Looked Bet-
ter In His Life; I Fear Nothing; Darlene.

505. JAM SESSION   (1944)
STARS:   Ann Miller, The Pied Pipers
DIR:     Charles Barton

506. JAZZ SINGER, THE   (1927)
STARS:   Al Jolson, May McAvoy
DIR:     Alan Crosland
Blue Skies (Irving Berlin); Dirty Hands Dirty Face (Jimmy
Monaco - Al Jolson - Grant Clarke - Edgar Leslie); Kol Nidre;
Mother I Still Have You (Al Jolson - Louis Silvers); My Manny
(Walter Donaldson - Joe Young - Sam Lewis); Toot Toot Tootsie
Goodbye (Dan Russo - Ernie Erdman - Gus Kahn).
Soundtrak  ST-102-2.

507. THE JAZZ SINGER   (1953)
STARS:   Danny Thomas, Peggy Lee
DIR:     Michael Curtiz
SONGS:   Sammy Fain - Jerry Seelen
I Hear The Music Now; O Moon; Living The Life Of Love; What
Are New Yorkers Made Of; Also: Kol Nidrei (Trad.); This Is
A Very Special Day; Hush-A-Bye; Lover.
RCA  LPM-3118

508. JESUS CHRIST SUPERSTAR   (1973)
STARS:   Ted Neely, Carl Anderson
DIR:     Norman Jewison
SONGS:   Andrew Lloyd Weber - Tim Rice
Heaven On Their Minds; What's The Buzz?; Strange Thing Mys-
tifying; Then We Are Decided; Everything's Alright; This Jesus
Must Die; Hosanna; Simon Zealotes; Poor Jerusalem; Pilate's
Dream; The Temple; I Don't Know How To Love Him; Damned For
All Time; Blood Money; The Last Supper; Gethsemane; The Arrest;
Peter's Denial; Pilate And Christ; King Herod's Song; Could We
Start Again Please?; Judas' Death; Trial Before Pilate; Super-
star; The Crucifixion; John Nineteen Forty One.
MCA 2-11000

509. JIMMY AND SALLIE   (1933)

STARS: James Dunn, Claire Trevor
DIR: James Tinling
SONGS: Jay Gorney - Sidney Clare

510. JITTERBUGS (1943)
STARS: Laurel and Hardy
DIR: Mal St. Clair
SONGS: Lew Pollack - Charles Newman

511. JOHNNY APOLLO (1940)
STARS: Dorothy Lamour, Tyrone Power
DIR: Henry Hathaway

512. JOHNNY DOUGHBOY (1942)
STARS: Jane Withers, Jenry Wilcoxson
DIR: John F. Auer

513. JOLSON SINGS AGAIN (1949)
STARS: Larry Parks, Barbara Hale
DIR: Henry Levin

514. JOLSON STORY, THE (1946)
STARS: Larry Parks, Evelyn Keyes
DIR: Alfred E. Green

515. JOSETTE (1938)
STARS: Simone Simon, Don Ameche
DIR: Allan Dwan
SONGS: Harry Revel - Mack Gordon

516. JOY OF LIVING (1938)
STARS: Irene Dunne, Douglas Fairbanks Jr.
DIR: Tay Garnett
SONGS: Jerome Kern - Dorothy Fields
You Couldn't Be Cuter; Just Let Me Look At You; What's Good
About Good Night?; A Heavenly Party.
Jerome Kern In Hollywood, 1934 - 1938: JJA 19747D

517. JUKE BOX JENNIE (1942)
STARS: Harriet Hilliard, Ken Murray
DIR: Harold Young

518. JUMBO (1962)
STARS: Doris Day, Stephen Boyd
DIR: Charles Walters
SONGS: Richard Rodgers - Lorenz Hart
Over And Over Again; Circus On Parade; Why Can't I?; This Can't
Be Love; The Most Beautiful Girl In The World; My Romance; Lit-
tle Girl Blue; What Is A Circus?; Sawdust; Spangles, And Dreams.
Col. CSP - AOS - 2260

519. JUMPING JACKS (1952)
STARS: Dean Martin, Jerry Lewis
DIR: Norman Taurog

SONGS:  Jerry Livingston - Mack David
Do The Parachute Jump; What Have You Done For Me Lately?; The
Big Blue Sky Is The Place For Me; I Know A Dream When I See
One; I Can't Resist A Boy In Uniform; Keep A Little Dream Handy.

520.  JUNIOR PROM  (1946)
      STARS:  Freddie Stewart, June Preisser
      DIR:    Arthur Dreifuss

521.  JUPITER'S DARLING  (1955)
      STARS:  Esther Williams, Howard Keel
      DIR:    George Sidney
      SONGS:  Burton Lane - Harold Adamson
      I Have A Dream; If This Be Slav'ry; The Life Of An Elephant;
      I Never Trust A Woman; Don't Let This Night Get Away; Hanni-
      bal's Victory March; Horatio's Narrative (Saul Chaplin - George
      Wells).

522.  JUST AROUND THE CORNER  (1938)
      STARS:  Shirley Temple, Joan Davis
      DIR:    Irving Cummings
      SONGS:  Harold Spina - Walter Bullock

523.  JUST FOR YOU  (1952)
      STARS:  Bing Crosby, Jane Wyman
      DIR:    Elliott Nugent
      SONGS:  Harry Warren - Leo Robin
      The Live Oak Tree; Checkin' My Heart; I'll Si-Si In Bahia; On
      The 10:10 (From Ten, Ten Tennessee); Maiden Of Guadalupe; A
      Flight Of Fancy; Zing A Little Zong; He's Just Crazy For Me;
      Call Me Tonight; Just For You; The Ol' Spring Fever.
      Decca  DL-4263

524.  JUST IMAGINE  (1930)
      STARS:  Maureen O'Sullivan, El Brendel
      DIR:    David Butler
      SONGS:  Ray Henderson - B. G. DeSylva - Lew Brown

525.  KANSAS CITY KITTY  (1944)
      STARS:  Joan Davis, Jane Frazee
      DIR:    Del Lord

526.  KEEP 'EM FLYING  (1941)
      STARS:  Abbott and Costello
      DIR:    Arthur Lubin
      SONGS:  Gene DePaul - Don Raye

527.  KENTUCKY MOONSHINE  (1938)
      STARS:  The Ritz Brothers
      DIR:    David Butler

528.  KID FROM BROOKLYN, THE  (1946)
      STARS:  Danny Kaye, Virginia Mayo
      DIR:    Norman Z. McLeod

529. KID FROM SPAIN, THE   (1932)
     STARS:  Eddie Cantor, Lyda Roberti
     DIR:    Leo McCarey
     SONGS:  Harry Ruby - Bert Kalmar

530. KID MILLIONS   (1934)
     STARS:  Eddie Cantor, Ann Sothern
     DIR:    Roy Del Ruth

531. KING AND I, THE   (1956)
     STARS:  Yul Brynner, Deborah Kerr
     DIR:    Walter Lang
     SONGS:  Richard Rodgers - Oscar Hammerstein II
     My Lord And Master; I Whistle A Happy Tune; Hello Young Lovers;
     The March Of The Siamese Children; Shall I Tell You What I
     Think Of You; A Puzzlement; We Kiss In A Shadow; I Have Dreamed;
     Something Wonderful; Shall We Dance?; The Small House Of Uncle
     Thomas; The Song Of The King; Getting To Know You.
     Capitol  SW-740

532. KING KELLY OF THE U.S.A.   (1934)
     STARS:  Guy Robertson, Irene Ware
     DIR:    Leonard Fields
     SONGS:  Joe Sanders - Bernie Grossman

533. KING OF BURLESQUE   (1935)
     STARS:  Warner Baxter, Jack Oakie
     DIR:    Sidney Lanfield

534. KING OF JAZZ   (1930)
     STARS:  Paul Whiteman, John Boles
     DIR:    John Murray Anderson
     Happy Feet; A Bench In The Park; My Bridal Veil; Song Of The
     Dawn; I Like To Do Things For You; Music Has Charms; My Lover
     (Milton Ager - Jack Yellen); It Happened In Monterey; Ragamuf-
     fin Romeo (Mabel Wayne - Billy Rose); So The Bluebirds And The
     Blackbirds Got Together (Harry Barris - Billy Moll).
     Col.  C2L-43

535. KING SOLOMON OF BROADWAY   (1935)
     STARS:  Edmund Lowe, Dorothy Page
     DIR:    Alan Crosland

536. KING STEPS OUT, THE   (1936)
     STARS:  Grace Moore, Franchot Tone
     DIR:    William Perlberg
     SONGS:  Fritz Kreisler - Dorothy Fields

537. KISMET   (1955)
     STARS:  Howard Keel, Ann Blyth
     DIR:    Vincente Minnelli
     SONGS:  Alexander Borodin - Robert Wright and George Forrest.
     Rhymes Have I; Fate; Bored; And This Is My Beloved; Gesticulate;
     The Olive Tree; Not Since Nineveh; Rahadlakum; The Sands Of

141

Time; A Stranger In Paradise; Baubles, Bangles, and Beads;
Night Of My Nights.
MGM  3281

538.  KISS ME KATE  (1953)
      STARS:  Kathryn Grayson, Howard Keel
      DIR:    George Sidney
      SONGS:  Cole Porter
      Too Darn Hot; So In Love; We Open In Venice; Why Can't You
      Behave?; Were Thine That Special Face?; Tom, Dick Or Harry;
      Wunderbar; Always True To You In My Fashion; I Hate Men; I've
      Come To Wive It Wealthily In Padua; From This Moment On; Where
      Is The Life That Late I Led?; Brush Up Your Shakespeare; Kiss
      Me Kate.
      MGM  2-SES-44-ST

539.  KISS THE BOYS GOODBYE  (1941)
      STARS:  Mary Martin, Don Ameche
      DIR:    Victor Schertzinger
      SONGS:  Victor Schertzinger - Frank Loesser

540.  KISSING BANDIT, THE  (1948)
      STARS:  Frank Sinatra, Kathryn Grayson
      DIR:    Laslo Benedek
      SONGS:  Nacio Herb Brown - Earl Brent - Edward Heyman

541.  KLONDIKE ANNIE  (1936)
      STARS:  Mae West, Victor McLaglen
      DIR:    Raoul Walsh

542.  KNICKERBOCKER HOLIDAY  (1944)
      STARS:  Nelson Eddy, Charles Coburn
      DIR:    Harry Joe Brown

543.  KNOCK ON WOOD  (1954)
      STARS:  Danny Kaye
      DIR:    Norman Panama, Melvin Frank
      SONGS:  Sylvia Fine
      End Of Spring; Mon Ahan, O Han; All About You; Knock On Wood.
      Decca  DL-5527

544.  LA CONGA NIGHTS  (1940)
      STARS:  Hugh Herbert, Dennis O'Keefe
      DIR:    Lew Landers
      SONGS:  Frank Skinner - Sammy Lerner

545.  LADIES' MAN  (1947) ·
      STARS:  Eddie Bracken, Cass Daley
      DIR:    William D. Russell

546.  LADIES OF THE CHORUS  (1949)
      STARS:  Adele Jurgens, Marilyn Moore
      DIR:    Phil Karlson
      SONGS:  Lester Lee - Allan Roberts

547. LADY BE GOOD  (1941)
     STARS:  Eleanor Powell, Ann Sothern
     DIR:    Norman Z. McLeod

548. LADY IN THE DARK  (1944)
     STARS:  Ginger Rogers, Ray Milland
     DIR:    Michell Leisen

549. LADY LET'S DANCE  (1944)
     STARS:  Belita, James Ellison
     DIR:    Frank Woodruff

550. LADY OBJECTS, THE  (1938)
     STARS:  Lanny Ross, Gloria Stuart
     DIR:    Clifford Boughton
     SONGS:  Ben Oakland - Oscar Hammerstein II

551. LADY SINGS THE BLUES  (1972)
     STARS:  Diana Ross, Billy Dee Williams
     DIR:    Sidney J. Furie
     Lover Man (Jimmy Davis - Ram Ramirez - Jimmy Sherman); Don't
     Explain; God Bless The Child (B. Holiday - Arthur Herzog, Jr.);
     I Cried For You (Gus Arnheim - Abe Lyman - Arthur Freed); All
     Of Me (Gerald Marks - Seymour Simons); My Man (Maurice Yvain -
     Channing Pollack); You've Changed (Bill Carey - Carl Fisher);
     Them There Eyes (Maceo Pinkard - William Tracey - Doris Tauber);
     The Man I Love; Our Love Is Here To Stay (George and Ira Ger-
     shwin); Mean To Me (Roy Turk - Fred Ahlert); Fine And Mellow
     (B. Holiday); What A Little Moonlight Can Do (Harry Woods);
     Lady Sings The Blues (B. Holiday - H. Nicholas); T'aint No-
     body's Bizniss If I Do (Porter Grainger - E. Robbins); Gimme
     A Pigfoot And A Bottle Of Beer (Walter Wilson); Good Morning
     Heartache (I. Higgenbotham - Ervin Drake - Doris Fisher);
     Strange Fruit (Lester Allen).
     Motown  2-M7-758

552. LADY'S MORALS, A  (1930)
     STARS:  Grace Moore, Reginald Denny
     DIR:    Sydney Franklin

553. LARCENY WITH MUSIC  (1943)
     STARS:  Allan Jones, Kitty Carlisle
     DIR:    Edward Lilley

554. LAS VEGAS NIGHTS  (1941)
     STARS:  Bert Wheeler, Phil Regan
     DIR:    Frank Murphy
     LYRICS: Frank Loesser

555. LATIN LOVERS  (1953)
     STARS:  Lana Turner, Richardo Montalban
     DIR:    Mervyn LeRoy
     SONGS:  Nicholas Brodszky - Leo Robin

I Had To Kiss You; A Little More Of Your Amor; Come To My Arms; Carlotta, Ya Gotta Be Mine.

556. LAUGH IT OFF   (1939)
     STARS:   Johnny Downs, Constance Moore
     DIR:     Albert S. Rogell
     SONGS:   Ben Oakland - Sam Lerner

557. LAUGHING IRISH EYES   (1936)
     STARS:   Phil Regan, Walter Kelly
     DIR:     Joseph Santley
     SONGS:   Sammy Stept - Sidney Mitchell

558. LEMON DROP KID, THE   (1957)
     STARS:   Bob Hope, Marilyn Maxwell
     DIR:     Sidney Lanfield
     SONGS:   Jay Livingston - Ray Evans
     They Obviously Want Me To Sing; It Doesn't Cost A Dime To Dream
     Silver Bells.

559. LES GIRLS   (1957)
     STARS:   Gene Kelly, Mitzi Gaynor
     DIR:     George Cukor
     SONGS:   Cole Porter
     Les Girls; You're Just Too Too; Drinking Song; Why Am I So Gone
     On You; Ladies In Waiting; Ca C'est L'amour.
     MGM - 2 - SES - 51ST

560. LET FREEDOM RING   (1939)
     STARS:   Nelson Eddy, Virginia Bruce
     DIR:     John Conway

561. LET'S BE HAPPY   (1957)
     STARS:   Vera Ellen, Tony Martin
     DIR:     Henry Levin
     SONGS:   Nicholas Brodszky
     Tomorrow Man From Idaho; Rose Of The Heather; One Is A Lonely
     Number; Hold On To Love.

562. LET'S DANCE   (1950)
     STARS:   Betty Hutton, Fred Astaire
     DIR:     Norman Z. McLeod
     SONGS:   Frank Loesser
     Why Fight The Feeling?; Oh Them Dudes; Tunnel Of Love; Jack And
     The Beanstalk; The Hyacinth; Can't Stop Talking.

563. LET'S DO IT AGAIN   (1953)
     STARS:   Ray Milland, Jane Wyman
     DIR:     Alexander Hall
     SONGS:   Ned Washington - Lester Lee
     Anyone But You; Taking' A Slow Burn; These Are The Things I
     Remember; Gimme A Man Who Makes Music; Call Of The Wild.

564. LET'S FACE IT   (1943)

144

STARS:   Bob Hope, Betty Hutton
DIR:     Sidney Lanfield

565.  LET'S FALL IN LOVE  (1934)
STARS:   Ann Sothern, Edmund Lowe
DIR:     David Burton
SONGS:   Harold Arlen - Ted Koehler

566.  LET'S GO NATIVE  (1930)
STARS:   Jeanette MacDonald, Jack Oakie
DIR:     Leo McCarey
SONGS:   Richard Whiting - George Marion Jr.

567.  LET'S GO PLACES  (1930)
STARS:   Joseph Wagstaff, Lola Lane
DIR:     Frank Strayer

568.  LET'S MAKE LOVE  (1960)
STARS:   Marilyn Monroe, Yves Montand
DIR:     George Cukor
SONGS:   James Van Heusen - Sammy Cahn
You With The Crazy Eyes; Specialization; Let's Make Love; In-
curably Romantic; and My Heart Belongs To Daddy (Cole Porter).
Col. CSP-ACS-8327

569.  LET'S MAKE MUSIC  (1940)
STARS:   Bob Crosby, Jean Rogers
DIR:     Leslie Goodwins

570.  LET'S TALK IT OVER  (1934)
STARS:   Chester Morris, Mae Clark
DIR:     Kurt Newmann

571.  LIFE BEGINS IN COLLEGE  (1937)
STARS:   The Ritz Brothers, Joan Davis
DIR:     William A. Seiter

572.  LIFE OF THE PARTY  (1930)
STARS:   Winnie Lightner, Irene Delroy
DIR:     Roy Del Ruth

573.  LIFE OF THE PARTY  (1937)
STARS:   Joe Penner, Gene Raymond
DIR:     William A. Seiter

574.  LI'L ABNER  (1959)
STARS:   Peter Palmer, Leslie Parrish
DIR:     Melvin Frank
SONGS:   Gene DePaul - Johnny Mercer
A Typical Day; If I Had My Druthers; Jubilation T. Cornpone;
Don't Take That Rag Offen That Bush; There's Room Enough For
Us; Namely You; The Country's In The Very Best Of Hands; I'm
Past My Prime; Unnecessary Town; Otherwise; Put 'Em Back; Mat-
rimonial Stomp.
Col.  OS-2021

575. LILI (1953)
    STARS: Leslie Caron, Mel Ferrer
    DIR:   Charles Walters
    SONGS: Bronislaw Kaper - Helen Deutsch
    Adoration; Hi Lili, Hi-Lo; Lili And The Puppets.
    MGM E-187

576. LILLIAN RUSSELL (1940)
    STARS: Alice Faye, Don Ameche
    DIR:   Irving Cummings

577. LISTEN DARLING (1938)
    STARS: Judy Garland, Freddie Bartholomew
    DIR:   Edward L. Marin

578. LITTLE BIT OF HEAVEN, A (1940)
    STARS: Gloria Jean, Robert Stack
    DIR:   Andrew Marton

579. LITTLE BOY LOST (1953)
    STARS: Bing Crosby, Calude Dauphin
    DIR:   George Seaton
    SONGS: Johnny Burke - James Van Heusen
    The Magic Window; If It's All The Same To You; A Propos De
    Rien; Oh Susanna.
    Decca  DL-4264

580. LITTLE JOHNNY JONES (1929)
    STARS: Eddie Buzzell, Alice Day
    DIR:   Mervyn LeRoy

581. LITTLE MISS BROADWAY (1938)
    STARS: Shirley Temple, George Murphy
    DIR:   Irving Cummings
    SONGS: Harold Spina - Walter Bullock
    We Should Be Together; Be Optimistic; How Can I Thank You?; If
    All The World Were Paper; Swing Me An Old-Fashioned Song; I'll
    Build A Broadway For You; Little Miss Broadway; Hop, Skip,
    and Jump.
    20th Century - T-906e

582. LITTLE MISS BROADWAY (1947)
    STARS: Jean Porter, John Shelton
    DIR:   Arthur Dreifuss

583. LITTLE MISS MARKER (1934)
    STARS: Shirley Temple, Adolphe Menjou
    DIR:   Alexander Hall
    SONGS: Ralph Rainger - Leo Robin

584. LITTLE MISS ROUGHNECK (1938)
    STARS: Edith Fellows, Leo Carrillo
    DIR:   Aubrey Scotto
    SONGS: Ben Oakland - George Jessel - Milton Drake

146

85. LITTLE NELLIE KELLY  (1940)
    STARS:  Judy Garland, George Murphy
    DIR:    Norman Taurog

86. LITTLE PRINCE, THE  (1974)
    STARS:  Richard Kiley, Bob Fosse
    DIR:    Stanley Donen
    SONGS:  Frederick Loewe - Alan Jay Lerner
    I Need Air; Be Happy; I'm On Your Side; You're A Child; Little
    Prince; I Never Met A Rose; Why Is The Desert; Snake In The
    Grass; Closer And Closer And Closer.
    ABC-854

87. LIVING IT UP  (1954)
    STARS:  Dean Martin, Jerry Lewis
    DIR:    Norman Taurog
    SONGS:  Jule Styne - Bob Hilliard
    Ev'ry Street's A Boulevard; How Do You Speak To An Angel?;
    Money Burns A Hole In My Pocket; That's What I Like; Champagne
    And Wedding Cake.

88. LOOK FOR THE SILVER LINING  (1949)
    STARS:  June Haver, Ray Bolger
    DIR:    David Butler

89. LORD BYRON OF BROADWAY  (1930)
    STARS:  Ethelind Terry, Cliff Edwards
    DIR:    William Nigh and Harry Beaumont

90. LOST HORIZON  (1973)
    STARS:  Liv Ullman, Peter Finch
    DIR:    Charles Jarrott
    SONGS:  Burt Bacharach - Hal David
    Lost Horizon; Share The Joy; The World Is A Circle; Living
    Together, Growing Together; I Might Frighten Her Away; The
    Things I Will Not Miss; If I Could Go Back; Where Knowledge
    Ends; Question Me An Answer; I Come To You; Reflections.
    Bell 1300

91. LOST IN A HAREM  (1944)
    STARS:  Abbott and Costello
    DIR:    Charles Riesner

92. LOTTERY BRIDE  (1930)
    STARS:  Jeanette MacDonald, Zasu Pitts
    DIR:    Paul Stein

93. LOTTERY LOVER  (1935)
    STARS:  Lew Ayers, Pat Patterson
    DIR:    William Thiele
    SONGS:  Jay Gorney - Don Hartman

94. LOUD SPEAKER  (1934)
    STARS:  Ray Walter, Jacqueline Wells

DIR:     Joseph Santley

595.  LOUISIANA HAYRIDE  (1944)
      STARS:  Judy Canova, Ross Hunter
      DIR:    Charles Barton

596.  LOUISIANA PURCHASE  (1941)
      STARS:  Bob Hope, Vera Zorina
      DIR:    Irving Cummings
      SONGS:  Irving Berlin

597.  LOVE AND HISSES  (1937)
      STARS:  Walter Winchell, Ben Bernie
      DIR:    Sidney Lanfield
      SONGS:  Harry Revel - Mack Gordon

598.  LOVE AMONG THE MILLIONAIRES  (1930)
      STARS:  Clara Bow, Stanley Smith
      DIR:    Frank Tuttle
      SONGS:  Abel Baer - L. Wolfe Gilbert

599.  LOVE AND LEARN  (1947)
      STARS:  Jack Carson, Robert Hutton
      DIR:    Frederick De Cordova

600.  LOVE FINDS ANDY HARDY  (1938)
      STARS:  Judy Garland, Mickey Rooney
      DIR:    George B. Seitz

601.  LOVE IN BLOOM  (1935)
      STARS:  George Burns, Gracie Allen
      DIR:    Elliott Nugent
      SONGS:  Harry Revel - Mack Gordon

602.  LOVE IN THE ROUGH  (1930)
      STARS:  Dorothy Jardon, Robert Montgomery
      DIR:    Charles F. Reisner
      SONGS:  Jimmy McHugh - Dorothy Fields

603.  LOVE ME OR LEAVE ME  (1955)
      STARS:  James Cagney, Doris Day
      DIR:    Charles Vidor
      Never Look Back  (Chilton Price); I'll Never Stop Loving You
      (Nicholas Brodszky - Sammy Cahn); Also: It All Depends On You
      (Ray Henderson - B. G. DeSylva - Lew Brown); You Made Me Love
      You (James Monaco - Joseph McCarthy); Stay On The Right Side
      (Rube Bloom - Ted Koehler); Mean To Me (Fred Ahlert - Roy Turk
      Everybody Loves My Baby (Jack Palmer - Spencer Williams);
      Shakin' The Blues Away (Irving Berlin); Ten Cents A Dance
      (Richard Rodgers - Lorenz Hart); Sam, The Accordian Man; At Su
      down (Walter Donaldson); Love Me Or Leave Me (Walter Donald-
      son - Gus Kahn).
      Col. CSP-ACS-8773

604. LOVE ME TONIGHT   (1932)
   STARS:  Maurice Chevalier, Jeanette MacDonald
   DIR:    Rouben Mamoulian
   SONGS:  Richard Rodgers - Lorenz Hart

605. LOVE ON TOAST   (1938)
   STARS:  John Payne, Stella Ardler
   DIR:    E. A. Dupont

606. LOVE PARADE, THE   (1929)
   STARS:  Maurice Chevalier, Jeanette MacDonald
   DIR:    Ernst Lubitsch

607. LOVE THY NEIGHBOR   (1940)
   STARS:  Jack Benny, Mary Martin
   DIR:    Mark Sandrich
   SONGS:  Jimmy Van Heusen - Johnny Burke

608. LOVELY TO LOOK AT   (1952)
   STARS:  Kathryn Grayson, Red Skelton
   DIR:.   Mervyn LeRoy
   SONGS:  Jerome Kern - Otto Harbach, Oscar Hammerstein II,
   Dorothy Fields, Jimmy McHugh
   Opening Night; Lafayette; I'll Be Hard To Handle; Yesterdays;
   I Won't Dance; Lovely To Look At; You're Devastating; Smoke
   Gets In Your Eyes; The Most Exciting Night; The Touch Of Your
   Hand.
   MGM-2-SES-50ST

609. LOVER COME BACK   (1946)
   STARS:  Lucille Ball, George Brent
   DIR:    William Seiter

610. LUCKY BOY   (1929)
   STARS:  George Jessel, Margaret Quimby
   DIR:    Norman Taurog and Charles C. Wilson

611. LUCKY ME   (1954)
   STARS:  Doris Day, Robert Cummings
   DIR:    Jack Donahue
   SONGS:  Sammy Fain - Paul Francis Webster
   I Speak To The Stars; Men; Parisian Pretties; Blue Bells Of
   Broadway; High Hopes; I Love You Dearly; I Wanna Sing Like An
   Angel.

612. LULLABY OF BROADWAY   (1951)
   STARS:  Doris Day, Gene Nelson
   DIR:    David Butler
   You're Dependable (Sy Miller - Jerry Seelen); I Love The Way
   You Say Good Night (Eddie Pola - George Wyle); Just One Of
   Those Things (Cole Porter); You're Getting To Be A Habit With
   Me; Lullaby Of Broadway (Harry Warren - Al Dubin); Zing Went
   The Strings Of My Heart (James Hanley); Please Don't Talk About
   Me When I'm Gone (Sammy Stept - Sidney Clare); In A Shanty In

149

Old Shanty Town (Joe Siras - Little Jack Little - Joe Young).

613. LULU BELLE   (1948)
STARS:   Dorothy Lamour, George Montgomery
DIR:     Leslie Fenton

614. MAD ABOUT MUSIC   (1938)
STARS:   Deanna Durbin, Herbert Marshall
DIR:     Norman Taurog
SONGS:   Jimmy McHugh - Harold Adamson

615. MAKE A WISH   (1937)
STARS:   Bobby Breen, Basil Rathbone
DIR:     Kurt Neumann
LYRICS: Paul Francis Webster

616. MAKE BELIEVE BALLROOM   (1949)
STARS:   Jerome Courtland, Ruth Warrick
DIR:     Joseph Santley

617. MAKE MINE LAUGHS   (1949)
STARS:   Ray Bolger, Anne Shirley
DIR:     Richard Fleischer

618. MAME   (1974)
STARS:   Lucille Ball, Beatrice Arthur
DIR:     Gene Saks
SONGS:   Jerry Herman
It's Today; Open A New Window; Man In The Moon; My Best Girl;
We Need A Little Christmas; Mame; Loving You; Letter; Bosom
Buddies; If He Walked Into My Life; Gooch's Song.
Warner Bros.   W2773

619. MAMMY   (1930)
STARS:   Al Jolson, Louise Dresser
DIR:     Michael Curtiz
SONGS:   Irving Berlin

620. MAN ABOUT TOWN   (1939)
STARS:   Jack Benny, Betty Grable
DIR:     Mark Sandrich
LYRICS:  Frank Loesser

621. MAN I LOVE, THE   (1946)
STARS:   Ida Lupino, Robert Alda
DIR:     Raoul Walsh

622. MAN OF LA MANCHA   (1972)
STARS:   Peter O'Toole, Sophia Loren
DIR:     Arthur Hiller
SONGS:   Mitch Leigh - Joe Darion
Man Of La Mancha, Dulcinea; It's All The Same; I Really Like
Him; I'm Only Thinking Of Him; The Barber's Song; Little Bird,
Little Bird; The Golden Helmet Of Mambrino; The Impossible

Dream; The Dubbing; A Little Gossip; Aldonza; The Psalm; The
Quest.
United Artists UA 9906

623. MANHATTAN ANGEL   (1949)
STARS:  Gloria Jean, Ross Ford
DIR:    Arthur Dreifuss

624. MANHATTAN MERRY-GO-ROUND   (1931)
STARS:  Phil Regan, Leo Carrillo
DIR:    Charles F. Reiser

625. MANHATTAN PARADE   (1932)
STARS:  Winnie Lightner, Charles Butterworth
DIR:    Lloyd Bacon

626. MANY HAPPY RETURNS   (1934)
STARS:  Guy Lombardo, Burns and Allen
DIR:    Norman McLeod

627. MARIANNE   (1929)
STARS:  Marion Davies, Lawrence Gray
DIR:    Robert Z. Leonard

628. MARRIED IN HOLLYWOOD   (1929)
STARS:  J. Harold Murray, Norma Terris
DIR:    Marcel Silver
LYRICS: Harlan Thompson

629. MARY LOU   (1948)
STARS:  Robert Lowery, Joan Barton
DIR:    Arthur Dreifuss

630. MARY POPPINS   (1964)
STARS:  Julie Andrews, Dick Van Dyke
DIR:    Robert Stevenson
SONGS:  Richard M. and Robert B. Sherman
Spoonful Of Sugar; Jolly Holiday; Love To Laugh; Feed The
Birds, Chim-Chim-Cheree; Step In Time; Sister Sufragette, Stay
Awake; A Man Has Dreams; Supercalifragilisticexpialidocious;
The Life I Lead; Fidelity Fiduciary Bank.
Buena Vista STER-4026

631. MAYOR OF 44th STREET   (1942)
STARS:  George Murphy, Anne Shirley
DIR:    John Paddy
SONGS:  Harry Revel - Mort Greene

632. MAYTIME   (1937)
STARS:  Jeanette MacDonald, Nelson Eddy
DIR:    Robert Z. Leonard

633. MEET DANNY WILSON   (1952)
STARS:  Frank Sinatra, Alex Nicol

151

DIR:      Joseph Pervey
When You're Smiling (Larry Shay - Joe Goodwin - Mark Fisher);
All Of Me (Gerald Marks - Seymour Simons); That Old Black
Magic (Harold Arlen - Johnny Mercer); How Deep Is The Ocean?;
(Irving Berlin); A Good Man Is Hard To Find (Eddie Green);
She's Funny That Way (Richard Whiting - Neil Moret); You're
A Sweetheart (Jimmy McHugh - Harold Adamson); Lonesome Man
Blues (Sy Oliver); I've Got A Crush On You (George and Ira
Gershwin).

634.   MEET ME AFTER THE SHOW   (1951)
       STARS:  Betty Grable, MacDonald Carey
       DIR:      Richard Sale
       SONGS:  Jule Styne - Leo Robin
       Let Go Of My Heart; Meet Me After The Show; Bettin' On A Man;
       It's A Hot Night In Alaska; No Talent Joe; I Feel Like Danc-
       ing.

635.   MEET ME IN LAS VEGAS   (1956)
       STARS:  Dan Dailey, Cyd Charisse
       DIR:      Roy Rowland
       SONGS:  Nicholas Brodsky - Sammy Cahn
       If You Can Dream; Gal With The Yaller Shoes; Hell Hath No Fury;
       My Lucky Charm; I Refuse To Sing Rock And Roll; Frankie And
       Johnny Ballet (arr. Johnny Green).

636.   MEET ME IN ST. LOUIS   (1944)
       STARS:  Judy Garland, Margaret O'Brien
       DIR:      Vincente Minnelli
       The Trolley Song; Skip To My Lou; The Boy Next Door; Have Your-
       self A Merry Christmas (Hugh Martin - Ralph Blane); Meet Me In
       St. Louis (Kerry Mills - Andrew B. Sterling).
       MCA MCFM-2588 (import)

637.   MEET ME ON BROADWAY   (1946)
       STARS:  Marjorie Reynolds, Fred Brady
       DIR:      Leigh Jason
       SONGS:  Saul Chaplin - Edgar De Lange

638.   MEET MISS BOBBY SOX   (1944)
       STARS:  Bob Crosby, Lynn Merrick
       DIR:      Glenn Tryon

639.   MEET THE BOY FRIEND   (1937)
       STARS:  David Carlisle, Carol Hughes
       DIR:      Ralph Staub
       SONGS:  Roy Ingraham - Harry Tobias

640.   MEET THE PEOPLE   (1944)
       STARS:  Lucille Ball, Dick Powell
       DIR:      Charles Riesner

641.   MELODY AND MOONLIGHT   (1940)
       STARS:  Johnny Downs, Barbara Allen

```
         DIR:    Joseph Santley
         SONGS:  Jule Styne - Sol Meyer - George H. Brown

642.  MELODY CRUISE  (1933)
      STARS:  Charles Ruggles, Phil Harris
      DIR:    Mark Sandrich
      SONGS:  Will Jason - Val Burton

643.  MELODY FOR TWO  (1937)
      STARS:  James Melton, Patricia Ellis
      DIR:    Louis King

644.  MELODY IN SPRING  (1934)
      STARS:  Ann Sothern, Lanny Ross
      DIR:    Norman McLeod
      SONGS:  Lewis Gensler - Harlan Thompson

645.  MELODY LANE  (1929)
      STARS:  Eddie Leonard, Josephine Dunn
      DIR:    Robert F. Hill

646.  MELODY LANE  (1941)
      STARS:  Merry Macs
      DIR:    Charles Lamont
      SONGS:  Norman Berens - Jack Brooks

647.  MELODY PARADE  (1943)
      STARS:  Mary Beth Hughes, Eddie Quillan
      DIR:    Arthur Dreifuss
      SONGS:  Edward Kay - Eddie Cherkose

648.  MERRY ANDREW  (1958)
      STARS:  Danny Kaye, Pier Angeli
      DIR:    Michael Kidd
      SONGS:  Saul Chaplin - Johnny Mercer
      The Pipes Of Pan; Chin Up, Stout Fellow; You Can't Always Have
      What You Want; Everything Is Ticketty-Boo; The Square Of The
      Hypoteneuse; Salud
      Capitol T-1016

649.  MERRY MONIHANS, THE  (1944)
      STARS:  Donald O'Connor, Peggy Ryan
      DIR:    Charles Lamont

650.  MERRY WIDOW, THE  (1934)
      STARS:  Jeanette MacDonald, Maurice Chevalier
      DIR:    Ernst Lubitsch
      SONGS:  Frank Lehar - Gus Kahn, Lorenz Hart

651.  MERRY WIDOW, THE  (1952)
      STARS:  Lana Turner, Fernando Lamas
      DIR:    Curtis Bernhardt
      SONGS:  Franz Lehar - Paul Francis Webster
```

Vilia; Maxim's; Night; Merry Widow Waltz; Girls, Girls, Girls;
Can-Can.
MGM E-3228

652. MERRY-GO-ROUND OF 1938  (1937)
     STARS:  Bert Lahr, Jimmy Savo
     DIR:    Irving Cummings
     SONGS:  Jimmy McHugh - Harold Adamson

653. MEXICANA  (1945)
     STARS:  Tito Guizar, Constance Moore
     DIR:    Alfred Santell

654. MILKMAN, THE  (1950)
     STARS:  Donald O'Connor, Jimmy Durante
     DIR:    Charles T. Barton
     LYRICS: Jack Barnett (Composer follows in parentheses)
     It's Bigger Than Both Of Us; The Early Morning Song (Sammy
     Fain); Nobody Wants My Money; That's My Boy (Jimmy Durante)

655. MILLIONS IN THE AIR  (1935)
     STARS:  Willie and Eugene Howard
     DIR:    Ray McCarey

656. MINSTREL MAN  (1944)
     STARS:  Benny Fields, Gladys George
     DIR:    Joseph H. Lewis
     SONGS:  Harry Revel - Paul Francis Webster

657. MISS SADIE THOMPSON  (1953)
     STARS:  Rita Hayworth, Jose Ferrer
     DIR:    Curtis Bernhardt
     SONGS:  Lester Lee - Ned Washington
     The Heat Is On; Hear No Evil, See No Evil; Blue Pacific Blues;
     A Marine, A Marine (Lester Lee - Allan Roberts).

658. MISSISSIPPI  (1935)
     STARS:  Bing Crosby, W. C. Fields
     DIR:    Edward A. Sutherland
     SONGS:  Richard Rodgers - Lorenz Hart
     It's Easy To Remember (And So Hard To Forget); Soon; Down By
     The River; Roll Mississippi
     Decca DL-4250

659. MONEY FROM HOME  (1953)
     STARS:  Dean Martin, Jerry Lewis
     DIR:    George Marshall
     Be Careful Song; Love Is The Same (Joseph J. Lilley - Jack
     Brooks); Moments Like This (Burton Lane - Frank Loesser).

660. MONKEY BUSINESS  (1931)
     STARS:  The Marx Brothers, Thelma Todd
     DIR:    Norman McLeod

561. MONTE CARLO  (1930)
     STARS:   Jeanette MacDonald, Jack Buchanan
     DIR:     Ernst Lubitsch
     SONGS:   Richard Whiting - W. Franke Harling - Leo Robin

562. MOON OVER LAS VEGAS  (1944)
     STARS:   Anne Gwynne, David Bruce
     DIR:     Jean Yarbrough

563. MOON OVER MIAMI  (1941)
     STARS:   Don Ameche, Betty Grable
     DIR:     Walter Lang
     SONGS:   Ralph Rainger - Leo Robin

564. MOONLIGHT AND CACTUS  (1944)
     STARS:   The Andrews Sisters, Leo Carrillo
     DIR:     Edward F. Cline

565. MOONLIGHT AND PRETZELS  (1933)
     STARS:   Leo Carrillo, Mary Brian
     DIR:     Karl Freund

566. MOONLIGHT IN HAVANA  (1942)
     STARS:   Allan Jones, Jane Frazee
     DIR:     Anthony Mann
     SONGS:   Dave Franklin

567. MOONLIGHT IN HAWAII  (1941)
     STARS:   Jane Frazee, Johnny Downs
     DIR:     Charles Lamont
     SONGS:   Gene DePaul - Don Raye

568. MOONLIGHT IN VERMONT  (1943)
     STARS:   Gloria Jean, Ray Malone
     DIR:     Edward Lilley

569. MOTHER WORE TIGHTS  (1947)
     STARS:   Betty Grable, Dan Dailey
     DIR:     Walter Lang

570. MOULIN ROUGE  (1934)
     STARS:   Constance Bennett, Franchot Tone
     DIR:     Signey Lanfield
     SONGS:   Harry Warren - Al Dubin

571. MOUNTAIN MUSIC  (1937)
     STARS:   Martha Raye, Bob Burns
     DIR:     Robert Florey
     SONGS:   Sam Coslow

572. MR. BIG  (1943)
     STARS:   Gloria Jean, Donald O'Connor
     DIR:     Charles Lamont
     SONGS:   Buddy Pepper - Inez James

673. MR. DODD TAKES THE AIR  (1937)
     STARS:  Kenny Baker, Jane Wyman
     DIR:    Alfred E. Green
     SONGS:  Harry Warren - Al Dubin

674. MR. IMPERIUM  (1951)
     STARS:  Ezio Pinza, Lana Turner
     DIR:    Don Hartman
     Let Me Look At You; My Love And My Mule; Andiamo (Harold Ar-
     len - Dorothy Fields); You Belong To My Heart (Augustin Lara -
     Ray Gilbert).
     RCA LM-61

675. MR. MUSIC  (1950)
     STARS:  Bing Crosby, Nancy Olson
     DIR:    Richard Haydn
     SONGS:  Jimmy Van Heusen - Johnny Burke
     Mr. Music; Wasn't I There?; Milady; Once More The Blue And
     White; Life Is So Peculiar; High On The List; Accidents Will
     Happen; Then You'll Be Home; Wouldn't It Be Funny?

676. MURDER AT THE VANITIES  (1934)
     STARS:  Carl Brisson, Victor McLaglen
     DIR:    Mitchell Leisen
     SONGS:  Arthur Johnston - Sam Coslow - Johnny Burke

677. MUSIC FOR MADAME  (1937)
     STARS:  Nino Martini, Joan Fontaine
     DIR:    John Blystone

678. MUSIC FOR MILLIONS  (1944)
     STARS:  Margaret O'Brien, Jose Iturbi
     DIR:    Henry Koster

679. MUSIC GOES ROUND, THE  (1936)
     STARS:  Harry Richman, Rochelle Hudson
     DIR:    Victor Schertzinger
     SONGS:  Harry Akst - Harry Richman - Lew Brown

680. MUSIC IN MANHATTAN  (1944)
     STARS:  Anne Shirley, Dennis Day
     DIR:    John H. Auer
     SONGS:  Lew Pollack - Herb Magidson

681. MUSIC IN MY HEART  (1940)
     STARS:  Tony Martin, Rita Hayworth
     DIR:    Joseph Santley
     SONGS:  Robert Wright - Chet Forrest

682. MUSIC IN THE AIR  (1934)
     STARS:  Gloria Swanson, John Boles
     DIR:    Joe May
     SONGS:  Jerome Kern - Oscar Hammerstein II
     Music In The Air; I Am So Eager; I've Told Ev'ry Little  Star;

156

Melodies Of May; One More Dance; The Song Is You; We Belong
Together; There's A Hill Beyond A Hill
<u>Jerome Kern In Hollywood</u>, <u>1934-1938</u>: JJA 19747D

683. MUSIC IS MAGIC (1935)
     STARS: Alice Faye, Bebe Daniels
     DIR:   George Marshall

684. MUSIC MAN, THE (1962)
     STARS: Robert Preston, Shirley Jones
     DIR:   Morton Da Costa
     SONGS: Meredith Willson
     Rock Island; Iowa Stubborn; Trouble; Piano Lesson; Goodnight
     My Someone; Seventy-Six Trombones; Sincere; The Sadder-But-
     Wiser Girl; Pickalittle; Marian The Librarian; Being In Love;
     Wells Fargo Wagon; It's You; Shippoopi; Lida Rose; Will I Ever
     Tell You?; Gary, Indiana; Til There Was You.
     Warner Bros. BS-1459

685. MY BLUE HEAVEN (1950)
     STARS: Betty Grable, Dan Dailey
     DIR:   Henry Koster
     Live Hard, Work Hard, Love Hard; The Friendly Islands; It's
     Deductible; Hallowe'n; Don't Rock The Boat Dear; What A Man;
     I Love A New Yorker; Cosmo Cosmetics (Harold Arlen - Ralph
     Blane); My Blue Heaven (Walter Donaldson - George Whiting).

686. MY DREAM IS YOURS (1949)
     STARS: Jack Carson, Doris Day
     DIR:   Michael Curtiz

687. MY FAIR LADY (1964)
     STARS: Rex Harrison, Audrey Hepburn
     DIR:   George Cukor
     SONGS: Frederick Loewe - Alan Jay Lerner
     Why Can't The English?; Wouldn't It Be Loverly; I'm An Ordinary
     Man; With A Little Bit Of Luck; Just You Wait; The Rain In
     Spain; I Could Have Danced All Night; Ascot Gavotte; On The
     Street Where You Live; The Embassy Waltz; You Did It; Show Me;
     Get Me To The Church On Time; A Hymn To Him; Without You; I've
     Grown Accustomed To Her Face.
     Col. KOS-2600

688. MY FRIEND IRMA (1949)
     STARS: Marie Wilson, John Lund
     DIR:   George Marshall
     SONGS: Jay Livingston - Ray Evans

689. MY FRIEND IRMA GOES WEST (1950)
     STARS: John Lund, Marie Wilson
     DIR:   Hal Wallis
     SONGS: Jay Livingston - Ray Evans
     Baby Obey Me; I'll Always Love You; Fiddle And Gittar Band.

690. MY GAL LOVES MUSIC  (1944)
     STARS:   Bob Crosby, Alan Mowbray
     DIR:     Edward Lilley
     SONGS:   Milton Rosen - Everett Carter

691. MY GAL SAL  (1942)
     STARS:   Rita Hayworth, Victor Mature
     DIR:     Irving Cummings

692. MY HEART GOES CRAZY  (1946)
     STARS:   Syd Field, Greta Gynt
     DIR:     Wesley Ruggles
     SONGS:   Jimmy Van Heusen - Johnny Burke

693. MY LIPS BETRAY  (1933)
     STARS:   Lilian Harvey, John Boles
     DIR:     John Blystone
     SONGS:   William Kernell

694. MY LUCKY STAR  (1938)
     STARS:   Sonja Henie, Richard Green
     DIR:     Roy Del Ruth
     SONGS:   Harry Revel - Mack Gordon

695. MY MAN  (1929)
     STARS:   Fanny Brice, Guinn Williams
     DIR:     Archie Mayo

696. MY SISTER EILEEN  (1955)
     STARS:   Betty Garrett, Janet Leigh
     DIR:     Richard Quine
     SONGS:   Jule Styne - Leo Robin
     Give Me A Band And A Baby; It's Bigger Than You And Me; There's
     Nothing Like Love; As Soon As They See Eileen; I'm Great; Mr.
     Gloom; What Happened To The Conga?

697. MY WEAKNESS  (1933)
     STARS:   Lew Ayres, Charles Butterworth
     DIR:     David Butler

698. MY WILD IRISH ROSE  (1947)
     STARS:   Dennis Morgan, Arlene Dahl
     DIR:     David Butler
     Wee Rose Of Killarney; Miss Lindy Lou; There's Room In My
     Heart For Them All; The Natchez And The Robert E. Lee (M. K.
     Jerome - Ted Koehler); Come Down Ma Evenin' Star (John Strom-
     berg - Robert B. Smith); My Nellie's Blue Eyes (William J.
     Scanlon); One Little Sweet Little Girl (Dan Sullivan); My Wild
     Irish Rose (Chauncey Olcott); A Little Bit Of Heaven (Ernest
     Ball - J. Keirn Brennan); Mother Machree (Ernest Ball - Chaun-
     cey Olcott - Rida Johnson Young).
     Col. ML-4272

699. MYRT AND MARGE  (1934)

```
        STARS:  Myrtle Vail, Donna Damerell
        DIR:    Al Boasberg
        SONGS:  M. K. Jerome - Joan Jasmin

700.  MYSTERY IN MEXICO  (1948)
        STARS:  William Lundigan, Jacqueline White
        DIR:    Robert Wise
        SONGS:  Jimmy Van Heusen - Johnny Burke

701.  NANCY GOES TO RIO  (1950)
        STARS:  Jane Powell, Ann Sothern
        DIR:    Robert Z. Leonard
        Love Is Like This (J. DeBarro - Ray Gilbert); Ca-Boom Pa Pa;
        Yipsee-I-O (Ray Gilbert); Time And Time Again (Fred Spielman -
        Earl Brent); Nancy's Goin' To Rio (Earl Brent - George Stoll);
        Magic Is The Moonlight (Maria Grever - Charles Pasquale).
        MGM 2-SES-53ST

702.  NAUGHTY BUT NICE  (1939)
        STARS:  Ann Sheridan, Dick Powell
        DIR:    Ray Enright
        SONGS:  Harry Warren - Johnny Mercer

703.  NAUGHTY MARIETTA  (1935)
        STARS:  Jeanette MacDonald, Nelson Eddy
        DIR:    W. S. Van Dyke
        SONGS:  Victor Herbert - Gus Kahn - Rida Johnson Young

704.  NAUGHTY NINETIES, THE  (1945)
        STARS:  Abbott and Costello
        DIR:    Jean Yarbrough

705.  NAVY BLUES  (1941)
        STARS:  Ann Sheridan, Jack Oakie
        DIR:    Lloyd Bacon
        SONGS:  Arthur Schwartz - Johnny Mercer

706.  NEPTUNE'S DAUGHTER  (1949)
        STARS:  Esther Williams, Red Skelton
        DIR:    Eddie Buzzell

707.  NEVER A DULL MOMENT  (1950)
        STARS:  Irene Dunne, Fred MacMurray
        DIR:    George Marshall
        SONGS:  Kay Swift
        Once You Find Your Guy; A Man With A Big Felt Hat; Sagebrush
        Lullaby.

708.  NEVER STEAL ANYTHING SMALL  (1959)
        STARS:  James Cagney, Shirley Jones
        DIR:    Charles Lederer
        SONGS:  Allie Wrubel - Maxwell Anderson
        Never Steal Anything Small; I Haven't A Thing To Wear; It
        Takes Love To Build A Home; Helping Our Friends; I'm Sorry--
        I Want A Ferrari.
```

709. NEW FACES OF 1937  (1937)
     STARS:  Joe Penner, Milton Berle
     DIR:    Leigh Janson

710. NEW FACES  (1954)
     STARS:  Ronny Graham, Alice Ghostly
     DIR:    Harry Horner
     Love Is A Simple Thing; Time For Tea; Penny Candy; Monotonous;
     He Takes Me Off His Income Tax (Arthur Siegal - June Carroll);
     Boston Beguine (Sheldon Harnick); Lucky Pierre; Don't Fall
     Asleep; I'm In Love With Miss Logan (Ronny Graham); Lizzie
     Borden (Michael Brown).  Added to film: C'est Si Bon; Santa
     Baby, Uskadara.

711. **NEW MOON**  (1930)
     STARS:  Grace Moore, Lawrence Tibbett
     DIR:    John Conway
     SONGS:  Sigmund Romberg - Frederic Arnold Kummer - Oscar
     Hammerstein II
     Marianne; Softly As In A Morning Sunrise; Stout-Hearted Men;
     One Kiss; Wanting You; Funny Little Sailor Man; Lover Come
     Back To Me.
     Raviola 69 (Listed as _Parisian Belle)_

712. NEW MOON, THE  (1940)
     STARS:  Jeanette MacDonald, Nelson Eddy
     DIR:    Robert Z. Leonard

713. NEW MOVIETONE FOLLIES OF 1930  (1930)
     STARS:  El Brendel, Marjorie White
     DIR:    Benjamin Stoloff

714. NEW ORLEANS  (1947)
     STARS:  Dorothy Patrick, Arturo De Cordova
     DIR:    Arthur Lubin

715. NICE GIRL?  (1941)
     STARS:  Deanna Durbin, Franchot Tone
     DIR:    William A. Seiter

716. NIGHT AND DAY  (1946)
     STARS:  Cary Grant, Alexis Smith
     DIR:    Michael Curtiz
     SONGS:  Cole Porter

717. NIGHT AT EARL CARROLL'S, A  (1940)
     STARS:  Ken Murray, Rose Hobart
     DIR:    Kurt Neumann

718. NIGHT CLUB GIRL  (1944)
     STARS:  Vivian Austin, Edward Norris
     DIR:    Edward Cline

719. NIGHT IS YOUNG, THE  (1935)

STARS:   Ramon Novarro, Evelyn Laye
DIR:     Dudley Murphy
SONGS:   Sigmund Romberg - Oscar Hammerstein II

720.  NIGHT THEY RAIDED MINSKY'S, THE   (1968)
STARS:   Jason Robards, Norman Wisdom
DIR:     William Friedkin
SONGS:   Charles Strouse - Lee Adams
The Night They Raided Minsky's' Take 10 Terrific Girls; You
Rat You; How I Loved Her; Perfect Gentlemen; Penny Arcade.
United Artists UAS-5191

721.  NO LEAVE, NO LOVE   (1946)
STARS:   Van Johnson, Keenan Wynn
DIR:     Charles Martin

722.  NO, NO NANETTE   (1930)
STARS:   Alexander Gray, Bernice Claire
DIR:     Clarence Badger

723.  NO, NO NANETTE   (1940)
STARS:   Anna Neagle, Richard Carlson
DIR:     Herbert Wilcox
SONGS:   Vincent Youmans - Otto Harbach - Irving Caesar

724.  NOBODY'S BABY   (1937)
STARS:   Patsy Kelly, Lyda Roberti
DIR:     Gus Meins
SONGS:   Marvin Hatley - Walter Bullock

725.  NORTHWEST OUTPOST   (1947)
STARS:   Nelson Eddy, Ilona Massey
DIR:     Allan Dwan
SONGS:   Rudolf Friml - Edward Heyman

726.  OH, JOHNNY HOW YOU CAN LOVE   (1940)
STARS:   Tom Brown, Peggy Moran
DIR:     Charles Lamont
SONGS:   Frank Skinner - Paul Gerard Smith

727.  OH! SAILOR BEHAVE!   (1930)
STARS:   Irene Delroy, Charles King
DIR:     Archie Mayo
SONGS:   Joe Burke - Al Dubin

728.  OH! WHAT A LOVELY WAR   (1969)
STARS:   John Mills, John Gielgud
DIR:     Richard Attenborough
World War I Songs: Girls And Boys Come Out To Play; Oh! It's
A Lovely War; Are We Downhearted? No!; The Bells of Hell; We
Don't Want To Lose You; Belgium Put The Kibosh On The Kaiser;
We're 'Ere Because We're 'Ere; Silent Night; Christmas Day
In The Cookhouse; Gassed; I'll Make A Man Of You; Comrades;
There's A Long, Long Trail; Goodbye-ee; Hush! Here Comes A

Whizzbang; I Don't Want To Be A Soldier; Adieu La Vie; They Were Only Playing Leapfrog; When This Lousy War Is Over; The Moon Shines Bright On Charlie Chaplin; Mademoiselle From Armentieres; Forward Joe Soap's Army; I Want To Go Home; Far Far From Vipers; We Are Fred Karno's Army; Pack Up Your Troubles; Whiter Than The Whitewash On The Wall; Never Mind; If You Want The Old Battalion; Keep The Home Fires Burning; They Didn't Believe Me.
Paramount PAS-5008

729.  OH YOU BEAUTIFUL DOLL   (1949)
      STARS:  S. Z. Sakall, June Haver
      DIR:    John M. Stahl
      SONGS:  Fred Fisher

730.  OKLAHOMA   (1955)
      STARS:  Gordon MacRae, Shirley Jones
      DIR:    Fred Zinneman
      SONGS:  Richard Rodgers - Oscar Hammerstein II
      Oklahoma; Oh What A Beautiful Morning; The Surrey With The Fringe On Top; Kansas City; I Cain't Say No; Many A New Day; People Will Say We're In Love; Pore Jud; Out Of My Dreams; All Er Nothin'; The Farmer And The Cowman.
      Capitol SWAO-595

731.  OLD HOMESTEAD, THE   (1935)
      STARS:  Mary Carlisle, Lawrence Gray
      DIR:    William Nigh

732.  OLD HOMESTEAD, THE   (1942)
      STARS:  The Weaver Brothers

733.  OLD MAN RHYTHM   (1935)
      STARS:  Charles "Buddy" Rogers, George Barbier
      DIR:    Eddie Ludwig
      SONGS:  Lewis Gensler - Johnny Mercer

734.  OLIVER!   (1968)
      STARS:  Ron Moody, Mark Lester
      DIR:    Carol Reed
      SONGS:  Lionel Bart
      Food, Glorious Food; Oliver; Boy For Sale; Where Is Love; I'd Do Anything; Consider Yourself; Pick A Pocket Or Two; Be Back Soon; As Long As He Needs Me; Who Will Buy?; It's A Fine Life; Reviewing The Situation; Oom-Pah-Pah.
      Colgems 5501

735.  ON A CLEAR DAY YOU CAN SEE FOREVER   (1970)
      STARS:  Barbra Streisand, Yves Montand
      DIR:    Vincente Minnelli
      On A Clear Day; What Did I Have That I Don't Have; He Isn't You; Melinda; Go To Sleep; Hurry, It's Lovely Up Here; Come Back To Me; Love With All The Trimmings.
      Col. CSP-AS-30082

736. ON AN ISLAND WITH YOU  (1948)
     STARS:   Esther Williams, Peter Lawford
     DIR:     Richard Thorpe
     SONGS:   Nacio Herb Brown - Edward Heyman

737. ON MOONLIGHT BAY  (1951)
     STARS:   Doris Day, Gordon MacRae
     DIR:     Roy Del Ruth
     Love Ya (Peter De Rose - Charles Tobias); Christmas Story (Paul
     Walsh); On Moonlight Bay (Percy Wenrich - Edward Madden); Cud-
     dle Up A Little Closer (Karl Kortlander - Otto Harbach); Tell
     Me Why Nights Are Lonely (Max Kortlander - W. J. Callahan); I'm
     Forever Blowing Bubbles (John W. Kellette - Jean Kenbrovin);
     Every Little Movement Has A Meaning All Its Own (Karl Hoschna -
     Otto Harbach); Till We Meet Again (Richard Whiting - Ray Egan);
     Pack Up Your Troubles In Your Old Kit Bag (George Asaf - Felix
     Powell).

738. ON STAGE EVERYBODY  (1945)
     STARS:   Peggy Ryan, Johnny Coy
     DIR:     Jean Yarbrough

739. ON THE AVENUE  (1937)
     STARS:   Dick Powell, Alice Faye
     DIR:     Roy Del Ruth
     SONGS:   Irving Berlin

740. ON THE RIVIERA  (1951)
     STARS:   Danny Kaye, Gene Tierney
     DIR:     Walter Lang
     Happy Ending; On The Riviera; Popo The Puppet; Rhythm Of A New
     Romance (Sylvia Fine); Ballin' The Jack (Chris Smith).

741. ON THE SUNNY SIDE OF THE STREET  (1951)
     STARS:   Frankie Laine, Billy Daniels
     DIR:     Richard Quine
     I Get A Kick Out Of You (Cole Porter); The Love Of A Gypsy
     (Fred Karger - Morris Stoloff); On The Sunny Side Of The Street
     (Jimmy McHugh - Dorothy Fields); Come Back To Sorrento (Ernesto
     de Curtis); Let's Fall In Love (Harold Arlen - Tel Koehler);
     Too Marvelous For Words (Richard Whiting - Johnny Mercer); I
     Hadn't Anyone Till You (Ray Noble); I'm Gonna Live Till I Die
     (Walter Kent - Mann Curtis - Al Hoffman); I May Be Wrong But
     I Think You're Wonderful (Henry Sullivan - Harry Ruskin).

742. ON THE TOWN  (1949)
     STARS:   Gene Kelly, Frank Sinatra
     DIR:     Gene Kelly, Stanley Donen
     LYRICS: Betty Comden - Adolph Green
     I Feel Like I'm Not Out Of Bed Yet; New York, New York; Miss
     Turnstiles; Come Up To My Place; A Day In New York (Leonard
     Bernstein); and Prehistoric Man; Main Street; You're Awful; On
     The Town; Count On Me (Roger Edens).
     Show Biz 5603

163

743. ON WITH THE SHOW  (1929)
     STARS:  Betty Compson, Louise Fazenda
     DIR:    Alan Crosland
     SONGS:  Harry Akst - Grant Clarke

744. ON YOUR TOES  (1939)
     STARS:  Zorina, Eddie Albert
     DIR:    Ray Enright
     SONGS:  Richard Rodgers - Lorenz Hart

745. THE ONE AND ONLY, GENUINE, ORIGINAL FAMILY BAND  (1968)
     STARS:  Walter Brennan, Lesley Ann Warren
     DIR:    Michael O'Herlihy
     SONGS:  Richard M. and Robert B. Sherman
     Dakota; The One And Only, Genuine, Original Family Band; Let's
     Put It Over With Grover; Drummin', Drummin', Drummin'; Ten
     Feet Off The Ground; 'Bout Time; Happiest Girl Alive; West Of
     The Wide Missouri; Oh Benjamin Harrison.
     Buena Vista STER-5002

746. ONE DARK NIGHT  (1939)
     STARS:  Mantan Moreland
     SONGS:  Lew Porter - Johnny Lange

747. ONE HOUR WITH YOU  (1932)
     STARS:  Maurice Chevalier, Jeanette MacDonald
     DIR:    Ernst Lubitsch/George Cukor
     SONGS:  Richard Whiting - Oscar Straus - Leo Robin

748. ONE IN A MILLION  (1936)
     STARS:  Sonja Henie, Adolphe Menjou
     DIR:    Sidney Lanfield
     SONGS:  Lew Pollack - Sidney Mitchell

749. ONE NIGHT IN THE TROPICS  (1940)
     STARS:  Abbott and Costello
     DIR:    A. Edward Sutherland
     SONGS:  Jerome Kern - Dorothy Fields

750. ONE SUNDAY AFTERNOON  (1948)
     STARS:  Dennis Morgan, Janis Paige
     DIR:    Raoul Walsh

751. ONE TOUCH OF VENUS  (1948)
     STARS:  Ava Gardner, Robert Walker
     DIR:    William A. Seiter
     SONGS:  Kurt Weill - Ogden Nash

752. OPPOSITE SEX, THE  (1956)
     STARS:  June Allyson, Dolores Gray
     DIR:    David Miller
     SONGS:  Nicholas Brodszky - Sammy Cahn
     Now! Baby, Now!; Dere's Yellow Gold On Da Trees; Rock And Roll
     Tumbleweed; A Perfect Love; Young Man With A Horn (Jimmy Mc-
     Hugh - Ralph Freed).

753.  ORCHESTRA WIVES   (1942)
      STARS:  George Montgomery, Ann Rutherford
      DIR:    Archie Mayo
      SONGS:  Harry Warren - Mack Gordon
      I've Got A Gal In Kalamazoo; Serenade In Blue; People Like
      You And Me; At Last; That's Sabotage.
      RCA LPT-3065

754.  OUT OF THIS WORLD   (1945)
      STARS:  Veronica Lake, Dianna Lynn
      DIR:    Hal Walker
      June Comes Around Every Year; Out Of This World (Harold Arlen -
      Johnny Mercer); I'd Rather Be Me (Sam Coslow - Felix Bernard -
      Eddie Cherkose); Ghost Of Mr. Chopin; All I Do Is Beat That
      Gol Darn Drum; It Takes A Little Bit More (Sam Coslow); Sailor
      With An 8-Day Pass (Bernie Wayne - Ben Raleigh).
      Decca DL-4259

755.  OUTSIDE OF PARADISE   (1938)
      STARS:  Phil Regan, Penny Singleton
      DIR:    John H. Auer
      SONGS:  Peter Tinturin - Jack Lawrence

756.  PAGAN LOVE SONG   (1950)
      STARS:  Esther Williams, Howard Keel
      DIR:    Robert Alton
      Sea Of The Moon; Singing In The Sun; Tahiti; House Of Singing
      Bamboo; Why Is Love So Crazy?; Etiquette (Harry Warren - Arthur
      Freed); Mata (Roger Edens); Pagan Love Song (Nacio Herb Brown -
      Arthur Freed).
      MGM 2-SES-43ST

757.  PAINT YOUR WAGON   (1969)
      STARS:  Clint Eastwood, Lee Marvin
      DIR:    Joshua Logan
      SONGS:  Frederick Loewe - Alan Jay Lerner
      I Talk To The Trees; I'm On My Way; They Call The Wind Maria;
      Hand Me Down That Can O'Beans; I Still See Elisa; Wandrin'
      Star; Whoop-ti-ay; There's A Coach Comin' In; and Gold Fever;
      A Million Miles Away Behind The Door; The First Thing You Know;
      Best Things; The Gospel Of No Name City (Andre Previn - Alan
      Jay Lerner).
      Paramount PMS-1001

758.  PAINTING THE CLOUDS WITH SUNSHINE   (1951)
      STARS:  Dennis Morgan, Virginia Mayo
      DIR:    Ralph Butler
      Tip-Toe Through The Tulips; Painting The Clouds With Sunshine
      (Joe Burke - Al Dubin); With A Song In My Heart (Richard Rod-
      gers - Lorenz Hart); Vienna Dreams (Rudolph Sieczy - Irving
      Caesar); Birth Of The Blues (Ray Henderson - B. G. DeSylva -
      Lew Brown); You're My Everything (Harry Warren - Mort Dixon);
      Jealousie (Jacob Gabe - Vera Bloom); Man Is A Necessary Evil;
      Mambo Man (Sonny Burke - Jack Elliott).

759. PAJAMA GAME (1957)
     STARS:  Doris Day, John Raitt
     DIR:    George Abbott, Stanley Donen
     SONGS:  Richard Adler - Jerry Ross
     Racing With The Clock; Once-A-Year Day; Hey There; Small Talk;
     The Pajama Game; I'll Never Be Jealous Again; I'm Not At All
     In Love;Hernando's Hideaway; Steam Heat; There Once Was A Man;
     7 1/2 Cents.
     Columbia OL-5210

760. PAL JOEY (1957)
     STARS:  Frank Sinatra, Rita Hayworth
     DIR:    George Sidney
     SONGS:  Richard Rodgers - Lorenz Hart
     That Terrific Rainbow; I Didn't Know What Time It Was; Zip;
     What Do I Care For A Dame?; Bewitched; My Funny Valentine; The
     Lady Is A Tramp; I Could Write A Book; There's A Small Hotel
     Capitol W-912

761. PALM SPRINGS (1936)
     STARS:  Frances Langford, Smith Ballew
     DIR:    Aubrey Scotto

762. PALMY DAYS (1931)
     STARS:  Eddie Cantor, Charlotte Greenwood
     DIR:    Edward Sutherland

763. PALOOKA (1934)
     STARS:  Jimmy Durante, Lupe Velez
     DIR:    Benjamin Stoloff

764. PAN-AMERICANA (1945)
     STARS:  Phillip Terry, Audrey Long
     DIR:    John H. Auer

765. PANAMA HATTIE (1942)
     STARS:  Ann Sothern, Red Skelton
     DIR:    Norman Z. McLeod

766. PARAMOUNT ON PARADE (1930)
     STARS:  Maurice Chevalier, Nancy Carroll
     DIR:    D. Arzner, E. Lubitsch, E. Goulding, V. Schertzinger

767. PARDNERS (1956)
     STARS:  Dean Martin, Jerry Lewis
     DIR:    Norman Taurog
     SONGS:  James Van Heusen - Sammy Cahn
     Pardners; Wind, the Wind; Me 'N' You 'N' The Moon; Buckskin
     Beauty.

768. PARDON MY SARONG (1942)
     STARS:  Abbott and Costello
     DIR:    Erle C. Kenton

769. PARIS  (1930)
     STARS:  Irene Bordoni, Jack Buchanan
     DIR:    Clarence Badger

770. PARIS FOLLIES OF 1956  (1955)
     STARS:  Margaret Whiting, Forrest Tucker
     DIR:    Leslie Goodwins
     SONGS:  Pony Sherrell - Phil Moody
     Can This Be Love?; Have You Ever Been In Paris?; I Love A Circus; I'm All Aglow Again; I'm In The Mood Tonight; The Hum Song (Sid Kuller).

771. PARIS HONEYMOON  (1939)
     STARS:  Bing Crosby, Franciska Gaal
     DIR:    Frank Tuttle
     SONGS:  Ralph Rainger - Leo Robin
     Work While You May; I Have Eyes; The Maiden By The Brook; Funny Old Hills; Joobalai; You're A Sweet Little Headache.
     Decca DL-4253

772. PARIS IN THE SPRING  (1935)
     STARS:  Mary Ellis, Tullio Carminati
     DIR:    Lewis Milestone
     SONGS:  Harry Revel - Mack Gordon

773. PENNIES FROM HEAVEN  (1936)
     STARS:  Bing Crosby, Madge Evans
     DIR:    Norman Z. McLeod
     SONGS:  Arthur Johnston - Johnny Burke

774. PEOPLE ARE FUNNY  (1946)
     STARS:  Jack Haley, Helen Walker
     DIR:    Sam White

775. PEPE  (1960)
     STARS:  Cantinflas, Maurice Chevalier
     DIR:    George Sidney
     SONGS:  Andre Previn - Dory Langdon
     That's How It Went All Right; Faraway Part Of Town; The Rumble; and; Pepe (Music by Hans Wiltstat); Lovely Day (Music by Agustin Lara).
     Colpix S-507

776. PERILS OF PAULINE  (1947)
     STARS:  Betty Hutton, John Lund
     DIR:    George Marshall

777. PETE KELLY'S BLUES  (1955)
     STARS:  Jack Webb, Peggy Lee
     DIR:    Jack Webb
     Pete Kelly's Blues (Ray Heindorf - Sammy Cahn); Sing Me A Rainbow; He Needs Me (Arthur Hamilton); Also: Gonna Meet My Sweetie Now; Somebody Loves Me; Oh, Didn't He Ramble; I Never Knew; Hard-Hearted Hannah; Bye, Bye Blackbird; Breezin' Along With

The Breeze; What Can I Say After I'm Sorry.
Col. CL-690.

778. PETTY GIRL, THE  (1950)
STARS:  Robert Cummings, Joan Caulfield
DIR:    Henry Levin
SONGS:  Harold Arlen - Johnny Mercer

779. PHANTOM PRESIDENT, THE  (1932)
STARS:  George M. Cohan, Claudette Colbert
DIR:    Norman Taurog
SONGS:  Richard Rodgers - Lorenz Hart

780. PIGSKIN PARADE  (1936)
STARS:  Stuart Erwin, Betty Grable, Judy Garland
DIR:    David Butler
SONGS:  Lew Pollack - Sidney Mitchell

781. PILLOW TALK  (1959)
STARS:  Rock Hudson, Doris Day
DIR:    Michael Gordon
SONGS:  Joe Lubin - I. J. Roth
Inspiration; I Need No Atmosphere; You Lied; Possess Me; and
Pillow Talk (Buddy Pepper - Inez James); Roly Poly (Sol Lake -
Elsa Doran).

782. PIN-UP GIRL  (1944)
STARS:  Betty Grable, Martha Raye
DIR:    Bruce Humberstone
SONGS:  Jimmy Monaco - Mack Gordon

783. PIRATE, THE  (1948)
STARS:  Judy Garland, Gene Kelly
DIR:    Vincente Minnelli
SONGS:  Cole Porter
You Can Do No Wrong; Love Of My Life; Mack The Black; Nina; Be
A Clown.
MGM 2-SES-43-ST

784. PLAYBOY OF PARIS  (1930)
STARS:  Maurice Chevalier, Frances Dee
DIR:    Ludwig Berger
SONGS:  Richard Whiting - Newell Chase - Leo Robin

785. PLAYMATES  (1941)
STARS:  Kay Kyser, Lupe Velez
DIR:    David Butler
SONGS:  Jimmy Van Heusen - Johnny Burke

786. POOR LITTLE RICH GIRL  (1936)
STARS:  Shirley Temple, Alice Faye
DIR:    Irving Cummings

SONGS: Harry Revel - Mack Gordon
Oh, My Goodness!; Buy A Bar Of Barry's; Military Man; When
I'm With You; But Definitely; You Gotta Eat Your Spinach Baby.
20th Century Fox   T-906e

787. POPPY  (1936)
STARS:  W. C. Fields, Rochelle Hudson

788. PORGY AND BESS  (1959)
STARS:  Sidney Portier, Dorothy Dandridge
DIR:    Otto Preminger
SONGS:  George Gershwin - Ira Gershwin - DuBose Heyward
Summertime; A Woman Is A Sometime Thing; They Pass By Singing;
Honey Man's Call; Gone, Gone, Gone; Oh Little Stars; Fill Up
De Saucer; My Man's Gone Now; The Train Is At The Station; I
Got Plenty O' Nuttin'; Bess, You Is My Woman Now; Oh, I Can't
Sit Down; I Ain't Got No Shame; It Ain't Necessarily So; What
You Want Wid Bess; It Takes A Long Pull To Get There; Straw-
berry Woman's Call; Crab Man's Call; I Loves You Porgy; Oh,
De Lawd Shake De Heaven; Dere's Somebody Knockin' At De Do';
A Red Headed Woman; Clara, Don't You Be Downhearted; There's
A Boat Dat's Leavin' Soon For New York; Good Mornin' Sister;
Bess, Oh Where's My Bess; Oh Lawd, I'm On My Way.
Col.  OS-5410

789. POT OF GOLD  (1940)
STARS:  James Stewart, Paulette Goddard
DIR:    George Marshall

790. POWER GIRL  (1942)
STARS:  Anne Shirley, George Murphy
DIR:    Norman Z. McLeod
SONGS:  Jule Styne - Kim Gannon

791. PRESENTING LILY MARS  (1943)
STARS:  Judy Garland, Van Heflin
DIR:    Norman Taurog

792. PRINCESS COMES ACROSS, THE  (1936)
STARS:  Carole Lombard, Fred MacMurray
DIR:    William K. Howard

793. PRIORITIES ON PARADE  (1942)
STARS:  Ann Miller, Johnny Johnston
DIR:    Albert S. Rogell
SONGS:  Jule Styne - Herb Magidson

794. PRIVATE BUCKAROO  (1942)
STARS:  The Andrews Sisters, Dick Foran
DIR:    Edward F. Cline

795. A PRIVATE AFFAIR  (1959)
STARS:  Sal Mineo, Gary Crosby

169

DIR:     Raoul Walsh
SONGS:   Jimmy McHugh - Jay Livingston - Ray Evans
It's The Same Old Army; 36-24-36; Warm And Willing.

796.  PUDDIN' HEAD   (1941)
      STARS:   Judy Canova, Francis Lederer
      DIR:     Joseph Santley
      SONGS:   Jule Styne - Sol Meyer - Eddie Cherkose

797.  PURPLE HEART DIARY   (1951)
      STARS:   Frances Langford, Judd Holdren
      DIR:     Richard Quine
      Where Are You From?; Hi, Fellow Tourists; Hold Me In Your Arms
      (Tony Romano - Barbara Hayden - Johnny Bradford); Bread And
      Butter Woman (Lester Lee - Allan Roberts); Tattle-Tale Eyes
      (Tony Romano - John Bradford).

798.  PUTTIN' ON THE RITZ   (1930)
      STARS:   Harry Richman, Joan Bennett
      DIR:     Edward H. Sloman
      Alice In Wonderland; Puttin' On The Ritz; Singing A Vagabond
      Song; With You (Irving Berlin); There's Danger In Your Eyes,
      Cherie (Pete Wendling - Jack Meskill - Harry Richman).
      PRW-1930

799.  QUEEN HIGH   (1930)
      STARS:   Ginger Rogers, Frank Morgan
      DIR:     Fred Newmeyer

800.  RADIO CITY REVELS   (1938)
      STARS:   Bob Burns, Jack Oakie
      DIR:     Benjamin Stoloff
      SONGS:   Allie Wrubel - Herb Magidson

801.  RAIN OR SHINE   (1930)
      STARS:   Joe Cook, Louise Fazenda
      DIR:     Frank Capra
      LYRICS:  Jack Yellen

802.  RAINBOW ISLAND   (1944)
      STARS:   Dorothy Lamour, Eddie Bracken
      DIR:     Ralph Murphy
      SONGS:   Burton Lane - Ted Koehler

803.  RAINBOW MAN   (1929)
      STARS:   Eddie Dowling, Frankie Darro
      DIR:     Fred Newmeyer

804.  RAINBOW ON THE RIVER   (1936)
      STARS:   Bobby Breen, May Robson
      DIR:     Kurt Neumann

805.  RAINBOW OVER BROADWAY   (1934)

STARS:   Joan Marsh, Frank Albertson
DIR:     Richard Thorpe
SONGS:   Harry Von Tilzer - Elizabeth Morgan - Neville Fleeson

306.   RAINBOW 'ROUND MY SHOULDER   (1952)
STARS:   Frankie Laine, Billy Daniels
DIR:     Richard Quine
Wonderful, Wasn't It?   (Don Rodney - Hal David); Girl In The
Wood (Terry Gilkyson - Neal Stuart); There's A Rainbow 'Round
My Shoulder (Dave Dreyer - Billy Rose - Al Jolson); Wrap Your
Troubles In Dreams (And Dream Your Troubles Away) (Billy Moll -
Ted Koehler - Harry Barris); She's Funny That Way (Richard
Whiting - Neil Moret); Bye, Bye Blackbird (Ray Henderson -
Mort Dixon); The Last Rose Of Summer (Thomas Moore); Bubble,
Bubble, Bubble (Pink Champagne) (George Forrest - Robert
Wright).

307.   RAMONA   (1936)
STARS:   Loretta Young, Don Ameche
DIR:     Henry King

308.   RASCALS   (1938)
STARS:   Jane Withers, Rochelle Hudson
DIR:     H. Bruce Humberstone
SONGS:   Harry Akst - Sidney Clare

309.   READY, WILLING AND ABLE   (1937)
STARS:   Ruby Keeler, Lee Dixon
DIR:     Ray Enright
SONGS:   Richard Whiting - Johnny Mercer

310.   REBECCA OF SUNNYBROOK FARM   (1938)
STARS:   Shirley Temple, Randolph Scott
DIR:     Allan Dwan

311.   RECKLESS   (1935)
STARS:   Jean Harlow, William Powell
DIR:     Victor Fleming

312.   RECKLESS AGE, THE   (1944)
STARS:   Gloria Jean, Henry Stephenson
DIR:     Felix E. Feist

313.   RED GARTERS   (1954)
STARS:   Rosemary Clooney, Jack Carson
DIR:     George Marshall
SONGS:   Jay Livingston - Ray Evans
Red Garters; Man And Woman; Bad News; A Brave Man; A Dime And
Dollar; This Is Greater Than I Thought; Meet A Happy Guy; It
Was A Great Love Story; Good Intentions; Ladykiller.
Col. CL-6282

314.   RED HEAD FROM MANHATTAN   (1943)

171

```
                STARS:   Lupe Velez, Michael Duane
                DIR:     Lew Landers

815.    RED HEADS ON PARADE  (1935)
                STARS:   John Boles, Dixie Lee
                DIR:     Norman McLeod
                SONGS:   Jay Gorney - Don Hartman

816.    RED, HOT AND BLUE  (1949)
                STARS:   Betty Hutton, Victor Mature
                DIR:     John Farrow
                SONGS:   Frank Loesser

817.    RED-HEADED WOMAN  (1932)
                STARS:   Jean Harlow, Chester Morris
                DIR:     Jack Conway

818.    RENFREW OF THE MOUNTED  (1937)
                STARS:   James Newell, Carol Hughes
                DIR:     Al Herman
                SONGS:   Robert Lively - Betty Laidlow

819.    RHAPSODY IN BLUE  (1945)
                STARS:   Robert Alda, Joan Leslie
                DIR:     Irving Rapper
                SONGS:   George and Ira Gershwin

820.    RHYTHM INN  (1951)
                STARS:   Jane Frazee, Kirby Grant
                DIR:     Paul Landres
        Love (Edward J. Kay - Bill Raynor); Chi Chi (Armida); Return
        Trip; B Flat Blues; What Does It Matter? (Edward J. Kay); With
        A Twist Of The Wrist (Irvin Graham); I Love You That Is (Pat-
        rick Lewis - Jack Segal - Dewey Bergman); Window Wiper's Song
        (Jay Livingston - Ray Evans - Olsen and Johnson); It's A Big
        Wide Wonderful World (John Rox).
```

821.    RHYTHM OF THE ISLANDS  (1943)
                STARS:   Allan Jones, Jane Frazee
                DIR:     Roy William Neill

822.    RHYTHM ON THE RANGE  (1936)
                STARS:   Bing Crosby, Frances Farmer
                DIR:     Norman Taurog
        I Can't Escape From You (Richard Whiting - Leo Robin); Empty
        Saddles (Billy Hill); I'm An Old Cowhand (Johnny Mercer); If
        You Can't Sing It You'll Have To Swing It (Mr. Paganini) (Sam
        Coslow); The House Jack Built For Jill (Frederick Hollander -
        Leo Robin); Drink It Down (Ralph Rainger - Leo Robin); Hang
        Up My Saddle; Rhythm On The Range (Richard Whiting - Walter
        Bullock); Memories (Frederick Hollander - Richard Whiting).
        Decca DL-4251

823.    RHYTHM ON THE RIVER  (1940)

STARS:  Bing Crosby, Mary Martin
DIR:    Victor Schertzinger
Only Forever; When The Moon Comes Over Madison Square Garden;
Ain't It A Shame About Mame?; Rhythm On The River; That's For
Me; What Would Shakespeare Have Said (Jimmy Monaco - Johnny
Burke); I Don't Want To Cry Anymore (Victor Schertzinger -
Johnny Burke).
Decca DL-4251

824.  RHYTHM PARADE  (1942)
      STARS:  Nils T. Grunland, Gale Storm
      DIR:    Dave Gould, Howard Bretherton

825.  RICH, YOUNG AND PRETTY  (1951)
      STARS:  Jane Powell, Vic Damone
      DIR:    Norman Taurog
      SONGS:  Nicholas Brodszky - Sammy Cahn
      Dark Is The Night; Wonder Why?; I Can See You; We Never Talk
      Much; How D'Ya Like Your Eggs In The Morning?; Tonight For
      Sure; Paris; C'est Fini; My Little Nest Of Heavenly Blue (Franz
      Lehar - S. Spaeth); There's Danger In Your Eyes, Cherie (Pete
      Wendling - H. Richman - Jack Meskill).
      MGM 2-SES-53ST

826.  RIDE 'EM COWBOY  (1942)
      STARS:  Abbott and Costello
      DIR:    Arthur Lubin
      SONGS:  Gene DePaul - Don Raye

827.  RIDING HIGH  (1943)
      STARS:  Dorothy Lamour, Dick Powell
      DIR:    George Marshall

828.  RIDING HIGH  (1950)
      STARS:  Bing Crosby, Coleen Gray
      DIR:    Frank Capra
      SONGS:  Jimmy Van Heusen - Johnny Burke
      The Horse Told Me; Some Place On Anywhere Road; Sure Thing;
      Sunshine Cake.
      Decca DL-4261

829.  RIO RITA  (1929)
      STARS:  Bebe Daniels, John Boles
      DIR:    Luther Reed

830.  RIO RITA  (1942)
      STARS:  Abbott and Costello
      DIR:    S. Sylvan Simon

831.  RISE AND SHINE  (1941)
      STARS:  Jack Oakie, Linda Darnell
      DIR:    Allan Dwan
      SONGS:  Ralph Rainger - Leo Robin

832. ROAD SHOW  (1941)
     STARS:  Adolphe Menjou, Carole Landis
     DIR:    Hal Roach Jr., Gordon Douglas

833. ROAD TO BALI  (1953)
     STARS:  Bing Crosby, Bob Hope
     DIR:    Hal Walker
     SONGS:  James Van Heusen - Johnny Burke
     Chicago Style; Road To Bali; Hoot Mon; Moonflowers; To See You;
     Merry-Go-Run-Around.

834. ROAD TO HONG KONG  (1962)
     STARS:  Bing Crosby, Bob Hope
     DIR:    Norman Panama
     SONGS:  Jimmy Van Heusen - Sammy Cahn
     Teamwork; It's The Only Way To Travel; Warmer Than A Whisper;
     We're On The Road To Hong Kong; Let's Not Be Sensible.
     Liberty LOS-17002

835. ROAD TO MOROCCO, THE  (1942)
     STARS:  Bing Crosby, Bob Hope
     DIR:    David Butler
     SONGS:  Jimmy Van Heusen - Johnny Burke
     Ain't Got A Dime To My Name; Aladdin's Daughter; Moonlight
     Becomes You; Constantly.
     Decca DL-4257

836. ROAD TO RIO, THE  (1947)
     STARS:  Bing Crosby, Bob Hope
     DIR:    Norman Z. McLeod
     SONGS:  Jimmy Van Heusen - Johnny Burke
     Apalachicola, Florida; But Beautiful; You Don't Have To Know
     The Language; Experience.
     Decca DL-4260

837. ROAD TO SINGAPORE, THE  (1931)
     STARS:  William Powell, Mae Marsh
     DIR:    Alfred E. Green

838. ROAD TO SINGAPORE  (1940)
     STARS:  Bing Crosby, Bob Hope
     DIR:    Victor Schertzinger
     LYRICS: Johnny Burke (Composer follows in parentheses)
     Sweet Potato Piper; Kaigoon; Too Romantic (Jimmy Monaco); The
     Moon And The Willow Tree; Captain Custard (Victor Schertzinger).
     DL-6015

839. ROAD TO UTOPIA, THE  (1945)
     STARS:  Bing Crosby, Bob Hope
     DIR:    Hal Walker
     SONGS:  Jimmy Van Heusen - Johnny Burke
     Personality; Put It There Pal; Road To Morocco; Would You?;
     Good Time Charley; It's Anybody's Spring; Welcome To My Dream.
     Decca DL-4254

840. ROAD TO ZANZIBAR, THE (1941)
    STARS: Bing Crosby, Bob Hope
    DIR:   Victor Schertzinger
    SONGS: Jimmy Van Heusen - Johnny Burke
    You're Dangerous; Birds Of A Feather; It's Always You; You
    Lucky People You.
    DL-4255

841. ROBERTA (1935)
    STARS: Fred Astaire, Ginger Rogers
    DIR:   William A. Seiter
    Let's Begin; The Touch Of Your Hand; Smoke Gets In Your Eyes;
    Yesterdays (Jerome Kern - Otto Harbach); I'll Be Hard To Han-
    dle (Kern - Dorothy Fields); I Won't Dance (Kern - Oscar Ham-
    merstein II - Harbach - Fields - Jimmy McHugh); Lovely To Look
    At (Kern - Fields - McHugh).
    Jerome Kern In Hollywood, 1934-1938   JJA 19747D

842. ROBIN AND THE SEVEN HOODS (1964)
    STARS: Frank Sinatra, Dean Martin
    DIR:   Gordon Douglas
    SONGS: James Van Heusen - Sammy Cahn
    Don't Be A Do-Badder; Charlotte Couldn't Charleston; My Kind
    Of Town; All For One And One For All; Any Man Who Loves His
    Mother; Mr. Booze; Bang-Bang Style.
    Reprise S-2021

843. ROCK-A-BYE BABY (1958)
    STARS: Jerry Lewis, Marilyn Maxwell
    DIR:   Frank Tashlin
    SONGS: Harry Warren - Sammy Cahn
    Dormi-Dormi-Dormi; Rock-A-Bye Baby; Why Can't He Care For Me?;
    The White Virgin Of The Nile; Love Is A Lonely Thing; The Land
    Of La-La-La.

844. ROGUE SONG, THE (1930)
    STARS: Lawrence Tibbett, Catherine Dale Owen
    DIR:   Lionel Barrymore

845. ROMAN SCANDALS (1933)
    STARS: Eddie Cantor, Ruth Etting
    DIR:   Frank Tuttle
    SONGS: Harry Warren - Al Dubin

846. ROMANCE IN THE DARK (1938)
    STARS: Gladys Swarthout, John Boles
    DIR:   H. C. Potter

847. ROMANCE ON THE HIGH SEAS (1948)
    STARS: Jack Carson, Janis Paige
    DIR:   Michael Curtiz
    SONGS: Jule Styne - Sammy Cahn

848. ROOKIES ON PARADE (1941)

175

```
         STARS:   Bob Crosby, Ruth Terry
         DIR:     Joseph Santley

849.     ROSALIE    (1937)
         STARS:   Eleanor Powell, Nelson Eddy
         DIR:     W. S. Van Dyke
         SONGS:   Cole Porter

850.     ROSE MARIE    (1936)
         STARS:   Nelson Eddy, Jeanette MacDonald
         DIR:     W. S. Van Dyke

851.     ROSE MARIE    (1954)
         STARS:   Ann Blyth, Howard Keel
         DIR:     Mervyn LeRoy
         MUSIC:   Rudolf Friml
         Rose Marie; Indian Love Call; Song Of The Mounties; Totem Tom
         Tom (lyrics: Otto Harbach, Oscar Hammerstein II); The Right
         Place For A Girl; Free To Be Free; Love And Kisses; I Have
         Love (lyrics: Paul Francis Webster); and The Mountie Who Never
         Got His Man (George Stoll - Herbert Baker).
         MGM 2-SES-41ST

852.     ROSE OF THE RANCHO    (1936)
         STARS:   Gladys Swarthout, John Boles
         DIR:     Marion Gering
         SONGS:   Ralph Rainger - Leo Robin

853.     ROSE OF WASHINGTON SQUARE    (1939)
         STARS:   Tyrone Power, Alice Faye
         DIR:     Gregory Ratoff

854.     ROSIE THE RIVETER    (1944)
         STARS:   Jane Frazee, Frank Albertson
         DIR:     Joseph Santley

855.     ROYAL WEDDING    (1951)
         STARS:   Fred Astaire, Jane Powell
         DIR:     Stanley Donen
         SONGS:   Burton Lane - Alan Jay Lerner
         You're All The World To Me; How Could You Believe Me When I
         Said I Love You When You Know I've Been A Liar All My Life;
         Sunday Jumps; What A Lovely Day For A Wedding; I Left My Hat
         In Haiti; Too Late Now; The Happiest Day Of My Life; Every
         Night At Seven; Open Your Eyes.
         MGM 2-SES-53ST

856.     RUMBA    (1935)
         STARS:   Carole Lombard, George Raft
         DIR:     Marion Gering
         SONGS:   Ralph Rainger - Leo Robin

857.     SAFETY IN NUMBERS    (1930)
         STARS:   Charles "Buddy" Rogers, Josephine Dunn
```

DIR:     Victor Schertzinger
SONGS:   Richard Whiting - George Marion Jr.

858.  SAILOR BEWARE   (1951)
      STARS:  Dean Martin, Jerry Lewis
      DIR:      Hal Walker
      SONGS:  Jerry Livingston - Mack David
      Today, Tomorrow, Forever; Merci Beaucoup; Never Before; The
      Old Calliope; Sailors' Polka.

859.  SALLY   (1929)
      STARS:  Marilyn Miller, Alexander Gray
      DIR:      John Francis Dillon

860.  SALLY, IRENE AND MARY   (1938)
      STARS:  Alice Faye, Tony Martin
      DIR:      William A. Seiter

861.  SALUTE FOR THREE   (1943)
      STARS:  Betty Rhodes, MacDonald Carey
      DIR:      Ralph Murphy

862.  SAN ANTONIO ROSE   (1941)
      STARS:  Jane Frazee, Robert Paige
      DIR:      Charles Lamont

863.  SAN FRANCISCO   (1936)
      STARS:  Jeanette MacDonald, Clark Gable
      DIR:      W. S. Van Dyke

864.  SAY IT WITH SONGS   (1929)
      STARS:  Al Jolson, Davey Lee
      DIR:      Lloyd Bacon
      SONGS:  Ray Henderson - B. G. DeSylva - Lew Brown

865.  SAY ONE FOR ME   (1959)
      STARS:  Bing Crosby, Debbie Reynolds
      DIR:      Frank Tashlin
      SONGS:  James Van Heusen - Sammy Fain
      Say One For Me; Chico's Choo-Choo; The Secret Of Christmas;
      You Can't Love 'Em All; The Night Rock 'N' Roll Died; He's
      Starting To Get To Me; The Girl Most Likely To Succeed; I
      Couldn't Care Less.
      Col. CS-8147

866.  SCARED STIFF   (1953)
      STARS:  Dean Martin, Jerry Lewis
      DIR:      George Marshall
      SONGS:  Jerry Livingston - Mack David
      When Someone Wonderful Thinks You're Wonderful; I Don't Care
      If The Sun Don't Shine; What Have You Done For Me Lately?;
      San Domingo; The Enchilada Man; Mama, Eu Quero (Jararaca -
      Paiva - Stillman).

177

867. SECOND CHORUS  (1940)
     STARS:  Fred Astaire, Paulette Goddard
     DIR:    Henry C. Potter

868. SECOND FIDDLE  (1939)
     STARS:  Sonja Henie, Tyrone Power
     DIR:    Sidney Lanfield
     SONGS:  Irving Berlin
     I Poured My Heart Into A Song; Song Of The Metronome; When Win-
     ter Comes; Back To Back; I'm Sorry For Myself; An Old-Fash-
     ioned Tune Always Is New.
     Irving Berlin; 1909-1939: JJA-19744D

869. SECOND GREATEST SEX  (1955)
     STARS:  Jeanne Crain, George Nader
     DIR:    George Marshall
     SONGS:  Pony Sherrell - Phil Moody
     What Good Is A Woman Without A Man; My Love Is Yours; Send Us
     A Miracle; How Lonely Can I Get? (Joan Whitney - Alex Kramer);
     Second Greatest Sex (Jay Livingston - Ray Evans).

870. SEE MY LAWYER  (1945)
     STARS:  Olsen and Johnson
     DIR:    Edward F. Cline

871. SENORITA FROM THE WEST  (1945)
     STARS:  Allan Jones, Bonita Granville
     DIR:    Frank Strayer

872. SENSATIONS OF 1945  (1944)
     STARS:  W. C. Fields, Eleanor Powell
     DIR:    Andrew Stone
     SONGS:  Al Sherman - Harry Tobias

873. SEVEN BRIDES FOR SEVEN BROTHERS  (1954)
     STARS:  Howard Keel, Jane Powell
     DIR:    Stanley Donen
     SONGS:  Gene DePaul - Johnny Mercer
     Wonderful, Wonderful Day; Barn Raising Ballet; Bless Yore Beau-
     tiful Hide; June Bride; When You're In Love; It's Spring,
     Spring, Spring; June Bride; Lonesome Polecat; Sobbin' Women;
     Goin' Courtin'.
     MGM-2-SES-41ST

874. SEVEN DAYS ASHORE  (1944)
     STARS:  Wally Brown, Goldon Oliver
     DIR:    John H. Auer
     SONGS:  Lew Pollack - Mort Greene

875. SEVEN DAYS LEAVE  (1942)
     STARS:  Lucille Ball, Victor Mature
     DIR:    Tom Whelan
     SONGS:  Jimmy McHugh - Frank Loesser

876. SEVEN LITTLE FOYS, THE   (1955)
STARS:   Bob Hope, James Cagney
DIR:     Melville Shavelson
I'm The Greatest Father Of Them All; Nobody; I'm Tired; You're
Here; My Love; Chinatown, My Chinatown (Jean Schwartz - Wil-
liam Jerome); Mary's A Grand Old Name; Yankee Doodle Dandy
(George M. Cohan).
RCA LPM-3275

877. 1776   (1972)
STARS:   William Daniels, Ken Howard
DIR:     Peter H. Hunt
SONGS:   Sherman Edwards
Molasses To Rum; The Lees Of Old Virginia; Is Anybody There?;
He Plays The Violin; The Egg; But, Mr. Adams; Mama, Look Sharp;
Sit Down John; Yours, Yours, Yours; Till Then; Piddle, Twiddle,
And Resolve.
Col. BOS-3310

878. SHADY LADY, THE   (1933)
STARS:   Phyllis Haver, Robert Armstrong
DIR:     Edward H. Griffith
SONGS:   Sammy Stept - Bud Green

879. SHADY LADY   (1945)
STARS:   Charles Coburn, Robert Paige
DIR:     George Waggner

880. SHALL WE DANCE?   (1937)
STARS:   Ginger Rogers, Fred Astaire
DIR:     Mark Sandrich
SONGS:   George and Ira Gershwin
Let's Call The Whole Thing Off; Shall We Dance?; I've Got Be-
ginner's Luck; Slap That Bass; They Can't Take That Away From
Me; They All Laughed.
EMI   EMTC-102

881. SHE COULDN'T SAY NO   (1930)
STARS:   Winnie Lightner, Chester Morris
DIR:     Lloyd Bacon
SONGS:   Joe Burke - Al Dubin

882. SHE DONE HIM WRONG   (1933)
STARS:   Mae West, Cary Grant
DIR:     Lowell Sherman

883. SHE LEARNED ABOUT SAILORS   (1934)
STARS:   Alice Faye, Lew Ayers

884. SHE LOVES ME NOT   (1934)
STARS:   Bing Crosby, Miriam Hopkins
DIR:     Elliott Nugent

179

885. SHE MARRIED A COP   (1939)
     STARS:   Phil Regan, Jean Parker
     DIR:     Sidney Salkow
     SONGS:   Burton Lane - Ralph Freed

886. SHE'S A SWEETHEART   (1944)
     STARS:   Jane Frazee, Larry Parks
     DIR:     Del Lord

887. SHE'S BACK ON BROADWAY   (1953)
     STARS:   Virginia Mayo, Steve Cochran
     DIR:     Gordon Douglas
     SONGS:   Carl Sigman - Bob Hilliard
     I'll Take You As You Are; I Think You're Wonderful; One Step
     Ahead Of Everybody; Behind The Mask; The Ties That Bind; Break-
     fast In Bed.

888. SHE'S WORKING HER WAY THROUGH COLLEGE   (1952)
     STARS:   Virginia Mayo, Ronald Reagan
     DIR:     Bruce Humberstone
     Love Is Still For Free; I'll Be Loving You; The Stuff That
     Dreams Are Made Of; She's Working Her Way Through College; Am
     I In Love?; Give 'Em What They Want (Vernon Duke - Sammy Cahn);
     With Plenty Of Money And You (Harry Warren - Al Dubin).

889. SHINE ON HARVEST MOON   (1944)
     STARS:   Dennis Morgan, Ann Sheridan
     DIR:     David Butler
     SONGS:   M. K. Jerome - Kim Gannon

890. SHIP AHOY   (1942)
     STARS:   Eleanor Powell, Red Skelton
     DIR:     Eddie Buzzell

891. SHIP CAFE   (1935)
     STARS:   Carl Brisson, Arline Judge
     DIR:     Robert Florey

892. SHIPMATES FOREVER   (1935)
     STARS:   Dick Powell, Ruby Keeler
     DIR:     Frank Borzage
     SONGS:   Harry Warren - Al Dubin

893. SHOCKING MISS PILGRIM, THE   (1947)
     STARS:   Betty Grable, Dick Haymes
     DIR:     George Seaton
     SONGS:   George and Ira Gershwin

894. SHOOT THE WORKS   (1934)
     STARS:   Jack Oakie, Dorothy Dell
     DIR:     Wesley Ruggles

895. SHOW BOAT   (1929)

STARS:   Laura LaPlante, Otis Harlan
DIR:     Harry Pollard

896.   SHOW BOAT   (1936)
STARS:   Irene Dunne, Allan Jones
DIR:     James Whale
SONGS:   Jerome Kern - Oscar Hammerstein II
You Are Love; Bill; Gallivantin' Around; Ah Still Suits Me;
Can't Help Lovin' Dat Man; I Have The Room Above; Ol' Man River; Make Believe.
Col.  CSP-AC-55

897.   SHOW BOAT   (1951)
STARS:   Kathryn Grayson, Howard Keel
DIR:     George Sidney
SONGS:   Jerome Kern - Oscar Hammerstein II
Make Believe; Why Do I Love You?; Ol' Man River; Can't Help
Lovin' That Man; Bill (with P. G. Wodehouse; Cotton Blossom.
MGM 2-SES-42-ST

898.   SHOW BUSINESS   (1944)
STARS:   Eddie Cantor, George Murphy
DIR:     Edward L. Marin

899.   SHOW GIRL IN HOLLYWOOD   (1930)
STARS:   Alice White, Jack Mulhall
DIR:     Mervyn LeRoy
SONGS:   Sammy Stept - Bud Breen

900.   SHOW OF SHOWS   (1929)
STARS:   Irene Bordoni, Winnie Lightner
DIR:     John Adolfi

901.   SILK STOCKINGS   (1957)
STARS:   Fred Astaire, Cyd Charisse
DIR:     Rouben Mamoulian
SONGS:   Cole Porter
Red Blues; Too Bad; Ritz Roll And Rock; Paris Loves Lovers;
Josephine; Chemical Reaction; Fated To Be Mated; All Of You;
Siberia; Stereophonic Sound; Satin And Silk; Without Love.
MGM-2-SES-51-ST

902.   SILVER SKATES   (1943)
STARS:   Kenny Baker, Patricia Morison
DIR:     Leslie Goodwins

903.   SING A JINGLE   (1944)
STARS:   Allan Jones, June Vincent
DIR:     Edward C. Lilley

904.   SING AND BE HAPPY   (1937)
STARS:   Tony Martin, Leah Ray
DIR:     James Tinling
SONGS:   Harry Akst - Sidney Clare

905. SING ANOTHER CHORUS   (1941)
     STARS:  Jane Frazee, Johnny Downs
     DIR:    Charles Lamont
     SONGS:  Milton Rosen - Everett Carter

906. SING BABY SING   (1936)
     STARS:  Alice Faye, Adolphe Menjou
     DIR:    Sidney Lanfield

907. SING, DANCE AND PLENTY HOT   (1940)
     STARS:  Ruth Terry, Johnny Downs
     DIR:    Lew Landers
     SONGS:  Jule Styne - Lew Brown

908. SING ME A LOVE SONG   (1936)
     STARS:  James Melton, Patricia Ellis
     DIR:    Ray Enright

909. SING YOU SINNERS   (1938)
     STARS:  Bing Crosby, Fred MacMurray
     DIR:    Wesley Ruggles

910. SING YOUR WAY HOME   (1945)
     STARS:  Jack Haley, Marcy McGuire
     DIR:    Anthony Mann
     SONGS:  Allie Wrubel - Herb Magidson

911. SING YOUR WORRIES AWAY   (1942)
     STARS:  Bert Lahr, June Havoc
     DIR:    Edward Sutherland
     SONGS:  Harry Revel - Mort Greene

912. SINGIN' IN THE CORN   (1946)
     STARS:  Judy Canova, Allen Jenkins
     DIR:    Del Lord

913. SINGIN' IN THE RAIN   (1952)
     STARS:  Gene Kelly, Donald O'Connor
     DIR:    Gene Kelly, Stanley Donen
     Would You?; Singing In The Rain; All I Do Is Dream Of You;
     I've Got A Feeling You're Fooling; Wedding Of The Painted Doll;
     Should I?; Make 'Em Laugh; You Were Meant For Me; You Are My
     Lucky Star; Fit As A Fiddle And Ready For Love; Good Morning
     (Nacio Herb Brown - Arthur Freed); Moses (Roger Edens - Adolph
     Green - Betty Comden).
     MGM-2-SES-40-ST

914. SINGING FOOL, THE   (1929)
     STARS:  Al Jolson, Betty Bronson
     DIR:    Lloyd Bacon

915. SINGING KID, THE   (1936)
     STARS:  Al Jolson, Sybil Jason
     DIR:    William Keighley

182

916.  SINGING MARINE, THE   (1937)
      STARS:  Dick Powell, Doris Weston
      DIR:    Ray Enright
      SONGS:  Harry Warren - Johnny Mercer - Al Dubin

917.  SINGING NUN, THE   (1966)
      STARS:  Debbie Reynolds
      DIR:    Henry Koster
      SONGS:  Soeur Sourire  - English Lyrics: Randy Newman
      Dominique; It's A Miracle; A Pied Piper's Song; Sister Adele;
      Beyond The Stars; Je Voudrais; Mets Ton Joli; Jupon; Avec Toi;
      Alleluia; Brother John; Raindrops; Lovely (music by Randy
      Sparks).
      MGM S-1E-7ST

918.  SINGING SHERIFF, THE   (1944)
      STARS:  Bob Crosby, Fay McKenzie
      DIR:    Leslie Goodwins

919.  SIS HOPKINS   (1941)
      STARS:  Judy Canova, Bob Crosby
      DIR:    Joseph Santley
      SONGS:  Jule Styne - Frank Loesser

920.  SITTING ON THE MOON   (1936)
      STARS:  Roger Pryor, Grace Bradley
      DIR:    Ralph Staub
      SONGS:  Sammy Stept - Sidney Mitchell

921.  SITTING PRETTY   (1933)
      STARS:  Jack Oakie, Jack Haley
      DIR:    Harry Joe Brown
      SONGS:  Harry Revel - Mack Gordon

922.  SKIRTS AHOY   (1952)
      STARS:  Esther Williams, Vivian Blaine
      DIR:    Sidney Lanfield
      The Navy Waltz; We Will Fight; Hilda Matilda; Hold Me Close To
      You; What Good Is A Guy Without A Girl?; What Makes A Wave?;
      I Got A Funny Feeling; Glad To Have You Aboard (Harry Warren -
      Ralph Blaine); Oh By Jingo (Albert Von Tilzer - Lew Brown).

923.  SKY'S THE LIMIT, THE   (1943)
      STARS:  Fred Astaire, Joan Leslie
      DIR:    Edward H. Griffith
      SONGS:  Harold Arlen - Johnny Mercer
      One For My Baby (And One More For The Road); My Shining Hour;
      I've Got A Lot In Common With You.
      Curtain Calls CC 100/19

924.  SLEEPY LAGOON   (1943)
      STARS:  Judy Canova, Dennis Day
      DIR:    Joseph Santley

183

925. SLEEPY TIME GAL  (1942)
    STARS:  Judy Canova, Tom Brown
    DIR:    Albert S. Rogell

926. SLIGHTLY FRENCH  (1949)
    STARS:  Dorothy Lamour, Don Ameche
    DIR:    Douglas Sirk

927. SLIGHTLY TERRIFIC  (1944)
    STARS:  Leon Errol, Anne Rooney
    DIR:    Edward F. Cline

928. SMALL TOWN GIRL  (1953)
    STARS:  Jane Powell, Ann Miller
    DIR:    Leslie Kardos
    SONGS:  Nicholas Brodszky - Leo Robin
    My Flaming Heart; The Fellow I'd Follow; Small Towns Are Smile
    Towns; I've Gotta Hear That Beat; The Lullaby Of The Lord; My
    Gaucho; Take Me To Broadway; Fine, Fine, Fine.

929. SMARTEST GIRL IN TOWN  (1936)
    STARS:  Ann Sothern Gene Raymond
    DIR:    Joseph Santley

930. SMILING IRISH EYES  (1929)
    STARS:  Colleen Moore, James Hall
    DIR:    William A. Seiter

931. SMILING LIEUTENANT, THE  (1931)
    STARS:  Maurice Chevalier, Claudette Colbert
    DIR:    Ernst Lubitsch
    SONGS:  Oscar Straus - Clifford Grey

932. SO DEAR TO MY HEART  (1948)
    STARS:  Bobby Driscoll, Beulah Bondi

933. SO LONG LETTY  (1929)
    STARS:  Charlotte Greenwood, Grant Withers
    DIR:    Lloyd Bacon

934. SO THIS IS COLLEGE  (1929)
    STARS:  Elliott Nugent, Robert Montgomery
    DIR:    Sam Wood

935. SO THIS IS PARIS  (1955)
    STARS:  Tony Curtis, Gloria DeHaven
    DIR:    Richard Quine
    SONGS:  Pony Sherrell - Phil Moody
    Two Of Us; Looking For Someone To Love; Wait Till Paris Sees
    Us; So This Is Paris; Dame's A Dame; If You Were There; I Can't
    Give You Anything But Love, Baby (Jimmy McHugh - Dorothy
    Fields).
    Decca DL-5553

936. SOMBRERO  (1953)
STARS:  Ricardo Montalban, Cyd Charisse
DIR:  Norman Foster
SONGS:  Leo Arnaud, Geronimo Villavino, Ruben Fuentes, Ruben
Mendez - Saul Chaplin
Ufemia; Night On Bear Mountain; Farruca Flamenco; Gypsy Dance.

937. SOMEBODY LOVES ME  (1952)
STARS:  Betty Hutton, Ralph Meeker
DIR:  Irving Brecher
Love Him; Thanks To You; Honey Oh My Honey (Jay Livingston -
Ray Evans); Jealous (Dick Finch - Tommy Malie - Jack Little);
June Night (Abel Baer - Cliff Friend); I Cried For You (Abe
Lyman - Arthur Freed - Gus Arnheim); Sorry I Made You Cry (N.J.
Clesi); On San Francisco Bay (Gertrude Hoffman - Vincent Bry-
an); Somebody Loves Me (George Gershwin - B. G. DeSylva); Rose
Room (Art Hickman - Harry Williams); Way Down Yonder In New
Orleans (J. Turner Layton - Henry Creamer); Smiles (Lee S. Rob-
erts - J. Will Callahan); I Can't Tell Why I Love You (Gus Ed-
wards - Will J. Cobb); Wang, Wang Blues (Henry Busse - Buster
Johnson - Gus Mueller); Dixie Dreams (Roy Turk - Grant Clarke -
George W. Meyer - Arthur Johnston); That Teasing Rag (Joe Jor-
dan); Toddling The Todalo (A. Baldwin Sloane - E. Ray Goetz);
A Dollar And Thirty Cents.
RCA LPM-3097

938. SOMETHING FOR THE BOYS  (1944)
STARS:  Carmen Miranda, Michael O'Shea
DIR:  Lewis Seiler
SONGS:  Jimmy McHugh - Frank Loesser - Harold Adamson

939. SOMETHING IN THE WIND  (1947)
STARS:  Deanna Durbin, Donald O'Connor
DIR:  Irving Pichell
SONGS:  Johnny Green - Leo Robin

940. SOMETHING TO SHOUT ABOUT  (1943)
STARS:  Don Ameche, Janet Blair
DIR:  Gregory Ratoff
SONGS:  Cole Porter

941. SOMETHING TO SING ABOUT  (1937)
STARS:  James Cagney, Evelyn Daw
DIR:  Victor Schertzinger
SONGS:  Victor Schertzinger

942. SON OF PALEFACE  (1952)
STARS:  Bob Hope, Jane Russell
DIR:  Frank Tashlin
What A Dirty Shame; California Rose; Wing Ding Tonight (Jay
Livingston - Ray Evans); Four-Legged Friend; Am I In Love?;
There's A Cloud In My Valley Of Sunshine (Lyle Moraine - Jack
Hope - Jack Brooks).

943. SONG AND DANCE MAN   (1936)
      STARS:  Claire Trevor, Paul Kelly
      DIR:    Allan Dwan
      SONGS:  Lew Pollack - Sidney Clare

944. SONG FOR MISS JULIE, A   (1945)
      STARS:  Shirley Ross, Barton Hepburn
      DIR:    William Rowland
      SONGS:  Louis Herscher - Marla Shelton

945. SONG IS BORN, A   (1948)
      STARS:  Danny Kaye, Hugh Herbert
      DIR:    Howard Hawks
      SONGS:  Gene DePaul - Don Raye

946. SONG O' MY HEART   (1930)
      STARS:  John McCormack, Alice Joyce
      DIR:    Frank Borzage

947. SONG OF LOVE   (1929)
      STARS:  Belle Baker, Ralph Graves
      DIR:    Erle C. Kenton

948. SONG OF NORWAY   (1970)
      STARS:  Florence Henderson, Toraly Maurstad
      DIR:    Andrew L. Stone
      SONGS:  Edvard Grieg - Robert Wright - George Forrest
      Ribbons And Wrappings; Wrong To Dream; John Heggerstrom; Song
      Of Norway; A Rhyme And A Reason; Hill Of Dreams; Betrothal;
      Hand In Hand; Three There Were; Christmas Time; A Welcome
      Toast; Solvejg's Song; National Anthem; Life Of A Wife Of A
      Sailor; Freddy And His Fiddle; Strange Music; Little House;
      I Love You; Be A Boy Again; Midsummer's Eve; Solitary Wanderer.
      ABC  OC-14.

949. SONG OF SCHEHERAZADE   (1947)
      STARS:  Jean Pierre Aumont, Yvonne De Carlo
      DIR:    Walter Reisch
      SONGS:  Rimsky - Korsakoff - Jack Brooks

950. SONG OF THE FLAME   (1930)
      STARS:  Alexander Gray, Bernice Claire
      DIR:    Alan Crosland

951. SONG OF THE ISLANDS   (1942)
      STARS:  Betty Grable, Victor Mature
      DIR:    Walter Lang

952. SONG OF THE OPEN ROAD   (1944)
      STARS:  Edgar Bergen, Jane Powell
      DIR:    S. Sylvan Simon
      SONGS:  Walter Kent - Kim Gannon

953. SONG OF THE SARONG   (1945)

STARS:   Nancy Kelly, William Gargan
DIR:     Harold Young

954. SONG OF THE WEST   (1930)
STARS:   John Boles, Vivienne Segal
DIR:     Ray Enright

955. SOUND OF MUSIC, THE   (1965)
STARS:   Julie Andrews, Christopher Plummer
DIR:     Robert Wise
SONGS:   Richard Rodgers - Oscar Hammerstein II
The Sound Of Music; Sixteen Going On Seventeen; I Have Confi-
dence; Maria; Climb Every Mountain; My Favorite Things; The
Lonely Goatherd; Processional; Something Good; Do-Re-Mi; So
Long Farewell; Edelweiss.
RCA LSOD-2005

956. SOUTH OF DIXIE   (1944)
STARS:   Ann Gwynne, David Bruce
DIR:     Jean Yarbrough

957. SOUTH PACIFIC   (1958)
STARS:   Rossano Brazzi, Mitzi Gaynor
DIR:     Joshua Logan
SONGS:   Richard Rodgers - Oscar Hammerstein II
Dites-Moi; A Cockeyed Optimist; Twin Soliloquies; Some Enchant-
ed Evening; You've Got To Be Taught; This Nearly Was Mine; I'm
Gonna Wash That Man Right Out Of My Hair; There Is Nothing
Like A Dame; Bali Ha'i; Younger Than Springtime; I'm In Love
With A Wonderful Guy; Happy Talk; Honey Bun; My Girl Back Home.
RCA LSO-1032

958. SPRING IS HERE   (1930)
STARS:   Alexander Gray, Bernice Claire
DIR:     John Francis Dillon

959. SPRING PARADE   (1940)
STARS:   Deanna Durbin, Robert Cummings
DIR:     Henry Koster

960. SPRINGTIME IN THE ROCKIES   (1942)
STARS:   Betty Grable, John Payne
DIR:     Irving Cummings
SONGS:   Harry Warren - Mack Gordon

961. ST. LOUIS BLUES   (1939)
STARS:   Dorothy Lamour, Lloyd Nolan
DIR:     Raoul Walsh

962. ST. LOUIS BLUES   (1958)
STARS:   Nat King Cole, Eartha Kitt
DIR:     Allen Reisner
SONGS:   W. C. Handy

187

Chantez Les Bas; Beale Street Blues; Hesitating Blues; Yellow
Dog Blues; Harlem Blues; Stay; Joe Turner's Blues; Memphis
Blues; Morning Star; Sheriff Honest John Baile (lyric: Mack
David]; Careless Love (lyric: Martha Koenig and Spencer Wil-
liams); Friendless Blues (lyric: Mercedes Gilbert).
Capitol SW-993

963. ST. LOUIS WOMAN   (1935)
STARS:  Jeanette Loff, Johnny Mack Brown
DIR:    Al Ray
SONGS:  Bob Lively - Betty Laidlow

964. STAGE DOOR CANTEEN   (1943)
STARS:  Kenny Baker, Talulah Bankhead
DIR:    Frank Borzage
The Machine Gun Song; Don't Worry Island; A Rookie And His
Rhythm; We Mustn't Say Goodbye; American Boy; Quick Sands;
Sleep Baby Sleep; We Meet In The Funniest Places; Marching
Through Berlin (Jimmy Monaco - Al Dubin); She's A Bombshell
From Brooklyn (Jimmy Monaco - Al Dubin - Sol Lesser); The
Girl I Love To Leave Behind (Richard Rodgers - Lorenz Hart).
Curtain Calls   CC 100/11-12

965. STAGE STRUCK   (1936)
STARS:  Dick Powell, Joan Blondell
DIR:    Busby Berkeley
SONGS:  Harold Arlen - E. Y. Harburg

966. STAND UP AND CHEER   (1934)
STARS:  Shirley Temple, Warner Baxter
DIR:    Hamilton MacFadden

967. STAR!  (1968)
STARS:  Julie Andrews, Daniel Massey
DIR:    Robert Wise
Star (James Van Heusen - Sammy Cahn); In My Garden Of Joy (Saul
Chaplin); Has Anyone Seen Our Ship; Forbidden Fruit; Someday
I'll Find You; Parisian Pierrot (Noel Coward); Someone To Watch
Over Me; Dear Little Boy; Do-Do-Do (George and Ira Gershwin);
My Ship; Jenny (Kurt Weill - Ira Gershwin); The Physician (Cole
Porter); Limehouse Blues (Philip Braham - Douglas Furber); 'N'
Everything (B. G. DeSylva - Gus Kahn). Also: Down At The Old
Bull And Bush; Piccadilly; Oh, It's A Lovely War.
20th Cent. Fox   DTCS 5102

968. STAR FOR A NIGHT   (1936)
STARS:  Claire Trevor, Jane Darwell
DIR:    Lewis Seiler
SONGS:  Harry Akst - Sidney Clare

969. STAR IS BORN, A   (1954)
STARS:  Judy Garland, James Mason
DIR:    George Cukor
SONGS:  Harold Arlen - Ira Gershwin

The Man That Got Away; Gotta Have Me Go With You; It's A New
World; Someone At Last; Born In A Trunk (arr. Leonard Gershe);
I'll Get By; You Took Advantage Of Me; Black Bottom; Swanee;
Peanut Vendor; My Melancholy Baby.
Harmony HS-11366

970. STARLIFT (1951)
STARS: Doris Day, Gordon MacRae
DIR: Roy Del Ruth
You're Gonna Lose Your Gal (Jimmy Monaco - Joe Young); Liza;
'S Wonderful (George and Ira Gershwin); You Ought To Be In
Pictures (Dana Suesse - Edward Heyman); You Do Something To Me;
What Is This Thing Called Love? (Cole Porter); It's Magic (Jule
Styne - Sammy Cahn); Good Green Acres Of Home (Sammy Fain -
Irving Kahal); I May Be Wrong But I Think You're Wonderful
(Henry Sullivan - Harry Ruskin); Look Out Stranger I'm A Texas
Ranger (Phil Harris - Ruby Ralesin); Noche Carib (Percy Faith).

971. STAR MAKER, THE (1939)
STARS: Bing Crosby, Louise Campbell
DIR: Roy Del Ruth
SONGS: Jimmy Monaco - Johnny Burke

972. STARS ARE SINGING, THE (1953)
STARS: Rosemary Clooney, Anna Maria Alberghetti
DIR: Norman Taurog
SONGS: Jay Livingston - Ray Evans
Heavenly Weather For Ducks; My Heart Is A Home; I Do, I Do, I
Do; Haven't Got A Worry To My Name; Cone On-A My House (Ross
Bagdasarian - William Saroyan).

973. STARS ON PARADE (1944)
STARS: Larry Parks, Lynn Merrick
DIR: Lew Landers

974. STARS OVER BROADWAY (1935)
STARS: James Melton, Jane Froman
DIR: William Keighley

975. STAR-SPAGNLED RHYTHM (1942)
STARS: Bing Crosby, Ray Milland
DIR: George Marshall
SONGS: Harold Arlen - Johnny Mercer
He Loved Me Till The All-Clear Came; On The Swing Shift; Sharp
As A Tack; I'm Doing It For Defense; That Old Black Magic; Hit
The Road To Dreamland; Old Glory; A Sweater, A Sarong And A
Peekaboo Bang.
Curtain Calls CC 100/20

976. START CHEERING (1938)
STARS: Jimmy Durante, Joan Perry
DIR: Albert S. Rogell

977. STATE FAIR (IT HAPPENED ONE SUMMER) (1945)

189

STARS: Jeanne Crain, Dana Andrews
DIR: Walter Lang
SONGS: Richard Rodgers - Oscar Hammerstein II

978. STATE FAIR (1962)
STARS: Pat Boone, Bobby Darin
DIR: Jose Ferrer
SONGS: Richard Rodgers - Oscar Hammerstein II
It's A Grand Night For Singing; It Might As Well Be Spring;
That's For Me; State Fair; Isn't It Kinda Fun; and It's The
Little Things In Texas; More Than Just A Friend; Willing And
Eager; Never Say No; This Isn't Heaven (lyrics by Richard Rod-
gers).
Dot 29011

979. STEP LIVELY (1944)
STARS: Frank Sinatra, George Murphy
DIR: Tom Whelan
SONGS: Jule Styne - Sammy Cahn

980. STEPPING HIGH (1928)

981. STOLEN HARMONY (1935)
STARS: George Raft, Grace Bradley
DIR: Alfred Werker
SONGS: Harry Revel - Mack Gordon

982. STOOGE, THE (1952)
STARS: Dean Martin, Jerry Lewis
DIR: Norman Taurog
A Girl Named Mary And A Boy Named Bill (Jerry Livingston -
Mack David); Just One More Chance (Sam Coslow - Arthur John-
ston); Who's Your Little Whozis? (Walter Hirsch - Ben Bernie -
Al Goering); With My Eyes Wide Open I'm Dreaming (Harry Revel -
Mack Gordon); Louise (Richard Whiting - Leo Robin); I'm Yours
(Johnny Green - E. Y. Harburg).

983. STOP THE WORLD--I WANT TO GET OFF (1966)
STARS: Tony Tanner, Millicent Martin
DIR: Philip Saville
SONGS: Anthony Newley - Leslie Bricusse
I Wanna Be Rich; Gonna Build A Mountain; Meilinki Meilchick;
Typically Nippon; All American; Someone Nice Like You; I Be-
lieved It All; ABC Song; Typically English; Lumbered; Glorious
Russian; Family Fugue; Nag, Nag, Nag; Mumbo Jumbo; What Kind
Of Fool Am I?; Once In My Lifetime.
Warner Bros. WS-1643

984. STORK CLUB (1945)
STARS: Betty Hutton, Barry Fitzgerald
DIR: Hal Walker

985. STORMY WEATHER (1943)

STARS: Ethel Waters, Lena Horne
DIR: Andrew Stone

986. STORY OF ROBIN HOOD, THE (1952)
STARS: Richard Todd, Joan Rice
DIR: Kenneth Annakin
Riddle De Diddle De Day; Whistle My Love (George Wyle - Eddie Pola); Robin Hood Ballads; The Sweet Rhyming Minstred; Come Swing Low Come Swing High (Elton Hayes - Lawrence E. Watkins).

987. STORY OF VERNON AND IRENE CASTLE, THE (1939)
STARS: Ginger Rogers, Fred Astaire
DIR: Henry C. Potter

988. STOWAWAY (1936)
STARS: Shirley Temple, Robert Young
DIR: William A. Seiter

989. STRAIGHT, PLACE AND SHOW (1938)
STARS: The Ritz Brothers, Ethel Merman
DIR: David Butler

990. STREET GIRL, THE (1929)
STARS: Betty Compson, Jack Oakie
DIR: Wesley Ruggles
SONGS: Oscar Levant - Sidney Clare

991. STRICTLY DYNAMITE (1934)
STARS: Jimmy Durante, Lupe Velez
DIR: Elliott Nugent

992. STRICTLY IN THE GROOVE (1942)
STARS: Martha Tilton, The Dinning Sisters
DIR: Vernon Keays

993. STRIKE ME PINK (1936)
STARS: Eddie Cantor, Ethel Merman
DIR: Norman Taurog
SONGS: Harold Arlen - Lew Brown

994. STRIKE UP THE BAND (1940)
STARS: Judy Garland, Mickey Rooney
DIR: Busby Berkeley
Our Love Affair (Roger Edens-Arthur Freed); Nell Of New Rochelle; Do The Conga; Drummer Boy; Nobody (Roger Edens); Strike Up The Band (George and Ira Gershwin).
Curtain Calls CC 100/9-10.

995. STRIP, THE (1951)
STARS: Mickey Rooney, Sallie Forrest
DIR: Leslie Kardos

996. STUDENT PRINCE (1954)
STARS: Ann Blyth, Edmund Purdom
DIR: Richard Thorpe

191

SONGS: Sigmund Romberg - Dorothy Donnelly
Golden Days; Drink, Drink, Drink; Serenade; Deep In My Heart;
and I'll Walk With God; Beloved; Summer In Heidelberg (Nichola
Brodszky - Paul Francis Webster).

997. STUDENT TOUR (1934)
STARS: Jimmy Durante, Charles Butterworth
DIR: Charles Reisner

998. SULTAN'S DAUGHTER, THE (1943)
STARS: Ann Corio, Tim and Irene Ryan
DIR: A. Dreifuss
SONGS: K. Hajos - M. Greene

999. SUMMER HOLIDAY (1948)
STARS: Mickey Rooney, Gloria DeHaven
DIR: Rouben Mamoulian
SONGS: Harry Warren - Ralph Blane

1000. SUMMER STOCK (1950)
STARS: Judy Garland, Gene Kelly
DIR: Charles Walters
SONGS: Harry Warren - Mack Gordon
If You Feel Like Singing, Sing; Mem'ry Island; Dig-Dig-Dig
For Your Dinner; Friendly Star; Blue Jean Polka; You Wonderful
You (lyrics by Jack Brooks and Saul Chaplin); Heavenly Music
(Saul Chaplin); Get Happy (Harold Arlen - Ted Koehler).
MGM 2-SES-52ST

1001. SUN VALLEY SERENADE (1941)
STARS: Sonja Henie, John Payne
DIR: H. Bruce Humberstone
SONGS: Harry Warren - Mack Gordon

1002. SUNBONNET SUE (1945)
STARS: Gale Storm, Phil Regan
DIR: Ralph Murphy

1003. SUNNY (1930)
STARS: Marilyn Miller, Lawrence Gray
DIR: William A. Seiter
SONGS: Jerome Kern - Oscar Hammerstein II - Otto Harbach

1004. SUNNY (1941)
STARS: Anna Neagle, Ray Bolger
DIR: Herbert Wilcox
SONGS: Jerome Kern - Oscar Hammerstein II - Otto Harbach

1005. SUNNY SIDE UP (1929)
STARS: Janet Gaynor, Charles Farrell
DIR: David Butler
SONGS: Ray Henderson - B. G. DeSylva - Lew Brown

1006. SWANEE RIVER (1939)

STARS:  Don Ameche, Al Jolson

1007.   SWEATER GIRL   (1942)
        STARS:  Eddie Bracken, June Priesser
        DIR:    William Clemons

1008.   SWEET ADELINE   (1935)
        STARS:  Irene Dunne, Donald Woods
        DIR:    Mervyn LeRoy
        SONGS:  Jerome Kern - Oscar Hammerstein II
        We Were So Young; Play Us A Polka Dot; Sultan's Place; Lonely
        Feet; 'Twas Not So Long Ago; Don't Ever Leave Me; Down Where
        The Wurtzburger Flows; Pretty Little Jennie Lee; I'd Leave
        My Happy Home For You; Molly O'Donohue; Why Was I Born?; Here
        I Am.
        Jerome Kern In Hollywood, 1934-1938:  JJA-19747D

1009.   SWEET AND LOW DOWN   (1944)
        STARS:  Linda Darnell, Lynn Bari
        DIR:    Archie Mayo
        SONGS:  Jimmy Monaco - Mack Gordon

1010.   SWEET CHARITY   (1969)
        STARS:  Shirley MacLaine, Chita Rivera
        DIR:    Bob Fosse
        SONGS:  Cy Coleman - Dorothy Fields
        Sweet Charity; I Love To Cry At Weddings; It's A Nice Face;
        If My Friends Could See Me Now; Big Spender; My Personal Prop-
        erty; Rich Man's Frug; Where Am I Going?; There's Gotta Be
        Something Better Than This; Rhythm Of Life; I'm A Brass Band.
        Decca 71502

1011.   SWEET MUSIC   (1935)
        STARS:  Rudy Vallee, Ann Sothern
        DIR:    Alfred E. Green

1012.   SWEET ROSIE O'GRADY   (1943)
        STARS:  Betty Grable, Robert Young
        DIR:    Irving Cummings
        SONGS:  Harry Warren - Mack Gordon

1013.   SWEET SURRENDER   (1935)
        STARS:  Tamara, Frank Parker
        DIR:    Monte Brice

1014.   SWEETHEART OF THE CAMPUS   (1941)
        STARS:  Ruby Keeler, Ozzie Nelson
        DIR:    Edward Dmytryk

1015.   SWEETHEARTS   (1938)
        STARS:  Nelson Eddy, Jeanette MacDonald
        DIR:    W. S. Van Dyke
        SONGS:  Victor Herbert - Bob Wright - Chet Forrest

1016. SWEETHEARTS OF THE U.S.A.   (1944)
      STARS:  Una Merkel, Donald Novis
      DIR:    Lew Collins
      SONGS:  Lew Pollack - Charles Newman

1017. SWEETHEARTS ON PARADE   (1930)
      STARS:  Alice White, Lloyd Hughes
      DIR:    Marshall Neilan

1018. SWEETIE   (1929)
      STARS:  Nancy Carroll, Helen Kane
      DIR:    Frank Tuttle

1019. SWING FEVER   (1943)
      STARS:  Kay Kyser, Marilyn Maxwell
      DIR:    Tim Whelan

1020. SWING HIGH   (1930)
      STARS:  Helen Twelvetrees, Fred Scott
      DIR:    Joseph Santley
      SONGS:  Ted Snyder - Abner Silver - Mack Gordon

1021. SWING HIGH SWING LOW   (1937)
      STARS:  Carole Lombard, Fred MacMurray
      DIR:    Mitchell Leisen

1022. SWING IN THE SADDLE   (1944)
      STARS:  Jane Frazee, Guinn Williams
      DIR:    Lew Landers

1023. SWING PARADE OF 1946   (1946)
      STARS:  Gale Storm, Phil Regan
      DIR:    Phil Karlson

1024. SWING SISTER SWING   (1938)
      STARS:  Ken Murray, Johnny Downs
      DIR:    Joseph Santley
      SONGS:  Charles Henderson - Frank Skinner

1025. SWING TIME   (1936)
      STARS:  Ginger Rogers, Fred Astaire
      DIR:    George Stevens
      SONGS:  Jerome Kern - Dorothy Fields
      Waltz In Swing Time; A Fine Romance; The Way You Look Tonight;
      Pick Yourself Up; Never Gonna Dance; Bojangles Of Harlem.
      EMI EMTC-102.

1026. SWING YOUR LADY   (1938)
      STARS:  Humphrey Bogart, Frank McHugh
      DIR:    Ray Enright
      SONGS:  M. K. Jerome - Jack Scholl

1027. SWING YOUR PARTNER   (1943)

STARS: Lulubelle and Scotty, Vera Vague
DIR: Frank McDonald

1028. SWINGTIME JOHNNY (1944)
STARS: The Andrews Sisters, Harriet Hilliard
DIR: Edward F. Cline

1029. SWISS MISS (1938)
STARS: Laurel and Hardy
DIR: John Blystone
SONGS: Phil Charig - Arthur Quenzer

1030. SYNCOPATION (1929)
STARS: Morton Downey, Dorothy Lee
DIR: Burt Glennon

1031. SYNCOPATION (1942)
STARS: Adolphe Menjou, Jackie Cooper
DIR: William Dieterle

1032. TAHITI HONEY (1943)
STARS: Simone Simon, Dennis O'Keefe
DIR: John T. Auer
SONGS: Lew Pollack - Charles Newman

1033. TAKE A CHANCE (1933)
STARS: James Dunn, Cliff Edwards
DIR: Laurence Schwab, Monte Brice

1034. TAKE IT BIG (1944)
STARS: Jack Haley, Harriet Hilliard
DIR: Frank McDonald
SONGS: Lester Lee - Jerry Seelen

1035. TAKE ME OUT TO THE BALL GAME (1949)
STARS: Esther Williams, Frank Sinatra
DIR: Busby Berkeley
SONGS: Roger Edens - Adolph Green - Betty Comden
O'Brien To Ryan To Goldberg; Yes Indeed; The Right Girl For
Me; Strictly U.S.A.; It's Fate Baby It's Fate.
Curtain Calls CC 100/18

1036. TAKE ME TO TOWN (1953)
STARS: Ann Sheridan, Sterling Hayden
DIR: Douglas Sirk
Take Me To Town; The Tale Of Vermilion O'Toole (Lester Lee -
Dan Shapiro); Oh You Red Head (Frederick Herbert - Milton
Rosen).

1037. TALL, DARK AND HANDSOME (1941)
STARS: Cesar Romero, Virginia Gilmore
DIR: H. Bruce Humberstone

1038. TANNED LEGS (1929)

```
          STARS:  Ann Pennington, June Clyde
          DIR:    Marshall Neilan
          SONGS:  Oscar Levant - Sidney Clare

1039.  TARS AND SPARS  (1946)
          STARS:  Janet Blair, Alfred Drake
          DIR:    Alfred E. Green
          SONGS:  Jule Styne - Sammy Cahn

1040.  TEA FOR TWO  (1950)
          STARS:  Doris Day, Gordon MacRae
          DIR:    David Butler
          I Know That You Know (Vincent Youmans - Anne Caldwell); Crazy
          Rhythm (Joseph Meyer - Roger Wolfe Kahn - Irving Caesar); I
          Only Have Eyes For You (Harry Warren - Al Dubin); I Want To
          Be Happy; Tea For Two (Youmans - Irving Caesar); Do Do Do
          (George and Ira Gershwin); Oh Me Oh My (Youmans - Ira Gersh-
          win).
          Col. CL-6149

1041.  TERROR OF TINY TOWN  (1938)
          STARS:  Billy Curtis, Yvonne Moray
          DIR:    Sam Newfield
          SONGS:  Lew Porter - L. Wolfe Gilbert

1042.  TEXAS CARNIVAL  (1951)
          STARS:  Esther Williams, Red Skelton
          DIR:    Charles Walters

1043.  THANK YOUR LUCKY STARS  (1943)
          STARS:  Eddie Cantor, Bette Davis
          DIR:    David Butler
          SONGS:  Arthur Schwartz - Frank Loesser
          I'm Going North; Thank Your Lucky Stars; Love Isn't Born It's
          Made; I'm Riding For A Fall; How Sweet You Are; They're Either
          Too Young Or Too Old; The Dreamer; Good Night Good Neighbor;
          Ice Cold Katy; We're Staying Home Tonight; That's What You
          Jolly Well Get.
          Curtain Calls  CC 100/8

1044.  THANKS A MILLION  (1935)
          STARS:  Dick Powell, Ann Dvorak
          DIR:    Roy Del Ruth

1045.  THANKS FOR EVERYTHING  (1938)
          STARS:  Adolphe Menjou, Jack Oakie
          DIR:    William A. Seiter
          SONGS:  Harry Revel - Mack Gordon

1046.  THAT CERTAIN AGE  (1938)
          STARS:  Deanna Durbin, Melvyn Douglas
          DIR:    Edward Ludwig
          SONGS:  Jimmy McHugh - Harold Adamson
```

1047. THAT GIRL FROM PARIS   (1936)
      STARS:  Lili Pons, Jack Oakie
      DIR:    Leigh Jason
      SONGS:  Arthur Schwartz - Edward Heyman

1048. THAT LADY IN ERMINE   (1948)
      STARS:  Betty Grable, Douglas Fairbanks Jr.
      DIR:    Ernst Lubitsch

1049. THAT NIGHT IN RIO   (1941)
      STARS:  Alice Faye, Don Ameche
      DIR:    Irving Cummings
      SONGS:  Harry Warren - Mack Gordon
      I Yi Yi Yi Yi Yi Like You Very Much; The Baron Is In Confer-
      ence; Chica Chica Boom Chic; Boa Noite; They Met In Rio.
      Curtain Calls   CC 100/14

1050. THAT'S A GOOD GIRL   (1934)
      STARS:  Jack Buchanan, Elsie Randolph

1051. THAT'S MY GIRL   (1946)
      STARS:  Lynne Roberts, Donald Barry
      DIR:    George Blair

1052. THAT'S RIGHT, YOU'RE WRONG   (1939)
      STARS:  Kay Kyser, Adolphe Menjou
      DIR:    David Butler

1053. THAT'S THE SPIRIT   (1945)
      STARS:  Peggy Ryan, Jack Oakie
      DIR:    Charles Lamont

1054. THERE'S A GIRL IN MY HEART   (1949)
      STARS:  Lee Bowman, Elyse Knox
      DIR:    Arthur Dreifuss
      SONGS:  Robert Bilder

1055. THERE'S NO BUSINESS LIKE SHOW BUSINESS   (1954)
      STARS:  Ethel Merman, Donald O'Connor
      DIR:    Walter Lang
      SONGS:  Irving Berlin
      There's No Business Like Show Business; Alexander's Ragtime
      Band; When The Midnight Choo-Choo Leaves For Alabam'; Heat
      Wave; Play A Simple Melody; Sailor's Not A Sailor; Man Chases
      A Girl; After You Get What You Want You Don't Want It; Lady.
      Decca DL-8091

1056. THEY LEARNED ABOUT WOMEN   (1930)
      STARS:  Bessie Love, Joe Schenck
      DIR:    John Conway, Sam Wood

1057. THEY MET IN ARGENTINA   (1941)
      STARS: ·Maureen O'Hara, James Ellison
      DIR:    Leslie Goodwins

197

SONGS:   Richard Rodgers - Lorenz Hart

1058.  THIN ICE   (1937)
       STARS:   Sonja Henie, Tyrone Power
       DIR:     Sidney Lanfield
       SONGS:   Lew Pollack - Sidney Mitchell

1059.  THIS IS THE ARMY   (1943)
       STARS:   Ronald Reagan, George Murphy
       DIR:     Michael Curtiz
       SONGS:   Irving Berlin
       This Is The Army Mr. Jones; The Army's Made A Man Out Of Me;
       Mandy; I'm Getting Tired So I Can Sleep; What The Well-Dressed
       Men In Harlem Will Wear; Give A Cheer For The Navy; I Left My
       Heart At The Stage Door Canteen; God Bless America; Poor Lit-
       tle Me I'm On K. P.; Oh, How I Hate To Get Up In The Morning;
       American Eagles
       Decca DL-5108   (orig. cast)

1060.  THIS IS MY AFFAIR   (1937)
       STARS:   Robert Taylor, Barbara Stanwyck
       DIR:     William A. Seiter
       SONGS:   Harry Revel - Mack Gordon

1061.  THIS IS THE LIFE   (1935)
       STARS:   Sally Blaine, Sidney Toler
       DIR:     Marshall Neilan
       SONGS:   Sammy Stept - Sidney Clare

1062.  THIS IS THE LIFE   (1944)
       STARS:   Donald O'Connor, Susanna Foster
       DIR:     Felix Feist

1063.  THIS TIME FOR KEEPS   (1947)
       STARS:   Esther Williams, Jimmy Durante
       DIR:     Richard Thorpe

1064.  THIS WAY PLEASE   (1937)
       STARS:   Charles "Buddy" Rogers, Mary Livingston
       DIR:     Robert Florey

1065.  THOROUGHLY MODERN MILLIE   (1967)
       STARS:   Julie Andrews, Mary Tyler Moore
       DIR:     George Roy Hill
       Thoroughly Modern Millie; The Tapioca (James Van Heusen -
       Sammy Cahn); Jimmy (Jay Thompson); Also: Baby Face; Poor
       Butterfly; Do It Again; Stumbling; Jazz Baby; Rose Of Wash-
       ington Square; Jewish Wedding Song; Japanese Sandman.
       Decca DL-71500

1066.  THOSE REDHEADS FROM SEATTLE   (1953)
       STARS:   Rhonda Fleming, Gene Barry
       DIR:     Lewis R. Foster
       I Guess It Was You All The Time (Hoagy Carmichael - Johnny

Mercer); Mr. Banjo Man (Jay Livingston - Ray Evans); Baby
Baby Baby (Mack David - Jerry Livingston); Take Back Your
Gold (M. H. Rosenfeld - Louis W. Pritzkow); Chick-A-Boom
Bob Merrill).

1067. THOUSANDS CHEER (1943)
STARS:  Gene Kelly, Kathryn Grayson
DIR:    George Sidney

1068. THREE CHEERS FOR LOVE (1936)
STARS:  Eleanor Whitney, Robert Cummings
DIR:    Ray McCarey
SONGS:  Ralph Rainger - Leo Robin

1069. THREE FOR THE SHOW (1955)
STARS:  Betty Grable, Marge and Gower Champion
DIR:    H. C. Potter
Someone To Watch Over Me; I've Got A Crush On You (George
Gershwin - Ira Gershwin); Which One? (Lester Lee - Ned Wash-
ington); I've Been Kissed Before (Bob Russell - Lester Lee);
How Come You Do Me Like You Do (Gene Austin - Ray Bergere);
Down Boy (Hoagy Carmichael - Harold Adamson).
Mercury 25204

1070. THREE LITTLE GIRLS IN BLUE (1946)
STARS:  June Haver, George Montgomery
DIR:    Bruce Humberstone
SONGS:  Joseph Myrow - Mack Gordon

1071. THREE LITTLE SISTERS (1944)
STARS:  Mary Lee, Cheryl Walker
DIR:    Joseph Santley
SONGS:  Walter Kent - Kim Gannon

1072. THREE LITTLE WORDS (1950)
STARS:  Fred Astaire, Red Skelton
DIR:    Richard Thorpe
SONGS:  Harry Ruby - Bert Kalmar
Where Did You Get That Girl? (with Harry Puck); Come On Papa
(lyrics by Edgar Leslie); Thinking Of You; She's Mine All
Mine; My Sunny Tennessee (with Herman Ruby); Three Little
Words; So Long Oo-Long; Who's Sorry Now? (with Ted Snyder);
All Alone Monday; I Wanna Be Loved By You; Hooray For Captain
Spaulding; I Love You So Much; Up In The Clouds; Mr. and Mrs.
Hoofer; You Are My Lucky Star (Nacio Herb Brown - Arthur
Freed).
MGM 2-SES-45ST

1073. THREE MUSKETEERS (1939)
STARS:  The Ritz Brothers, Don Ameche
DIR:    Allan Dwan
SONGS:  Samuel Pokrass - Walter Bullock

1074. THREE SAILORS AND A GIRL (1953)

199

STARS: Jane Powell, Gordon MacRae
DIR: Roy Del Ruth
SONGS: Sammy Fain - Sammy Cahn
Show Me A Happy Woman And I'll Show A Miserable Man; You're
But Oh So Right; When It's Love; Lately Song; Face To Face;
Home Is Where The Heart Is; There Must Be A Reason; When My
Heart Sings; Kiss Me Or I'll Scream.
Capitol L-485

1075. THREE SISTERS (1930)
STARS: Louise Dresser, Tom Patricola
DIR: Paul Sloane
SONGS: Jerome Kern - Oscar Hammerstein II

1076. THRILL OF A LIFETIME, THE (1937)
STARS: Dorothy Lamour, Ben Blue
DIR: George Archainbaud

1077. THRILL OF A ROMANCE (1945)
STARS: Van Johnson, Esther Williams
DIR: Richard Thorpe

1078. THRILL OF BRAZIL (1946)
STARS: Evelyn Keyes, Keenan Wynn
DIR: S. Sylvan Simon

1079. THUMBS UP (1943)
STARS: Brenda Joyce, Richard Frazer
DIR: Joseph Santley

1080. TILL THE CLOUDS ROLL BY (1946)
STARS: Robert Walker, Judy Garland
DIR: Richard Whorf
MUSIC: Jerome Kern (lyricist follows in parentheses)
Cotton Blossom; Make Believe; Life Upon The Wicked Stage; Ol'
Man River; Can't Help Lovin' That Man; Where's The Mate For
Me?; The Last Time I Saw Paris; Why Was I Born?; One More
Dance; All The Things You Are (Oscar Hammerstein II); Smoke
Gets In Your Eyes; Sunny (Otto Harbach - Hammerstein II);
Yesterdays; She Didn't Say Yes; Who? (Harbach); Till The Cloud
Roll By; Cleopatterer; Leave It To Jane; Go Little Boat; The
Land Where The Good Songs Go (P. G. Wodehouse); How'd You Like
To Spoon With Me? (Edward Laska); They Didn't Believe Me (Her-
bert Reynolds); Look For The Silver Lining (B. G. DeSylva);
Long Ago And Far Away (Ira Gershwin); A Fine Romance (Dorothy
Fields).
MGM-2-SES-45ST

1081. TIME OUT FOR RHYTHM (1941)
STARS: Ann Miller, Rudy Vallee
DIR: Sidney Salkow
SONGS: Saul Chaplin - Sammy Cahn

1082. TIME, THE PLACE AND THE GIRL, THE (1929)

STARS: Betty Compson, Grant Withers
DIR: Herb Bretherton

1083. TIME, THE PLACE AND THE GIRL, THE    (1946)
STARS: Dennis Morgan, Jack Carson
DIR: David Butler
SONGS: Arthur Schwartz - Leo Robin

1084. TIN PAN ALLEY    (1940)
STARS: Alice Faye, Betty Grable
DIR: Walter Lang

1085. TO BEAT THE BAND    (1935)
STARS: Hugh Herbert, Helen Broderick
DIR: Benjamin Stoloff
SONGS: Matt Malneck - Johnny Mercer

1086. TOAST OF NEW ORLEANS, THE    (1950)
STARS: Mario Lanza, Kathryn Grayson
DIR: Norman Taurog
SONGS: Nicholas Brodszky - Sammy Cahn
Boom Biddy Boom Boom; The Tina-Lina; The Bayou Lullaby; I'll
Never Love You; Be My Love.

1087. TOM SAWYER    (1973)
STARS: Johnny Whitaker, Celeste Holm
DIR: Don Taylor
SONGS: Richard M. and Robert B. Sherman
Freebootin'; River Song; Gratification.
United Artists UA LA-057-G

1088. TOM THUMB    (1958)
STARS: Russ Tamblyn, Terry-Thomas
DIR: George Pal
After All These Years; Talented Shoes (Fred Spielman - Janice
Torre); Tom Thumb's Tune; Are You A Dream? (Peggy Lee); Yawn-
ing Song (Fred Spielman - Kermit Goell).
MGM-Lion L-70084

1089. TONIGHT AND EVERY NIGHT    (1945)
STARS: Rita Hayworth, Janet Blair
DIR: Victor Saville
SONGS: Jule Styne - Sammy Cahn

1090. TOO MANY BLONDES    (1941)
STARS: Rudy Vallee, Helen Parrish
DIR: Thornton Freeland

1091. TOO MANY GIRLS    (1940)
STARS: Lucille Ball, Richard Carlson
DIR: George Abbott
SONGS: Richard Rodgers - Lorenz Hart

1092. TOO MUCH HARMONY    (1933)

STARS:   Bing Crosby, Jack Oakie
DIR:     Edward Sutherland
SONGS:   Arthur Johnston - Sam Coslow
Cradle Me With A Ha-Cha Lullaby; Two Aristocrats; I Guess It
Had To Be That Way; Buckin' The Wind; Boo, Boo, Boo; Black
Moonlight; The Day You Came Along; Thanks.
Col. C2L-43

1093.  TOP BANANA  (1954)
STARS:   Phil Silvers, Rose Marie
DIR:     Alfred E. Green
SONGS:   Johnny Mercer

1094.  TOP HAT  (1935)
STARS:   Ginger Rogers, Fred Astaire
DIR:     Mark Sandrich
SONGS:   Irving Berlin
Top Hat, White Tie And Tails; No Strings; The Piccolino; Isn't
This A Lovely Day?; Cheek To Cheek.
EMI EMTC-102

1095.  TOP O' THE MORNING  (1949)
STARS:   Bing Crosby, Ann Blyth
DIR:     David Miller
SONGS:   Jimmy Van Heusen - Johnny Burke

1096.  TOP OF THE TOWN  (1937)
STARS:   George Murphy, Hugh Herbert
DIR:     Ralph Murphy
SONGS:   Jimmy McHugh - Harold Adamson

1097.  TOP SPEED  (1930)
STARS:   Joe E. Brown, Bernice Claire
DIR:     Mervyn LeRoy

1098.  TORCH SINGER  (1933)
STARS:   Claudette Colbert, Ricardo Cortez
DIR:     Alexander Hall, George Somnes
SONGS:   Ralph Rainger - Leo Robin

1099.  TORCH SONG  (1953)
STARS:   Joan Crawford, Michael Wilding
DIR:     Charles Walters
Two Faced Woman (Arthur Schwartz - Howard Dietz); You're All
The World To Me (Burton Lane - Alan Jay Lerner); Once In A
While (Michael Edwards - Bud Green); When A Fool Falls In
Love; I Don't Know Why (Fred Ahlert - Roy Turk); You Won't
Forget Me (Fred Spielman - Kermit Goell); Tenderly (Walter
Gross - Jack Lawrence); Follow Me (Adolph Deutsch); Blue Moon
(Richard Rodgers - Lorenz Hart).
MGM E-214

1100.  TRANSATLANTIC MERRY-GO-ROUND  (1934)

STARS: Jack Benny, Gene Raymond
DIR: Benjamin Stoloff

1101. TROCADERO (1944)
STARS: Rosemary Lane, Johnny Downs
DIR: William Nigh

1102. TROPIC HOLIDAY (1938)
STARS: Dorothy Lamour, Ray Milland
DIR: Theodore Reed

1103. TRUE TO LIFE (1943)
STARS: Mary Martin, Franchot Tone
DIR: George Marshall
SONGS: Hoagy Carmichael - Johnny Mercer

1104. TRUE TO THE ARMY (1942)
STARS: Judy Canova, Allan Jones
DIR: Albert S. Rogell

1105. TURN OFF THE MOON (1937)
STARS: Johnny Downs, Charles Ruggles
DIR: Lewis Seiler
SONGS: Sam Coslow

1106. TWENTY MILLION SWEETHEARTS (1934)
STARS: Dick Powell, Ginger Rogers
DIR: Ray Enright
SONGS: Harry Warren - Al Dubin

1107. TWENTY-THREE AND A HALF HOURS' LEAVE (1937)
STARS: James Ellison, Terry Walker
DIR: John G. Blystone
SONGS: Sammy Stept - Ted Koehler

1108. TWO BLONDES AND A RED HEAD (1947)
STARS: Jean Porter, Jimmy Lloyd
DIR: Arthur Dreifuss

1109. TWO FOR TONIGHT (1935)
STARS: Bing Crosby, Joan Bennett
DIR: Frank Tuttle
SONGS: Harry Revel - Mack Gordon

1110. TWO GALS AND A GUY (1951)
STARS: Robert Alda, Janet Paige
DIR: Alfred E. Green
SONGS: Marty Nevins - Hal David
Sun Showers; Laugh And Be Happy; We Have With Us Tonight; So
Long For Now.

1111. TWO GIRLS AND A SAILOR (1944)
STARS: Van Johnson, June Allyson
DIR: Richard Thorpe

Young Man With A Horn (George Stoll - Ralph Freed); A Tisket
A Tasket (Ella Fitzgerald - Al Feldman); You Dear (Sammy
Fain - Ralph Freed); Thrill Of A New Romance (Xavier Cugat -
Harold Adamson); In A Moment Of Madness; My Mother Told Me
(Jimmy McHugh - Ralph Freed); Sweet And Lovely (Harry Tobias -
Jules Lemair - Gus Arnheim); A Love Like Ours (Alberta Nich-
ols - Mann Holiner).
Sound/Stage 2307

1112.  TWO GIRLS ON BROADWAY  (1940)
       STARS:  Lana Turner, Joan Blondell
       DIR:    S. Sylvan Simon

1113.  TWO GUYS FROM TEXAS  (1948)
       STARS:  Dennis Morgan, Jack Carson
       DIR:    David Butler
       SONGS:  Jule Styne - Sammy Cahn

1114.  TWO HEARTS IN WALTZ TIME  (1930)
       STARS:  Walter Janssen, Oscar Karlweiss
       SONGS:  Robert Stolz - Joe Young

1115.  TWO LATINS FROM MANHATTAN  (1941)
       STARS:  Joan Davis, Jinx Falkenburg
       DIR:    Charles Barton

1116.  TWO SISTERS FROM BOSTON  (1946)
       STARS:  Kathryn Grayson, June Allyson
       DIR:    Henry Koster

1117.  TWO TICKETS TO BROADWAY  (1951)
       STARS:  Tony Martin, Janet Leigh
       DIR:    Charles V. Kern
       The Closer You Are; Baby You Won't Be Sorry; Big Chief Hole-
       In-The-Ground; It Began In Yucatan; That's The Tune; Are You
       Just A Beautiful Dream?; The Worry Bird; Pelican Falls; Let's
       Do Something New; New York (Let Me Sing) (Jule Styne - Leo
       Robin); Let's Make Comparisons (Bob Crosby - Sammy Cahn);
       There's No Tomorrow (Leo Corday - Al Hoffman).
       RCA LPM-39

1118.  TWO WEEKS WITH LOVE  (1950)
       STARS:  Jane Powell, Debbie Reynolds
       DIR:    Roy Rowland
       A Heart That's Free (Thomas Railey - Alfred Robyn); By The
       Light Of The Silvery Moon (Edward Madden - Gus Edwards); My
       Hero (S. Stange - Oscar Straus); Oceana Roll (Roger Lewis -
       Lucien Denni); That's How I Need You (Joe McCarthy - Joe Good-
       win); Row, Row, Row (William Jerome - Jimmy Monaco); Aba Daba
       Honeymoon (Arthur Fields - Walter Donavan).
       MGM-2-SES-49ST

1119.  UNDER PRESSURE  (1935)

STARS:  Edmund Lowe, Victor McLaglen
DIR:    Raoul Walsh
SONGS:  Dan Dougherty - Jack Yellen

1120. UNDER THE PAMPAS MOON   (1935)
STARS:  Warner Baxter, Ketti Gallian
DIR:    James Tinling
Querida Mia (Lew Pollack - Paul Francis Webster)

1121. UNDER YOUR SPELL   (1936)
STARS:  Lawrence Tibbett, Wendy Barrie
DIR:    Otto Preminger
SONGS:  Arthur Schwartz - Howard Dietz

1122. UNSINKABLE MOLLY BROWN, THE   (1964)
STARS:  Debbie Reynolds, Harve Presnell
DIR:    Charles Walters
SONGS:  Meredith Willson
Colorado Is My Home; I'll Never Say No; He's My Friend;
Soliloquy; I Ain't Down Yet; Belly Up To The Bar Boys;
MGM SE-4232

1123. UP IN ARMS   (1944)
STARS:  Danny Kaye, Dinah Shore
DIR:    Elliott Nugent
SONGS:  Harold Arlen - Ted Koehler

1124. UP IN CENTRAL PARK   (1948)
STARS:  Deanna Durbin, Dick Haymes
DIR:    William Seiter
SONGS:  Sigmund Romberg - Dorothy Fields

1125. VAGABOND KING, THE   (1930)
STARS:  Dennis King, Jeanette MacDonald
DIR:    Ludwig Berger

1126. VAGABOND KING, THE   (1956)
STARS:  Kathryn Grayson, Oreste
DIR:    Michael Curtiz
SONGS:  Rudolf Friml - W. H. Post - Brian Hooker
Vagabond King; Drinking Song; Song Of The Vagabonds; Scotch
Archers' Song; Lord I'm Glad I Know; Only A Rose; Some Day;
Love Me Tonight; Vive La You; and This Same Heart; Bon Jour
(lyrics by Johnny Burke).
RCA LSC-2509

1127. VAGABOND LOVER, THE   (1929)
STARS:  Rudy Vallee, Sally Blane
DIR:    Marshall Neilan

1128. VARIETY GIRL   (1947)
STARS:  Mary Hatcher, Olga San Juan
DIR:    George Marshall
SONGS:  Frank Loesser

1129. VARIETY SHOW  (1937)
STARS:  Dick Powell, Ted Healy
DIR:    William Keighley
SONGS:  Richard Whiting - Johnny Mercer

1130. VIENNESE NIGHTS  (1930)
STARS:  Vivienne Segal, Alexander Gray
DIR:    Alan Crosland
SONGS:  Sigmund Romberg - Oscar Hammerstein II

1131. VIRGINIA  (1941)
STARS:  Madeleine Carroll, Fred MacMurray
DIR:    Edward H. Griffith
SONGS:  Arthur Schwartz - Howard Dietz

1132. VOGUES OF 1938  (1937)
STARS:  Joan Bennett, Warren Baxter
DIR:    Irving Cummings

1133. WABASH AVENUE  (1950)
STARS:  Betty Grable, Victor Mature
DIR:    Henry Koster
SONGS:  Josef Myrow - Mack Gordon
Wilhelmina; May I Tempt You With A Big Red Apple?; Baby Say
You Love Me; Down On Wabash Avenue; Clean Up Chicago.

1134. WAIKIKI WEDDING  (1937)
STARS:  Bing Crosby, Bob Burns
DIR:    Frank Tuttle

1135. WAKE UP AND DREAM  (1934)
STARS:  Russ Columbo, June Knight
DIR:    Kurt Neumann
SONGS:  Jack Stern - Grace Hamilton - Russ Columbo

1136. WAKE UP AND DREAM  (1946)
STARS:  Clem Bevans, John Payne
DIR:    Lloyd Bacon

1137. WAKE UP AND LIVE  (1937)
STARS:  Walter Winchell, Alice Faye
DIR:    Sidney Lanfield
SONGS:  Harry Revel - Mack Gordon
I Love You Too Much Muchacha; Wake Up And Live; Never In A
Million Years; There's A Lull In My Life; It's Swell Of You;
Oh, But I'm Happy; I'm Bubbling Over.
Col. ACL-3068

1138. WALKING MY BABY BACK HOME  (1953)
STARS:  Donald O'Connor, Janet Leigh
DIR:    Lloyd Bacon
Man's Gotta Eat (Scat Man Crothers - F. E. Miller); and Glow
Worm; Honeysuckle Rose; Hop On The Band Wagon; South Rampart
Street Parade; Down In The South; De Camptown Races; Hi Lee,

Hi Lo; Muskrat Ramble; Leibenstraum Jumps; Walking My Baby
Back Home.

1139. WALKING ON AIR   (1936)
      STARS:  Gene Raymond, Ann Sothern
      DIR:    Joseph Santley
      SONGS:  Harry Ruby - Bert Kalmar

1140. WALLABY JIM OF THE ISLANDS   (1937)
      STARS:  George Houston, Ruth Coleman
      DIR:    Charles Lamont

1141. WAVE, A WAC AND A MARINE, A   (1944)
      STARS:  Elyse Knox, Anne Gillis
      DIR:    Phil Karlson
      SONGS:  Freddie Rich - Jacques Press - Eddie Cherkose

1142. WAY TO LOVE, THE   (1933)
      STARS:  Maurice Chevalier, Ann Dvorak
      DIR:    Norman Taurog

1143. WEEK-END IN HAVANA   (1941)
      STARS:  Alice Faye, Carmen Miranda
      DIR:    Walter Lang
      SONGS:  Harry Warren - Mack Gordon
      The Nango; When I Love I Love; Week-End In Havana; Man With
      The Lollipop Song; Tropical Magic; Romance And The Rhumba
      (music by Jimmy Monaco).
      Curtain Calls   CC 100/14

1144. WEEKEND PASS   (1944)
      STARS:  Martha O'Driscoll, Noah Beery
      DIR:    Jean Yarbrough

1145. WELCOME STRANGER   (1947)
      STARS:  Bing Crosby, Barry Fitzgerald
      DIR:    Elliott Nugent
      SONGS:  Jimmy Van Heusen - Johnny Burke
      As Long As I'm Dreaming; Smack In The Middle Of Maine; My
      Heart Is A Hobo, Smile Right Back At The Sun; Country Style.
      Decca DL-4260

1146. WE'RE NOT DRESSING   (1934)
      STARS:  Bing Crosby, Carole Lombard
      DIR:    Norman Taurog
      May I?; Love Thy Neighbor; She Walks Like You, She Talks Like
      You; Once In A Blue Moon; Goodnight Lovely Little Lady; It's
      Just A New Spanish Custom (Harry Revel - Mack Gordon); When
      The Golden Gate Was Silver (Ralph Rainger - Leo Robin); Live
      And Love Tonight (Arthur Johnston - Sam Coslow).
      Col. C2L-43

1147. WEST POINT STORY, THE   (1950)
      STARS:  James Cagney, Virginia Mayo

DIR:    Roy Del Ruth
SONGS:  Jule Styne - Sammy Cahn
Ten Thousand Four Hundred And Thirty-Two Sheep; The Corps;
By The Kissing Rock; It Could Only Happen In Brooklyn; You
Love Me; Long Before I Knew You; Military Polka.

1148. WEST SIDE STORY   (1961)
      STARS:  Natalie Wood, Richard Beymer
      DIR:    Robert Wise, Jerome Robbins
      SONGS:  Leonard Bernstein - Stephen Sondheim
      Jet Song; Dance At The Gym; Maria; One Hand, One Heart; The
      Rumble; I Feel Pretty; A Boy Like That; I Have A Love; Some-
      where; Cool; Gee, Officer Krupke; America; Tonight; Something'
      Coming.
      Col.  OS-2070

1149. WHARF ANGEL   (1934)
      STARS:  Victor McLaglen, Dorothy Dell
      DIR:    William C. Menzies, George Somnes

1150. WHAT'S BUZZIN' COUSIN?   (1943)
      STARS:  Ann Miller, Eddie "Rochester" Anderson
      DIR:    Charles Barton

1151. WHAT'S COOKING?   (1942)
      STARS:  The Andrews Sisters, Gloria Jean
      DIR:    Edward F. Cline

1152. WHEN A GIRL'S BEAUTIFUL   (1947)
      STARS:  Adele Jurgens, Marc Platt
      DIR:    Frank McDonald
      SONGS:  Lester Lee - Allan Roberts

1153. WHEN JOHNNY COMES MARCHING HOME   (1942)
      STARS:  Allan Jones, Gloria Jean
      DIR:    Charles Lamont

1154. WHEN MY BABY SMILES AT ME   (1948)
      STARS:  Betty Grable, Dan Dailey
      DIR:    Walter Lang

1155. WHERE DO WE GO FROM HERE?   (1945)
      STARS:  Fred MacMurray, Joan Leslie
      DIR:    Gregory Ratoff
      SONGS:  Kurt Weill - Ira Gershwin
      All At Once; Christopher Columbus; The Nina, The Pinta And
      The Santa Maria; If Love Remains; Song Of The Rhineland
      Heritage 0051

1156. WHERE'S CHARLEY?   (1952)
      STARS:  Ray Bolger, Allyn McLerie
      DIR:    David Butler
      SONGS:  Frank Loesser
      Once In Love With Amy; The New Ashmolean Marching Society;

Make A Miracle; Lovelier Than Ever; My Darling, My Darling;
At The Red Rose Cotillon; The Years Before Us; Serenade With
Asides; Where's Charley?; Better Get Out Of Here.

1157. WHITE CHRISTMAS  (1954)
      STARS:  Bing Crosby, Danny Kaye
      DIR:    Michael Curtiz
      SONGS:  Irving Berlin
      Best Things Happen While You're Dancing; Love You Didn't Do
      Right By Me; Mandy; Gee, I Wish I Was Back In The Army; Old
      Man; Choreography; What Can You Do With A General; Blue Skies;
      Sisters; Snow; White Christmas; Count Your Blessings
      Decca DL-8083

1158. WHO DONE IT?  (1942)
      STARS:  Abbott and Costello
      DIR:    Erle C. Kenton
      SONGS:  Gene DePaul - Don Raye

1159. WHOOPEE  (1930)
      STARS:  Eddie Cantor, Eleanor Hunt
      DIR:    Thornton Freeland
      SONGS:  Walter Donaldson - Gus Kahn
      The Wildest Of Cowboys Is He; Whoopee; Wedding Song; My Baby
      Just Cares For Me; Stetson; Song Of The Setting Sun; and
      I'll Still Belong To You (Nacio Herb Brown - Ed Eliscu).
      PRW-1930

1160. WHY GIRLS LEAVE HOME  (1945)
      STARS:  Lola Lane, Sheldon Leonard
      DIR:    William Berke
      SONGS:  Jay Livingston - Ray Evans

1161. WILLY WONKA AND THE CHOCOLATE FACTORY  (1971)
      STARS:  Gene Wilder, Jack Albertson
      DIR:    Mel Stuart
      SONGS:  Anthony Newley - Leslie Bricusse
      The Candy Man; I've Got A Golden Ticket; Oompa-Loompa-Domp-
      adee-Doo; Willy Wonka; Cheer Up Charlie; I Want It Now; Pure
      Imagination.
      Paramount 6012

1162. WINTERTIME  (1943)
      STARS:  Sonja Henie, Jack Oakie
      DIR:    John Braham
      SONGS:  Nacio Herb Brown - Leo Robin

1163. WITH A SONG IN MY HEART  (1952)
      STARS:  Susan Hayward, Thelma Ritter
      DIR:    Walter Lang
      With A Song In My Heart; Blue Moon (Richard Rodgers - Lorenz
      Hart); That Old Feeling (Sammy Fain - Lew Brown); I've Got A
      Feeling You're Fooling (Nacio Herb Brown - Arthur Freed); Tea
      For Two (Vincent Youmans - Irving Caesar); Deep In The Heart

Of Texas (Don Swander - June Hershey); Carry Me Back To Old
Virginny (James Bland); Dixie (Dan Emmett); They're Either
Too Young Or Too Old (Arthur Schwartz - Frank Loesser); It's
A Good Day (Dave Barbour - Peggy Lee); I'll Walk Alone (Jule
Styne - Sammy Cahn); Give My Regards To Broadway (George M.
Cohan); Alabamy Bound (Ray Henderson - B. G. DeSylva - Bud
Green); California Here I Come (Joseph Meyer - Al Jolson -
B. G. DeSylva); Chicago (Fred Fisher); America The Beautiful
(Samuel A. Wart - Katherine Lee Bates); I'm Through With Love
(Matt Malneck - Fud Livingston - Gus Kahn); Embraceable You
(George and Ira Gershwin); On The Gay White Way (Ralph Rain-
ger - Leo Robin); The Right Kind Of Love (Charles Henderson -
Don George); Montparnasse (Eliot Daniel - Alfred Newman);
Maine Stein Song (Lincoln Colcord - E. A. Fenstad); (Back
Home Again In Indiana (James F. Hanley - Ballard MacDonald;
Get Happy (Harold Arlen - Ted Koehler); Hoe That Corn (Jack
Woodford - Max Showalter); Jim's Toasted Peanuts; Wonderful
Home Sweet Home (Ken Darby).
Capitol L-309

1164.   WIZARD OF OZ, THE   (1939)
        STARS:   Judy Garland, Bert Lahr
        DIR:     Victor Fleming
        SONGS:   Harold Arlen - E. Y. Harburg
        Merry Old Land Of Oz; Ding, Dong The Witch Is Dead; If I Only
        Had A Heart; We're Off To See The Wizard; If I Only Had A
        Brain; Munchkinland; If I Only Had The Nerve; Over The Rain-
        bow.
        MGM SE-3996-STe

1165.   WONDER BAR   (1934)
        STARS:   Al Jolson, Kay Francis
        DIR:     Lloyd Bacon
        SONGS:   Harry Warren - Al Dubin

1166.   WONDERFUL WORLD OF THE BROTHERS GRIMM, THE   (1962)
        STARS:   Laurence Harvey, Karl Boehm
        DIR:     Henry Levin, George Pal
        SONGS:   Bob Merrill

1167.   WORDS AND MUSIC   (1929)
        STARS:   Lois Moran,  Helen Twelvetrees
        DIR:     James Tinling

1168.   WORDS AND MUSIC   (1948)
        STARS:   Mickey Rooney, Tom Drake
        DIR:     Norman Taurog
        SONGS:   Richard Rodgers - Lorenz Hart
        Thou Swell; The Lady Is A Tramp; Johnny One-Note; This Can't
        Be Love; With A Song In My Heart; There's A Small Hotel; On
        Your Toes; Slaughter On 10th Avenue; Mountain Greenery; Where
        Or When? Way Out West; Spring Is Here; Blue Moon; I Wish I
        Were In Love Again; The Girl Friend; Blue Room; Manhattan;
        Where's That Rainbow; My Heart Stood Still; Lover; I Married

An Angel; You Took Advantage Of Me; Ev'rything I Got.
MGM-2-SES-54ST

1169. YANKEE DOODLE DANDY  (1942)
      STARS:  Jimmy Cagney, Walter Huston
      DIR:    Michael Curtiz
      I Was Born In Virginia; You're A Grand Old Flag; The Warmest
      Baby In The Bunch; Forty-Five Minutes From Broadway; Give My
      Regards To Broadway; Harrigan; Mary's A Grand Old Name; Over
      There; So Long Mary; Yankee Doodle Dandy (George M. Cohan);
      All Aboard For Old Broadway (M. K. Jerome - Jack Scholl).
      Curtain Calls CC 100/13

1170. YES SIR THAT'S MY BABY  (1949)
      STARS:  Donald O'Connor, Gloria De Haven
      DIR:    George Sherman
      SONGS:  Walter Scharf - Jack Brooks

1171. YOKEL BOY  (1942)
      STARS:  Albert Dekker, Joan Davis
      DIR:    Joseph Santley

1172. YOLANDA AND THE THIEF  (1945)
      STARS:  Fred Astaire, Lucille Bremer
      DIR:    Vincente Minnelli
      SONGS:  Harry Warren - Arthur Freed

1173. YOU CAN'T HAVE EVERYTHING  (1937)
      STARS:  Alice Faye, Don Ameche
      DIR:    Norman Taurog

1174. YOU CAN'T RATION LOVE  (1944)
      STARS:  Betty Jane Rhodes, Johnny Johnston
      DIR:    Lester Fuller

1175. YOU CAN'T RUN AWAY FROM IT  (1956)
      STARS:  June Allyson, Jack Lemmon
      DIR:    Dick Powell
      SONGS:  Gene DePaul - Johnny Mercer
      Howdy Friends And Neighbors; Temporarily; You Can't Run Away
      From It; Scarecrow Ballet; Thumbin" A Ride.
      Decca 8396

1176. YOU WERE MEANT FOR ME  (1948)
      STARS:  Jeanne Crain, Dan Daily
      DIR:    Lloyd Bacon

1177. YOU WERE NEVER LOVELIER  (1942)
      STARS:  Rita Hayworth, Fred Astaire
      DIR:    William A. Seiter
      SONGS:  Jerome Kern - Johnny Mercer
      Dearly Beloved; Wedding In The Spring; The Shorty George; You
      Were Never Lovelier; I'm Old Fashioned; On The Beam.
      Vocalion VL-3710

1178. YOU'LL FIND OUT   (1940)
STARS:   Kay Kyser, Peter Lorre
DIR:     David Butler
SONGS:   Jimmy McHugh - Johnny Mercer

1179. YOU'LL NEVER GET RICH   (1941)
STARS:   Fred Astaire, Rita Hayworth
DIR:     Sidney Lanfield
SONGS:   Cole Porter
Dream Dancing; Wedding Cake Walk; Since I Kissed My Baby Good-
bye; Shooting The Works For Uncle Sam; So Near And Yet So Far;
Boogie Woogie Barcarole.
Vocalion VL-3710

1180. YOUNG AT HEART   (1955)
STARS:   Doris Day, Frank Sinatra
DIR:     Gordon Douglas
Young At Heart (Johnny Richards - Carolyn Leigh); Someone To
Watch Over Me (George Gershwin - Ira Gershwin); Ready, Wil-
ling, And Able (Floyd Huddleston - Al Rinker); Hold Me In
Your Arms (Ray Hendry - Charles Henderson - Don Pippin); You,
My Love (James Van Heusen - Mack Gordon); There's A Rising
Moon (Sammy Fain - Paul Francis Webster); Just One Of Those
Things (Cole Porter); 'Til My Love Comes Back To Me (Mendels-
sohn - P. F. Webster); One For My Baby (Harold Arlen - Johnny
Mercer).

1181. YOUNG PEOPLE   (1946)
STARS:   Shirley Temple, Jack Oakie
DIR:     Allan Dwan
SONGS:   Harry Revel - Mack Gordon

1182. YOU'RE A SWEETHEART   (1937)
STARS:   Alice Faye, George Murphy
DIR:     David Butler

1183. YOU'RE THE ONE   (1941)
STARS:   Bonnie Baker, Orrin Tucker
DIR:     Ralph Murphy
SONGS:   Jimmy McHugh - Johnny Mercer

1184. ZIEGFELD FOLLIES   (1946)
STARS:   Fred Astaire, Lucille Bremer
DIR:     Vincente Minnelli
(and George Sidney, Robert Lewis, Lemuel Ayers, Roy Del Ruth)
Here's To The Girls (Roger Edens - Ralph Freed); This Heart
Of Mine (Harry Warren - Arthur Freed); Madame Crematon (Roger
Edens - Kay Thompson); There's Beauty Everywhere (Earl Brent -
A Freed); Bring On The Wonderful Men (Edens - Brent); Love
(Hugh Martin - Ralph Blane); The Babbitt And The Bromide
(George - Ira Gershwin); Limehouse Blues (Philip Braham -
Douglas Furber).
Curtain Calls CC 100/15-16

1185.   ZIEGFELD GIRL   (1941)
        STARS:   James Stewart, Judy Garland
        DIR:     Robert Z. Leonard

1186.   ZIS BOOM BAH   (1941)
        STARS:   Mary Healy, Peter Lind Hayes
        DIR:     William Nigh

A CHRONOLOGY OF THE HOLLYWOOD MUSICAL

Jazz Singer, The

1928
Gang War
Stepping High

1929
Applause
Battle Of Paris
Blue Skies
Broadway
Broadway Babies
Broadway Melody
Broadway Scandals
Close Harmony
Cockeyed World, The
Cocoanuts
Dance Of Life
Desert Song, The
Devil May Care
Fox Movietone Follies
Glorifying The American Girl
Gold Diggers Of Broadway
Hallelujah
Hollywood Revue
Honky Tonk
Hot For Paris
Innocents Of Paris
Is Everybody Happy?
It's A Great Life
Little Johnny Jones
Love Parade, The
Lucky Boy
Marianne
Married In Hollywood
Melody Lane
My Man
On With The Show
Rainbow Man
Rio Rita
Sally
Say It With Songs
Show Boat
Show Of Shows
Singing Fool, The
Smiling Irish Eyes
So Long Letty
So This Is College
Song Of Love
Street Girl, The
Sunny Side Up

Sweetie
Syncopation
Tanned Legs
Time, The Place, And The Girl, The
Vagabond Lover, The
Words And Music

1930
Animal Crackers
Be Yourself
Big Boy
Big Pond, The
Bride Of The Regiment
Captain Of The Guard
Chasing Rainbows
Check And Double Check
Cheer Up And Smile
Children Of Pleasure
Cuckoos, The
Dancing Sweeties
Dangerous Nan McGrew
Dixiana
Follow The Leader
Follow Through
Free And Easy
Golden Dawn
Good News
Happy Days
Heads Up
High Society Blues
Hit The Deck
Hold Everything
Honey
Just Imagine
King Of Jazz
Lady's Morals, A
Let's Go Native
Let's Go Places
Life Of The Party
Lord Byron Of Broadway
Lottery Bride
Love Among The Millionaires
Love In The Rough
Mammy
New Moon
New Movietone Follies Of 1930
No, No Nanette
Oh! Sailor Beware!
Paramount On Parade
Paris
Playboy Of Paris
Puttin' On The Ritz

Queen High
Rain Or Shine
Rogue Song, The
Safety In Numbers
She Couldn't Say No
Show Girl In Hollywood
Song O' My Heart
Song Of The Flame
Song Of The West
Spring Is Here
Sunny
Sweethearts On Parade
Swing High
They Learned About Women
Three Sisters
Top Speed
Two Hearts In Waltz Time
Vagabond King, The
Viennese Nights
Whoopee

## 1931
Along Came Youth
Blonde Crazy
Bright Lights
Children Of Dreams
Connecticut Yankee, A
Cuban Love Song
Dance, Fools, Dance
Delicious
Fifty Million Frenchmen
Flying High
Holy Terror
Honeymoon Lane
Hot Heiress
Monkey Business
Palmy Days
Road To Singapore, The
Smiling Lieutenant, The

## 1932
Big Broadcast Of 1932, The
Big City Blues
Blondie Of The Follies
Careless Lady
Crooner, The
Girl Crazy
Kid From Spain, The
Love Me Tonight
Manhattan Parade
One Hour With You
Phantom President, The

Red-Headed Woman

## 1933
Adorable
Bedtime Story, A
Best Of Enemies
Broadway Bad
Broadway Through A Keyhole
Broadway To Hollywood
College Coach
College Humor
Dance, Girl, Dance
Dancing Lady
Duck Soup
Flying Down To Rio
Footlight Parade
Forty-Second Street
Girl Without A Room
Going Hollywood
Gold Diggers Of 1933
Hallelujah, I'm A Bum
Hello Everybody
I Loved You Wednesday
I'm No Angel
International House
It's Great To Be Alive
Jimmy And Sally
Melody Cruise
Moonlight And Pretzels
My Lips Betray
My Weakness
Roman Scandals
Shady Lady, The
She Done Him Wrong
Sitting Pretty
Take A Chance
Too Much Harmony
Torch Singer
Way To Love, The

## 1934
Babes In Toyland
Bachelor Of Arts
Belle Of The Nineties
Bottoms Up
Cat And The Fiddle, The
Cockeyed Cavaliers
College Rhythm
Dames
Down To Their Last Yacht
Embarrassing Moments
Flirtation Walk

Gay Divorcee, The
George White's Scandals
Gift Of Gab, The
Girl From Missouri
Happiness Ahead
Harold Teen
Here Is My Heart
Hips Hips, Hooray
Hollywood Party
I Am Suzanne
I Like It That Way
Kid Millions
King Kelly Of The U. S. A.
Let's Fall In Love
Let's Talk It Over
Little Miss Marker
Loud Speaker
Many Happy Returns
Melody In Spring
Merry Widow, The
Moulin Rouge
Murder At The Vanities
Music In The Air
Myrt And Marge
Palooka
Rainbow Over Broadway
She Learned About Sailors
She Loves Me Not
Shoot The Works
Stand Up And Cheer
Strictly Dynamite
Student Tour
That's A Good Girl
Transatlantic Merry-Go-Round
Twenty Million Sweethearts
Wake Up And Dream
We're Not Dressing
Wharf Angel
Wonder Bar

1935
After The Dance
All The King's Horses
Big Broadcast Of 1936
Brewster's Millions
Bright Lights
Broadway Gondolier
Broadway Hostess
Broadway Melody Of 1936
Coronado
Curly Top
Every Night At Eight
Folies Bergere

Frankie And Johnny
George White's Scandals
Girl Friend
Go Into Your Dance
Goin' To Town
Gold Diggers Of 1935
Here Comes The Band
Hooray For Love
I Dream Too Much
I Live For Love
In Caliente
In Person
King Of Burlesque
King Solomon Of Broadway
Lottery Lover
Love In Bloom
Millions In The Air
Mississippi
Music Is Magic
Naughty Marietta
Night Is Young, The
Old Homestead, The
Old Man Rhythm
Paris In The Spring
Reckless
Red Heads On Parade
Roberta
Rumba
Ship Cafe
Shipmates Forever
St. Louis Woman
Stars Over Broadway
Stolen Harmony
Sweet Adeline
Sweet Music
Sweet Surrender
Thanks A Million
This Is The Life
To Beat The Band
Top Hat
Two For Tonight
Under Pressure
Under The Pampas Moon

1936
Anything Goes
Banjo On My Knee
Big Broadcast Of 1937
Born To Dance
Cain And Mabel
Can This Be Dixie?
Captain January
Colleen

College Holiday
Collegiate
Dancing Feet
Dimples
Dizzy Dames
First Baby, The
Follow The Fleet
Follow Your Heart
Give Us This Night
Gold Diggers Of 1937
Great Ziegfeld, The
Hats Off
Hi Gaucho
King Steps Out, The
Klondike Annie
Laughing Irish Eyes
Music Goes Round, The
One In A Million
Palm Springs
Pennies From Heaven
Pigskin Parade
Poor Little Rich Girl
Poppy
Princess Comes Across, The
Rainbow On The River
Ramona
Rhythm On The Range
Rose Marie
Rose Of The Rancho
San Francisco
Show Boat
Sing Baby Sing
Sing Me A Love Song
Singing Kid, The
Sitting On The Moon
Smartest Girl In Town
Song And Dance Man
Stage Struck
Star For A Night
Stowaway
Strike Me Pink
Swing Time
That Girl From Paris
Three Cheers For Love
Under Your Spell
Walking On Air

1937
Ali Baba Goes To Town
Artists And Models
Blossoms On Broadway
Broadway Melody Of 1937
Champagne Waltz, The

Damsel In Distress
Day At The Races, The
Double Or Nothing
Every Day's A Holiday
Fifty-Second Street
Firefly, The
Hideaway Girl
High, Wide, And Handsome
Hit Parade
Hitting A New High
Hollywood Hotel
Holy Terror, The
I'll Take Romance
Life Begins In College
Life Of The Party
Love And Hisses
Make A Wish
Manhattan Merry-Go-Round
Maytime
Meet The Boy Friend
Melody For Two
Merry-Go-Round Of 1938
Mountain Music
Mr. Dodd Takes The Air
Music For Madame
New Faces Of 1937
Nobody's Baby
On The Avenue
Ready, Willing And Able
Renfrew Of The Mounted
Rosalie
Shall We Dance?
Sing And Be Happy
Singing Marine, The
Something To Sing About
Swing High Swing Low
Thin Ice
This Is My Affair
This Way Please
Thrill Of A Lifetime, The
Top Of The Town
Turn Off The Moon
Twenty-Three And A Half Hours'
    Leave
Varsity Show
Vogues Of 1938
Waikiki Wedding
Wake Up And Live
Wallaby Jim Of The Islands
You Can't Have Everything
You're A Sweetheart

## 1938

Alexander's Ragtime Band
All-American Sweetheart
Artists And Models Abroad
Big Broadcast Of 1938
Breaking The Ice
Carefree
Cocoanut Grove
College Swing
Cowboy From Brooklyn
Doctor Rhythm
Everybody Sing
Fools For Scandal
Freshman Year, The
Gaiety Girls
Garden Of The Moon
Girl Of The Golden West
Give Me A Sailor
Going Places
Gold Diggers In Paris
Goldwyn Follies
Great Waltz, The
Happy Landing
Having A Wonderful Time
Hold That Coed
Josette
Joy Of Living
Just Around The Corner
Kentucky Moonshine
Lady Objects, The
Listen Darling
Little Miss Broadway
Little Miss Roughneck
Love Finds Andy Hardy
Love On Toast
Mad About Music
My Lucky Star
Outside Of Paradise
Radio City Revels
Rascals
Rebecca Of Sunnybrook Farm
Romance In The Dark
Sally, Irene And Mary
Sing You Sinners
Start Cheering
Straight Place And Show
Sweethearts
Swing Sister Swing
Swing Your Lady
Swiss Miss
Terror Of Tiny Town
Thanks For Everything
That Certain Age
Tropic Holiday

## 1939

At The Circus
Babes In Arms
Balalaika
Broadway Serenade
Cafe Society
Day At The Circus, A
East Side Of Heaven
First Love
Great Victor Herbert, The
Gulliver's Travels
Hawaiian Nights
Honolulu
Ice Follies Of 1939
Laugh It Off
Let Freedom Ring
Man About Town
Naughty But Nice
On Your Toes
One Dark Night
Paris Honeymoon
Rose Of Washington Square
Second Fiddle
She Married A Cop
St. Louis Blues
Star Maker, The
Story Of Vernon And Irene Castle
Swanee River
That's Right, You're Wrong
Three Musketeers
Wizard Of Oz, The

## 1940

Argentine Nights
Barnyard Follies
Bitter Sweet
Bluebird, The
Boys From Syracuse
Broadway Melody
Buck Benny Rides Again
Captain Caution
Dance Girl Dance
Down Argentine Way
Go West
Hit Parade Of 1941
I Can't Give You Anything But
    Love Baby
If I Had My Way
I'm Nobody's Sweetheart Now
Irene
It's A Date
Johnny Apollo
La Conga Nights

Let's Make Music
Lillian Russell
Little Bit Of Heaven, A
Little Nellie Kelly
New Moon, The
Love Thy Neighbor
Melody And Moonlight
Music In My Heart
Night At Earl Carroll's, A
No, No Nanette
Oh, Johnny How You Can Love
One Night In The Tropics
Pot Of Gold
Rhythm On The River
Road To Singapore
Second Chorus
Sing, Dance, And Plenty Hot
Spring Parade
Strike Up The Band
Tin Pan Alley
Too Many Girls
Two Girls On Broadway
You'll Find Out
Young People

Playmates
Puddin' Head
Rise And Shine
Road Show
Road To Zanzibar, The
Rookies On Parade
San Antonio Rose
Sing Another Chorus
Sis Hopkins
Sun Valley Serenade
Sunny
Sweetheart Of The Campus
Tall, Dark, And Handsome
That Night In Rio
They Met In Argentina
Time Out For Rhythm
Too Many Blondes
Two Latins From Manhattan
Virginia
Weekend In Havana
You'll Never Get Rich
You're The One
Ziegfeld Girl
Zis Boom Bah

1941
All-American Coed
Angels With Broken Wings
Babes On Broadway
Big Store, The
Birth Of The Blues
Blondie Goes Latin
Blues In The Night
Buck Privates
Cadet Girl
Chocolate Soldier, The
Dancing On A Dime
Fiesta
Four Jacks And A Jill
Go West Young Lady
Great American Broadcast
Hellzapoppin
In The Navy
Keep 'Em Flying
Kiss The Boys Goodbye
Lady Be Good
Las Vegas Nights
Louisiana Purchase
Melody Lane
Moon Over Miami
Moonlight In Hawaii
Navy Blues
Nice Girl?

1942
Almost Married
Behind The Eight Ball
Born To Sing
Broadway
Cairo
Call Out The Marines
Don't Get Personal
Fleet's In, The
Footlight Serenade
For Me And My Gal
Get Hep To Love
Give Out Sisters
Hard Way, The
Hi Neighbor
Holiday Inn
I Married An Angel
Ice Capades Revue
Iceland
Johnny Doughboy
Juke Box Jennie
Mayor Of 44th Street
Moonlight In Havana
My Gal Sal
Old Homestead, The
Orchestra Wives
Panama Hattie
Pardon My Sarong

Powers Girl
Priorities On Parade
Private Buckaroo
Rhythm Parade
Ride 'Em Cowboy
Rio Rita
Road To Morocco, The
Seven Days Leave
Ship Ahoy
Sing Your Worries Away
Sleepy Time Gal
Song Of The Islands
Springtime In The Rockies
Star Spangled Rhythm
Strictly In The Groove
Sweater Girl
Syncopation
True To The Army
What's Cooking?
When Johnny Comes Marching Home
Who Done It?
Yankee Doodle Dandy
Yokel Boy
You Were Never Lovelier

## 1943
Always A Bridesmaid
Around The World
Best Foot Forward
Cabin In The Sky
Campus Rhythm
Career Girl
Chatterbox
Coney Island
Cowboy In Manhattan
Crazy House
Desert Song, The
Dixie
Dubarry Was A Lady
Follies' Girl
Follow The Band
Footlight Glamour
Gals, Inc.
Gang's All Here, The
Girl Crazy
Happy Go Lucky
Harvest Melody
Heat's On, The
Hello Frisco Hello
Here Comes Elmer
Hi Buddy
Higher And Higher
Hit Parade Of 1943

Hit The Ice
Hi'ya Chum
Hi'ya Sailor
Honeymoon Lodge
How's About It?
I Dood It
Is Everybody Happy?
Jitterbugs
Larceny With Music
Let's Face It
Melody Parade
Moonlight In Vermont
Mr. Big
Presenting Lily Mars
Red Head From Manhattan
Rhythm Of The Islands
Riding High
Salute For Three
Silver Skates
Sky's The Limit, The
Sleepy Lagoon
Something To Shout About
Stage Door Canteen
Stormy Weather
Sultan's Daughter, The
Sweet Rosie O'Grady
Swing Fever
Swing Your Partner
Tahiti Honey
Thank Your Lucky Stars
This Is The Army
Thousands Cheer
Thumbs Up
True To Life
What's Buzzin' Cousin?
Wintertime

## 1944
Allergic To Love
And The Angels Sing
Babes On Swing Street
Bathing Beauty
Beautiful But Broke
Belle Of The Yukon
Bowery To Broadway
Broadway Rhythm
Can't Help Singing
Carolina Blues
Casanova In Burlesque
Chip Off The Old Block
Cover Girl
Dixie Jamboree
Ever Since Eve

Follow The Boys
Four Jills In A Jeep
Ghost Catchers
Girl Rush
Going My Way
Greenwich Village
Hat Check Honey
Here Come The Waves
Hey Rookie
Hi, Good Lookin'
Hollywood Canteen
In Society
Jam Session
Kansas City Kitty
Knickerbocker Holiday
Lady In The Dark
Lady Let's Dance
Lost In A Harem
Louisiana Hayride
Meet Me In St. Louis
Meet Miss Bobby Sox
Meet The People
Merry Monihans, The
Minstrel Man
Moon Over Las Vegas
Moonlight And Cactus
Music For Millions
Music In Manhattan
My Gal Loves Music
Night Club Girl
Pin-Up Girl
Rainbow Island
Reckless Age, The
Rosie The Riveter
Sensations Of 1945
Seven Days Ashore
She's A Sweetheart
Shine On Harvest Moon
Show Business
Sing A Jingle
Singing Sheriff, The
Slightly Terrific
Something For The Boys
Song Of The Open Road
South Of Dixie
Stars On Parade
Step Lively
Sweet And Low Down
Sweethearts Of The U. S. A.
Swing In The Saddle
Swingtime Johnny
Take It Big
This Is The Life
Three Little Sisters

Trocadero
Two Girls And A Sailor
Up In Arms
Wave, A Wac, And A Marine, A
Weekend Pass
You Can't Ration Love


1945
Abbott And Costello In Hollywood
Anchors Aweigh
Bells Of St. Mary's, The
Blonde Ransom
Bring On The Girls
Delightfully Dangerous
Diamond Horseshoe
Doll Face
Dolly Sisters, The
Earl Carroll's Vanities
Easy To Look At
George White's Scandals Of 1945
Hangover Square
Here Come The Coeds
Honeymoon Ahead
I'll Tell The World
Incendiary Blonde
Mexicana
Naughty Nineties, The
On Stage Everybody
Pan-Americana
Rhapsody In Blue
Road To Utopia, The
See My Lawyer
Senorita From The West
Shady Lady
Sing You Way Home
Song For Miss Julie, A
Song Of The Sarong
State Fair
Stork Club
Sunbonnet Sue
That's The Spirit
Thrill Of Romance
Tonight And Every Night
Where Do We Go From Here?
Why Girls Leave Home
Yolanda And The Thief


1946
Bamboo Blonde
Betty Coed
Blue Skies
Centennial Summer

Cinderella Jones
Cross My Heart
Cuban Pete
Do You Love Me?
Down Missouri Way
Earl Carroll Sketch Book
Easy To Wed
Freddie Steps Out
Harvey Girls, The
High School Hero
If I'm Lucky
Jolson Story, The
Junior Prom
Kid From Brooklyn, The
Lover Come Back
Man I Love, The
Meet Me On Broadway
My Heart Goes Crazy
Night And Day
No Leave, No Love
People Are Funny
Singin' In The Corn
Swing Parade Of 1946
Tars And Spars
That's My Girl
Three Little Girls In Blue
Thrill Of Brazil
Till The Clouds Roll By
Time, The Place, And The Girl, The
Two Sisters From Boston
Wake Up And Dream
Ziegfeld Follies

1947
Beat The Band
Calendar Girl
Carnegie Hall
Carnival In Costa Rica
Cigarette Girl
Copacabana
Down To Earth
Fabulous Dorseys, The
Fiesta
Fun And Fancy Free
Good News
Hit Parade Of 1947
I Wonder Who's Kissing Her Now
I'll Be Yours
It Happened In Brooklyn
It Happened On Fifth Avenue
Ladies' Man
Little Miss Broadway

Love And Learn
Mother Wore Tights
My Wild Irish Rose
New Orleans
Northwest Outpost
Perils Of Pauline
Road To Rio, The
Shocking Miss Pilgrim, The
Something In The Wind
Song Of Scheherazade
This Time For Keeps
Two Blondes And A Red Head
Variety Girl
Welcome Stranger
When A Girl's Beautiful

1948
April Showers
Are You With It?
Campus Honeymoon
Casbah
Countess Of Monte Cristo, The
Date With Judy, A
Easter Parade
Feudin', Fussin', And A-Fightin'
Glamour Girl
I Surrender Dear
If You Knew Susie
Isn't It Romantic?
Kissing Bandit, The
Lulu Belle
Mary Lou
Mystery In Mexico
On An Island With You
One Sunday Afternoon
One Touch Of Venus
Pirate, The
Romance On The High Seas
So Dear To My Heart
Song Is Born, A
Summer Holiday
That Lady In Ermine
Two Guys From Texas
Up In Central Park
When My Baby Smiles At Me
Words And Music
You Were Meant For Me

1949
Always Leave Them Laughing
Barkleys Of Broadway, The
Beautiful Blonde From Bashful

Bend
Connecticut Yankee, A
Dancing In The Dark
Holiday In Havana
In The Good Old Summertime
Inspector General, The
It's A Great Feeling
Jolson Sings Again
Ladies Of The Chorus
Look For The Silver Lining
Make Believe Ballroom
Make Mine Laughs
Manhattan Angel
My Dream Is Yours
My Friend Irma
Neptune's Daughter
Oh You Beautiful Doll
On The Town
Red Hot, And Blue
Slightly French
Take Me Out To The Ball Game
There's A Girl In My Heart
Top O' The Morning
Yes Sir That's My Baby

1950
Annie Get Your Gun
At War With The Army
Buccaneer's Girl
Duchess Of Idaho
Fancy Pants
Hit Parade Of 1951
I'll Get By
Let's Dance
Milkman, The
Mr. Music
My Blue Heaven
My Friend Irma Goes West
Nancy Goes To Rio
Never A Dull Moment
Pagan Love Song
Petty Girl, The
Riding High
Summer Stock
Tea For Two
Three Little Words
Toast Of New Orleans, The
Two Weeks With Love
Wabash Avenue
West Point Story, The

1951
American In Paris, An
Call Me Mister
Casa Manana
Comin' Round The Mountain
Disc Jockey
Excuse My Dust
Footlight Varieties
G. I. Jane
Golden Girl
Here Comes The Groom
Honeychile
I'll See You In My Dreams
Lemon Drop Kid, The
Lullaby Of Broadway
Meet Me After The Show
Mr. Imperium
On Moonlight Bay
On The Riviera
On The Sunny Side Of The Street
Painting The Clouds With Sunshine
Purple Heart Diary
Rhythm Inn
Rich, Young, And Pretty
Royal Wedding
Sailor Beware
Show Boat
Star Lift
Strip, The
Texas Carnival
Two Gals And A Guy
Two Tickets To Broadway

1952
Aaron Slick From Punkin Crick
About Face
April In Paris
Because You're Mine
Belle Of New York, The
Everything I Have Is Yours
Hans Christian Andersen
I Dream Of Jeanie
Jack And The Beanstalk
Jumping Jacks
Just For You
Lovely To Look At
Meet Danny Wilson
Merry Widow, The
Rainbow 'Round My Shoulder
She's Working Her Way Through
    College
Singin' In The Rain
Skirts Ahoy

Somebody Loves Me
Son Of Paleface
Stooge, The
Story Of Robin Hood, The
Where's Charley?
With A Song In My Heart

1953
All Ashore
Bandwagon, The
By The Light Of The Silvery Moon
Caddy, The
Calamity Jane
Call Me Madam
Dangerous When Wet
Desert Song, The
Down Among The Sheltering Palms
Easy To Love
Eddie Cantor Story, The
Farmer Takes A Wife, The
5000 Fingers Of Dr. T
Gentlemen Prefer Blondes
Geraldine
Girl Next Door, The
Give A Girl A Break
Here Come The Girls
I Love Melvin
Jazz Singer, The
Kiss Me Kate
Latin Lovers
Let's Do It Again
Lili
Little Boy Lost
Miss Sadie Thompson
Money From Home
Road To Bali
Scared Stiff
She's Back On Broadway
Small Town Girl
Sombrero
Stars Are Singing, The
Take Me To Town
Those Redheads From Seattle
Three Sailors And A Girl
Torch Song
Walking My Baby Home

1954
Athena
Brigadoon
Carmen Jones
Country Girl, The

Deep In My Heart
Glenn Miller Story
Knock On Wood
Living It Up
Lucky Me
New Faces
Red Garters
Rose Marie
Seven Brides For Seven Brothers
Star Is Born, A
Student Prince
There's No Business Like Show
    Business
Top Banana
White Christmas

1955
Ain't Misbehavin'
Artists And Models
Daddy Long Legs
Gentlemen Marry Brunettes
Girl Rush
Guys And Dolls
Hit The Deck
It's Always Fair Weather
Jupiter's Darling
Kismet
Love Me Or Leave Me
My Sister Eileen
Oklahoma
Paris Follies Of 1956
Pete Kelly's Blues
Second Greatest Sex
Seven Little Foys, The
So This Is Paris
Three For The Show
Young At Heart

1956
Anything Goes
Benny Goodman Story
Best Things In Life Are Free,
    The
Birds And The Bees, The
Bundle Of Joy
Carousel
Court Jester, The
High Society
Hollywood Or Bust
King And I, The
Meet Me In Las Vegas
Opposite Sex, The

227

**Pardners**
**Vagabond** King, The
**You** Can't Run Away From It

1957
April Love
Funny Face
Helen Morgan Story
Les Girls
Let's Be Happy
Pajama Game
Pal Joey
Silk Stockings

1958
Damn Yankees
Gigi
Girl Most Likely, The
Merry Andrew
Rock-A-Bye Baby
South Pacific
St. Louis Blues
Tom Thumb

1959
Blue Angel, The
Five Pennies, The
Gene Krupa Story, The
Li'l Abner
Never Steal Anything Small
Pillow Talk
Porgy And Bess
Private's Affair, A
Say One For Me

1960
Bells Are Ringing
Can-Can
Cinderfella
Let's Make Love
Pepe

1961
Babes In Toyland
Flower Drum Song
West Side Story

1962
Gypsy
Jumbo
Music Man, The
Road To Hong Kong
State Fair
Wonderful World Of The Brothers
    Grimm, The

1963
Bye Bye Birdie
How The West Was Won

1964
Mary Poppins
My Fair Lady
Robin And The Seven Hoods
Unsinkable Molly Brown, The

1965
Sound Of Music, The

1966
Funny Thing Happened On The Way
    To The Forum, A
Singing Nun, The
Stop The World--I Want To Get
    Off

1967
Camelot
Doctor Dolittle
Happiest Millionaire, The
How To Succeed In Business With-
    out Really Trying
Thoroughly Modern Millie

1968
Chitty Chitty Bang Bang
Finian's Rainbow
Funny Girl
Half A Sixpence
Night They Raided Minsky's, The
Oliver!
One And Only, Genuine, Original
    Family Band
Star!

228

**1969**
Hello Dolly
Oh! What A Lovely War
Paint Your Wagon
Sweet Charity

**1970**
Darling Lili
On A Clear Day You Can See For-
    ever
Song Of Norway

**1971**
Bedknobs And Broomsticks
Boy Friend, The
Fiddler On The Roof
Willy Wonka And The Chocolate
    Factory

**1972**
Cabaret
Great Waltz, The
Lady Sings The Blues
Man Of La Mancha
1776

**1973**
Godspell
Jesus Christ Superstar
Lost Horizon
Tom Sawyer

**1974**
Huckleberry Finn
Little Prince, The
Mame

**1975**
At Long Last Love
Funny Lady

COMPOSERS AND LYRICISTS

Garrett, Buddy, 426
Gaunt, Percy, 1002
Gay, Byron, 853
Geisel, Theodore (Dr. Seuss), 283
Gensler, Lewis, 409, 644, 733, 799, 891
George, Don, 56, 96, 269, 638, 649, 774, 918, 1163
Gershe, Leonard, 312, 969
Gershwin, George, 17, 18, 50, 208, 225, 312, 334, 335, 336, 398, 478, 513, 514, 547, 551, 621, 633, 788, 819, 880, 893, 937, 967, 994, 1040, 1069, 1155, 1163, 1180, 1184
Gershwin, Ira, 17, 18, 50, 193, 195, 208, 225, 312, 334, 335, 344, 366, 398, 514, 547, 548, 551, 621, 633, 788, 819, 880, 893, 967, 994, 1040, 1050, 1069, 1080, 1163, 1180, 1184
Gibson, Andy, 985
Gilbert, L. Wolfe, 15, 57, 201, 385, 467, 514, 598, 610, 766, 837, 987, 1041
Gilbert, Mercedes, 962
Gilbert, Ray, 664, 674, 701
Gilkyson, Terry, 806
Gillespie, Haven, II, 398, 903, 995
Glogau, Jack, 1082
Glover, Charles W., 946
Goell, Kermit, 251, 292, 1028, 1088, 1099
Goering, Al, 894, 982
Goetz, E. Ray, 18, 26, 576, 937, 1082
Gold, Ray, 346
Golden, Ray, 31, 79, 366, 989
Goodhart, Al, 120, 180, 218, 512
Goodwin, Joe, 162, 442, 589, 633, 729, 900, 1118
Gordon, Barbara, 301
Gordon, Irving, 457
Gordon, Mack, 8, 56, 88, 119, 124, 137, 183, 185, 231, 242, 246, 305, 321, 339, 369, 401, 434, 466, 473, 478, 511, 515, 576, 588, 597, 600, 601, 617, 669,

694, 753, 761, 771, 782, 786, 792, 810, 853, 860, 884, 894, 921, 947, 951, 960, 981, 982, 988, 1000, 1001, 1009, 1012, 1020, 1045, 1049, 1060, 1070, 1083, 1109, 1133, 1137, 1143, 1146, 1154, 1173, 1180, 1181
Gordon, Roz, 233
Gorney, Jay, 26, 53, 261, 350, 397, 410, 507, 593, 665, 815, 846, 966
Gottler, Archie, 83, 106, 176, 306, 385, 464, 567, 572, 649, 774, 837, 902, 1084, 1167
Gottlieb, Hilda, 180
Gould, Morton, 226
Goulding, Edmund, 86
Crage, Bill, 168, 812, 1062
Graham, Irvin, 820
Graham, Ronny, 710
Grainger, Porter, 551
Grandee, George, 210
Grant, Bert, 242
Grant, Ian, 322
Gray, George, 1064
Gray, Glen, 505
Grayson, Phil, 416
Green, Adolph, 65, 368, 502, 742, 913, 1035
Green, Bud, 72, 322, 478, 878, 898, 899, 930, 1030, 1099
Green, Eddie, 633
Green, Johnny, 45, 52, 175, 244, 259, 267, 280, 398, 457, 621, 635, 867, 976, 982
Greene, Joe, 870
Greene, Mort, 47, 55, 57, 138, 304, 617, 631, 764, 874, 911, 998, 1150
Greenwood, Charlotte, 934
Greer, Jesse, 54, 165, 442, 627, 934
Grever, Maria, 701
Grey, Clifford, 125, 230, 267, 398, 427, 428, 548, 552, 588, 606, 844, 859, 931
Grey, Lanny, 664
Grieg, Edvard, 948
Grier, Jimmy, 269, 406
Grofe, Ferde, 763, 1067
Groner, Duke, 1023
Gross, Walter, 1099
Grossman, Bernie, 532, 715, 947
Grouya, Ted, 549, 638

Gruber, Edmund L.,  397, 471
Guizar, Tito,  76
Guizar, Jose,  774

Hagan, Earle,  323
Haggart, Bob,  569
Hajos, Karl,  804, 998
Haley, Ed,  1002
Hall, Fred,  314
Hall, Rich,  1031
Hamilton, Arthur,  777
Hamilton, Grace,  1135
Hammerstein II, Oscar,  151,
    155, 160, 166, 227, 228,
    229, 286, 347, 364, 371,
    398, 419, 435, 469, 480,
    531, 547, 550, 588, 608,
    621, 623, 682, 712, 719,
    730, 749, 811, 841, 850,
    851, 895, 896, 897, 954,
    955, 957, 964, 977, 978,
    995, 1003, 1004, 1008,
    1075, 1080, 1130
Hanbrich, Earl,  16
Handman, Lou,  422
Handy, W. C.,  81, 413, 494,
    495, 505, 962
Hanighen, Bernie,  867
Hanley, James F.,  117, 150,
    313, 385, 418, 448, 569,
    577, 612, 695, 713, 803,
    853, 883, 946, 1013, 1079,
    1163
Harbach, Otto,  81, 159, 228,
    229, 279, 305, 364, 588,
    608, 723, 737, 749, 850,
    851, 987, 1003, 1004, 1080
Harburg, E. Y.,  26, 27, 37,
    40, 43, 128, 133, 144, 222,
    250, 261, 278, 294, 314,
    350, 363, 398, 438, 487,
    495, 640, 665, 765, 791,
    799, 829, 830, 867, 887,
    915, 965, 982, 1033, 1067,
    1164
Harline, Leigh,  55
Harling, W. Franke,  445
    661
Harnick, Sheldon,  273, 710
Harriman, Al,  732
Harris, Charles K.,  576

Harris, Harry,  263, 341, 495
Harris, Phil,  970
Harris, Will J.,  824
Harrison, Annie F.,  56
Hart, Lorenz,  37, 40, 98, 188,
    215, 295, 297, 323, 380, 396,
    420, 441, 454, 468, 518, 603,
    604, 640, 650, 658, 668, 744,
    758, 760, 779, 958, 964,
    1057, 1062, 1091, 1099, 1163,
    1168
Hartman, Don,  218, 593, 815
Hassel, Minor,  449
Hatley, Marvin,  724
Hayden, Barbara,  797
Hayes, Elton,  986
Hayton, Lennie,  94
Hazard, Dick,  233
Heath, E. P.,  477
Heath, Hy,  413, 638, 789, 1052
Heelan, Will,  704
Heindorf, Ray,  17, 29, 438, 599,
    777
Henderson, Charles,  6, 238, 242,
    381, 398, 576, 709, 1024,
    1027, 1163, 1180, 1182
Henderson, Ray,  70, 78, 81, 107,
    168, 176, 204, 294, 295, 325,
    326, 327, 367, 368, 385, 398,
    443, 514, 524, 588, 603, 609,
    758, 806, 864, 898, 914,
    1005, 1163
Hendry, Ray,  1180
Heneker, David,  378
Herbert, Frederick,  1036
Herbert, Victor,  41, 42, 370,
    588, 703, 1015
Herman, Jerry,  399, 618
Herman, Woody,  254, 1151
Hermann, Bernard,  381
Hernandez, Rafael,  202
Herpin, Jamblan,  520
Herscher, Louis,  141, 156, 821,
    944
Hershey, June,  414, 1163
Herzog, Arthur Jr.,  551
Heuberger, Al,  262
Heyman, Edward,  24, 45, 226, 237,
    280, 328, 398, 540, 560, 621,
    660, 725, 736, 884, 970,
    1013, 1047
Heyward, Du Bose,  788
Hickman, Art,  649, 937
Higgenbotham, Al,  551

240

Kalman, Emmerich, 364, 477
Kalmar, Bert, 22, 104, 164,
   177, 203, 252, 266, 323,
   352, 384, 421, 529, 625,
   987, 995, 1044, 1072, 1097,
   1139
Kander, John, 127, 314
Kaper, Bronislaw, 46, 170,
   223, 266, 352, 401, 575,
   576, 863
Karger, Fred, 9, 435, 582, 741
Kassel, Art, 794
Katz, Bill, 221
Kay, Arthur, 628
Kay, Edward J., 416, 647, 820,
   824
Kaye, Buddy, 290, 311, 1153
Kellette, John W., 737
Kenbrovin, Jean, 737
Kendis, James, 474, 1002
Kennedy, Jimmy, 718
Kennett, Karl, 125
Kenny, Charles, 290, 495
Kenny, Nick, 86, 290
Kent, Walter, 29, 96, 157,
   247, 254, 486, 595, 624,
   638, 741, 871, 952, 1051,
   1071
Kern, James, 1052
Kern, Jerome, 143, 159, 160,
   195, 398, 419, 463, 516,
   547, 588, 608, 621, 682,
   749, 811, 841, 859, 895,
   896, 897, 1003, 1004, 1008,
   1025, 1075, 1080, 1177
Kernell, William, 309, 316,
   503, 693, 807, 946, 1167
Kharito, Nicholas, 721
Killion, Leo, 862
King, Charles E., 471, 645
King, Jack, 15, 766, 811
King, Robert, 1082
King, Wayne, 903
Kirk, Leslie, 1063
Kisco, Charles, 1021
Klages, Ray, 165, 442, 627,
   934, 1082
Klatzkin, David, 570
Klein, Lew, 474
Klein, Lou, 209, 1002
Klemm, Gustave, 903
Knight, Fuzzy, 328
Knight, Vic, 413
Knight, Vickie, 794

Knopf, Ed H., 811
Koehler, Ted, 33, 73, 204, 232,
   280, 438, 478, 533, 565, 603,
   625, 698, 741, 802, 806, 926,
   976, 985, 1000, 1023, 1107,
   1123, 1163
Koenig, Martha, 962
Kornblum, L. B., 467
Korngold, Erich, 347
Kortlander, Max, 495, 737
Krakeur, Jack, 886, 1014
Kramer, Alex, 638, 869, 956
Kraushaar, Raoul, 414
Kreisler, Fritz, 536
Kroll, Bobby, 738
Krupa, Gene, 327
Kuller, Sid, 31, 79, 366, 770,
   989
Kummer, Frederic Arnold, 711


Lacalle, Joseph M., 281
Lacerdo, 830
Laidlow, Betty, 818, 963, 1140
Lake, Sol, 781
Lane, Burton, 33, 43, 62, 95,
   131, 161, 177, 181, 184, 215,
   216, 244, 250, 267, 272, 278,
   289, 344, 407, 415, 438, 521,
   530, 554, 605, 640, 659, 735,
   763, 765, 791, 802, 811, 855,
   885, 887, 929, 961, 991,
   1021, 1063, 1067, 1099
Lane, Ken, 290
Lanfield, Sidney, 1006
Langdon, Dory, 775
Lange, Johnny, 413, 638, 746,
   985, 1052, 1186
Langford, Frances, 322
Lara, Agustin, 58, 477, 674, 775,
   1102
Laska, Edward, 1080
LaTouche, John, 94, 128, 198,
   461, 478
Lava, Bill, 918
Lawnhurst, Vee, 605, 789
Lawrence, Jack, 624, 664, 755,
   924, 973, 1062, 1099, 1144
Layton, J. Turner, 302, 495, 937
Layva, Lamberto, 274
Leader, Mickey, 738
LeBarron, William, 152, 370

242

243

449, 569, 620, 961, 1023, 1085, 1100, 1163
Malotte, Albert Hay, 58, 412, 946
Mancini, Henry, 220
Manners, Diane, 331
Manners, Maxine, 432
Manners, Zeke, 346
Marcotte, Don, 436
Marion, George, Jr., 4, 15, 295, 467, 566, 792, 857, 1018
Markes, Larry, 57, 163, 292
Marks, Clarence J., 895
Marks, Gerald, 83, 150, 551, 633, 988
Markush, Fred, 411, 738
Marsh, Roy K., 449, 992
Marshall, Henry, 125, 750
Marshall, James T., 457
Marshall, Mayes, 973
Martin, Charles, 721, 1022
Martin, Hugh, 2, 31, 68, 116, 338, 342, 368, 636, 1067, 1184
Martinez Durango, Leocadio, 275
Marvell, Holt, 330
Marvin, Johnny, 51
Marx, Chico, 660
Masters, Frankie, 1052
Matos, M. G., 13
McCarron, Charles, 776
McCarthy, Joseph, 242, 310, 401, 418, 489, 493, 514, 567, 577, 603, 649, 729, 794, 829, 830, 853, 987, 1031, 1118, 1149, 1185
McCree, Junie, 487, 595, 704
McGavish, James, 401
McHugh, Jimmy, 32, 49, 105, 112, 135, 176, 201, 209, 215, 221, 238, 241, 246, 265, 280, 288, 292, 305, 308, 322, 337, 386, 420, 425, 430, 452, 460, 463, 476, 495, 505, 533, 602, 608, 614, 633, 652, 662, 741, 752, 774, 795, 817, 841, 875, 935, 938, 939, 985, 992, 995, 1046, 1082, 1096, 1104, 1108, 1111, 1112, 1178, 1182, 1183
McKenna, William J., 401

McLeod, Victor, 582
McMichael, Ted, 862
Melson, Henrietta, 1002
Mencher, Murray, 332, 571, 577, 1182
Mendelssohn, Felix, 462, 1180
Mendez, Ruben, 936
Menéndez, Nilo, 269, 274, 717
Mercer, Johnny, 17, 20, 62, 81, 92, 180, 196, 205, 219, 220, 267, 284, 320, 358, 359, 391, 405, 408, 439, 454, 569, 574, 616, 633, 648, 702, 705, 733, 741, 754, 778, 809, 822, 827, 867, 873, 916, 923, 975, 1063, 1085, 1093, 1100, 1103, 1129, 2275, 1177, 1178, 1180, 1183
Merrill, Blanche, 695
Merrill, Bob, 313, 1066, 1166
Merson, Billy, 514
Meskill, Jack, 332, 713, 798, 825, 1077
Meyer, George W., 66, 83, 108, 937
Meyer, Joseph, 217, 314, 326, 513, 514, 572, 610, 853, 1040, 1050, 1163, 1176
Meyer, Sol, 163, 414, 471, 641, 732, 796, 854, 861
Meyers, Billy, 479, 483, 817
Meyers, Henry, 397, 410
Miller, Jean, 432
Miller, F. E., 1138
Miller, Ned, 318, 457
Miller, Sidney, 30, 44, 168, 413, 664, 668, 738, 918, 1053, 1062
Miller, Sy, 426, 612
Mills, Irving, 73, 164, 176, 406, 915, 985
Mills, Kerry, 636
Milton, Jay, 774
Mitchell, Charles, 992
Mitchell, George, 613
Mitchell, Sidney, 83, 109, 176, 213, 249, 296, 306, 385, 464, 527, 557, 567, 571, 572, 748, 780, 810, 837, 903, 906, 920, 1058, 1167
Mitchell, Teepee, 331, 1101
Mizzy, Vic, 44, 258, 486, 525, 794
Mockridge, Cyril J., 985, 1120

Moll, Billy, 534, 806
Monaco, Jimmy, 73, 240, 242,
   255, 443, 474, 489, 506,
   514, 567, 603, 782, 794,
   822, 837, 838, 909, 964,
   970, 971, 987, 1009, 1031,
   1118, 1143, 1149
Montgomery, Reggie, 162, 367
Moody, Phil, 770, 869, 935
Mooney, Harold, 664
Moore, Billy, Jr., 308
Moore, Charles, 401
Moore, McElbert, 582
Moore, Phil, 292, 1022, 1101
Moore, Thomas, 806
Moraine, Lyle, 942
Morales, Noro, 436
Morales, Obdulio, 438
Moret, Neil, 237, 633, 731,
   806
Morey, Larry, 932
Morgan, Elizabeth, 805
Morley, James, 210
Morros, Boris, 152
Morse, Dolly, 26, 329
Mueller, Gus, 937
Muir, Lewis E., 401, 487, 489,
   514, 987
Mundy, Jimmy, 438
Murphy, C. W., 401
Murphy, Johnny, 1028
Murphy, Ralph, 1002
Murphy, Spud
Murphy, Stanley, 125, 401
Muse, Clarence, 5
Myddleton, George, 73
Myers, Richard, 461, 1030
Myrow, Josef, 56, 124, 137,
   339, 466, 475, 478, 669,
   1070, 1133, 1154
Mysels, Sammy, 569


Napton, Johnny, 291
Nash, Ogden, 751
Neal, Larry, 438
Neiburg, Al J., 375, 956
Neill, Larry, 200
Nelson, Ozzie, 449, 992
Nemo, Henry, 251
Neuman, Sam, 148, 236
Nevins, Marty, 1110

Newley, Anthony, 983, 1161
Newman, Alfred, 91, 254, 455,
   511, 576, 807, 1163
Newman, Charles, 11, 257, 411,
   510, 549, 582, 794, 1014,
   1016, 1017, 1032, 1052
Newman, Lionel, 56, 238, 365,
   381, 511
Newman, Randy, 917
Newman, Rex, 267
Nicholas, H., 551
Nichols, Alberta, 1111
Nicholls, Horatio, 769
Niesen, Gertrude, 717, 846
Noble, James, 1151
Noble, Johnny, 291, 461, 499
Noble, Ray, 74, 100, 311, 322,
   505, 741, 891, 1176
Nolan, Bob, 992
Nolan, Jimmy, 718
Norlin, Lloyd, 11
Norman, Jose, 202
Norman, Pierre, 78, 218, 432,
   660
North, Bobby, 768
Norton, George, 81, 398


Oakes, Clarence P., 457
Oakland, Ben, 12, 45, 57, 79,
   161, 314, 393, 435, 469, 480,
   550, 556, 573, 584, 623, 898,
   976
O'Connor, Shamus, 478
O'Flynn, Charles, 837
O'Hara, Geoffrey, 176, 1084
Ohman, Phil, 145, 560, 924
O'Keefe, Walter, 217
Olcott, Chauncey, 698
Oliver, Sy, 633
Olsen and Johnson, 156, 820
Oppenheim, Dave, 131, 549, 824,
   902
Original Dixieland Jazz Band,
   494, 718
Orred, Meta, 56
Owens, Harry, 951, 1134
Owens, Jack, 414, 862

247

Thompson, Kay, 721, 1077, 1184
Thompson, Ken, 1023
Tierney, Harry, 234, 493, 829, 830
Timberg, Sammy, 375
Timm, W. A., 457
Tinturin, Peter, 624, 755
Tobias, Charles, 3, 54, 168, 203, 332, 394, 571, 599, 737, 794, 889, 933, 976, 992, 1171, 1182
Tobias, Harry, 86, 131, 237, 332, 481, 499, 639, 718, 731, 872, 985, 992, 1111
Tobias, Henry, 774, 992
Tomlin, Pinky, 269, 406, 499, 535, 985
Torbett, Dave, 1031
Torme, Mel, 932
Torre, Janice, 487, 1088
Touzet, Rene, 435
Trace, Al, 718
Tracey, Bill, 732
Tracey, William G., 401, 487, 551
Trent, Jo, 162, 318, 442
Trivers, Barry, 264
Troup, Bob, 323, 1115
Tucker, Henry, 489
Tugend, Harry, 81
Turk, Roy, 73, 83, 209, 292, 309, 478, 551, 570, 603, 627, 937, 1099, 1176
Twohig, Dan, 903
Twomey, Kay, 512


Udall, Lyn, 125
Unger, Stella, 221
Utera, Adolph, 269


Valdez, Miguelito, 435
Vallee, Rudy, 71, 350, 398
Van and Schenck, 1056
VanAlstyne, Egbert, 116, 125, 302, 479, 495, 513, 853
Van Heusen, Jimmy, 20, 25, 64, 66, 189, 200, 235, 262, 357, 548, 577, 579, 607,
675, 692, 700, 767, 785, 828, 833, 834, 835, 836, 839, 840, 842, 865, 967, 1065, 1093, 1145, 1180
Van Steeden, Peter, 664
Vajvoda, J., 457
Vermelho, 960
Villavino, Geronimo, 936
Violinsky, Sol, 660
Vodery, Will, 467
Von Tilzer, Albert, 704, 908, 922, 1154
Von Tilzer, Harry, 81, 242, 332, 401, 407, 487, 489, 495, 514, 595, 704, 805, 824, 1149


Waggner, George, 237, 261, 367, 879
Walker, Raymond, 776
Wallace, Oliver, 311
Waller, Fats, 26, 323, 985, 1067, 1084, 1176
Walsh, Raoul, 961
Walsh, William, 311
Walters, Serge, 228, 229
Ward, Edward, 96, 101, 103, 118, 162, 211, 261, 274, 330, 632, 722, 769, 900, 950
Ward, Samuel A., 1163
Warfield, Charles, 1053
Warren, Blackie, 308
Warren, Harry, 34, 50, 62, 80, 88, 110, 129, 132, 173, 179, 196, 206, 231, 246, 299, 303, 305, 314, 319, 320, 321, 322, 351, 358, 359, 361, 362, 363, 369, 391, 401, 451, 473, 478, 484, 513, 514, 523, 612, 643, 669, 670, 673, 686, 702, 753, 756, 758, 843, 845, 888, 892, 908, 916, 922, 951, 958, 960, 974, 999, 1000, 1001, 1012, 1022, 1040, 1042, 1049, 1083, 1106, 1143, 1165, 1172, 1184
Warren, Robert, 296
Washington, Ned, 103, 289, 307, 337, 407, 422, 563, 653, 657, 717, 722, 837, 846, 900, 924, 1069, 1102
Watkins, Lawrnece E., 986
Watson, Johnny, 1051

251